A. CRAIG BAIRD, Litt.D., Wabash College, is Distinguished Visiting Professor of Speech at Southern Illinois University and also Professor Emeritus of Speech at the University of Iowa, annually teaching one semester at each institution. Dr. Baird previously held teaching positions at Columbia University, Ohio Wesleyan University, the University of Missouri, and Dartmouth College. He is co-author, with Lester Thonssen, of *Speech Criticism*, published by The Ronald Press Company.

RHETORIC
A Philosophical Inquiry

A. CRAIG BAIRD
University of Iowa

THE RONALD PRESS COMPANY • NEW YORK

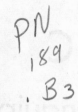

Library of Congress Catalog Card Number: 65–12742
PRINTED IN THE UNITED STATES OF AMERICA

To

Marion and Barbara

Preface

"A book on so old a subject as rhetoric," said John F. Genung in 1887, "can scarcely hope to give the world much that is new." But rhetorical communication, still living and highly influential in human affairs, needs fresh definition, interpretation, and perspective to meet the conditions of this later age. Rhetoric continues its association with stylistic artificiality and pomposity and, now and then, with written composition in schools and colleges. Kenneth Burke, on the contrary, has remarked that "wherever there is meaning, there is persuasion." Plainly, the term needs further explication if its values and methods are worthy of survival and intellectual support.

This volume attempts to frame and develop a philosophy of rhetoric. Philosophy, as I apply it here, is a method of inquiry into important problems in any field, an approach of intellectual severity and independence. Such inquiry deals with causes and results, with facts and inferences, with comprehensiveness of treatment. The philosopher attempts to relate the separate aspects of knowledge and experience to a common character and end. In addition, he would explore the relationship of knowledge to ultimate values. He inquires into the responsibilities of the communicator and the measures of his social and moral effectiveness.

This present writing grows out of my courses and seminars in "The Philosophical Foundations of Public Address" (or rhetoric) at the University of Missouri for four years, and at Southern Illinois University for five years. These courses and seminars in turn were closely allied with those I have been giving for many years at the University of Iowa in speech criticism and ancient and modern rhetoric. In each course I drew upon the various areas of that subject that gave it method and substance. These principal categories of experience and learning include logic, psychology, ethics, politics, science, literature, language, formal learning, communication itself, and metaphysics. Most of these divisions compose the traditional divisions of philosophy. They form the successive chapters of this book. Unitedly, these academic divisions represent the organon of learning as related to a genuine philosophy of communication. Philosophy is the foundational direction toward which each area moves as it penetrates into the basic principles of its field.

Two sections at the end of the text offer projects and problems suggested in the successive chapters, and a list of background readings to supplement the specific references in the chapters.

My outstanding obligation is to my colleague, Dr. Lester Thonssen, for his original and definitive contribution to speech criticism. The present book attempts to supplement or provide further background for *Speech Criticism,* in the writing of which Lester Thonssen and I collaborated.

My debt to my speech colleagues at the University of Iowa and elsewhere is beyond measure. I have drawn heavily on such writers as Professors Donald Bryant, Loren Reid, Bower Aly, Wilbur S. Howell, Herbert Wichelns, James H. McBurney, Richard Murphy, Karl Wallace, John Hoshor, Everett Hunt, Franklin Knower, Carroll Arnold, Hoyt Hudson, Fred Haberman, Otto Dieter, Marie Hochmuth Nichols, Norwood Brigance, Orville Hitchcock, Ota Thomas Reynolds, Clarence Edney, Margaret Wood, Douglas Ehninger, Waldo Braden, Gregg Phifer, and Gordon Hostettler.

Dr. H. Clay Harshbarger at the State University of Iowa and Ralph Micken at Southern Illinois University gave helpful counsel and encouragement in the evolution of this book.

I freely and fully recognize my reliance on the representative rhetoricians of the past. Since my writing motive has been to adapt the later insights to these traditional theories, I have tried to apply some philosophical judgment in the synthesis of the older and later concepts.

This volume, I hope, may be of service to undergraduate as well as graduate students in courses or seminars in Communicating, English Composition, Rhetoric, Speech, and Public Speaking.

A. CRAIG BAIRD

Iowa City, Iowa
January, 1965

Contents

RHETORIC
A Philosophical Inquiry

1

Boundaries and Applications

Communication in the Space Age

The space age, as speakers and writers have reminded us since 1950, is also the age of communication. The wide distribution and volume of talk and related publications give to this period of post-1960 communicative distinction. In this later twentieth century, the verbal overflow within our nation and without is something new even though Americans have always been speechmakers if not pamphleteers. Around the globe this stepped-up communication is obvious.

Why this accelerated flow of language? The rapid electronic expansion and related transportation and other technical developments partly account for this rapid multiplication of the number and range of voices and personalities. The launching of the Telstar satellite, July 10, 1962, with its transatlantic television broadcasts via the satellite, and the opening of worldwide space communications since then mark the advances.

Role of Communication

A direct link is obvious between cultural and all other progress and oral and written exchange. As Cicero reflected in his *De Oratore:*

For it is by this one gift [speech] that we are distinguished from brute animals, that we converse together, and can express our thoughts by speech. Who therefore would not justly make this an object of admiration, and think it worthy of his utmost exertions, to surpass mankind themselves in that single excellence by which they claim their superiority over brutes? . . . What other power could either have assembled mankind, when dispersed into one place, or have brought them from wild and savage life to the present humane and civilized state of society; or when cities were established have described for them laws, judicial institutions, and rights? [1]

[1] Cicero, *De Oratore*, I, viii, in *Cicero on Oratory and Orators, with Letters to Quintus and Brutus,* tr. J. S. Watson (London, H. G. Bohn, 1855). Note that classical references give book and chapter numbers in upper- and lower-case Roman numerals, respectively; page and line numbers are Arabic in all references.

Speech is an essential civilizing agency. In the home, in factories, on farms, wherever industry, labor, and management carry on the economic life of the community or nation, speaking effectiveness is basic. As Andrew Weaver of the University of Wisconsin stated, "In the United States there are more than twenty thousand different ways of earning a living and effective speech is essential to every one."

Many critics have condemned oral communication as useless and sometimes dangerous. Quintilian stated their case and his rebuttal:

> They say that eloquence frees the wicked, condemns the good, that its greatest use is in making falsehood prevail against truth. The comic poets accused Socrates of teaching how to make the worse appear the better cause, as Plato accuses Tisias and Gorgias. Greece and Rome, these critics say, were upset by harmful eloquence. Sparta banished it, Athens forbade orators to arouse passions. With equal truth they could decry generals, magistrates, medicine, philosophy, since all these are sometimes hurtful. Let us give up foods, houses, swords, fire, water; they sometimes do damage.[2]

As Quintilian suggested, the efficiency of the political community depends partly on the responsible utterances of its members. History, including that of America, in its economic, political, social, and cultural expression, is the record of speechmaking leaders who have importantly influenced attitudes and events. Such speakers are intimately associated with the historical changes. As Rufus Choate said, "It is the peculiarity of some schools of eloquence that they embody and utter, not merely the individual genius and character of the speaker, but a national consciousness—a national era, mood, a hope, a despair—in which you listen to the spoken history of the time."

Such recognition of the necessary role of speech in community life Aristotle made clear at the outset of his *Rhetoric*. To him rhetoric supported truth and justice in their maintenance of their natural superiority. To Aristotle, things that were true and just had a natural tendency to triumph. If error and injustice prevailed, then such unfortunate conditions were due to the weakness of the speakers themselves. Moreover, the influence and necessity of rhetoric were especially important in application to popular audiences that cannot follow complicated scientific demonstrations. To Aristotle, sheer and complicated expositions of the better course are insufficient. The presentation of the best decision must come through oral and written communication addressed to the understanding and comprehensiveness of the people who determine the direction of the body politic.

---

[2] Quintilian, *The Institutio Oratoria of Quintilian*, II, xvi, tr. H. E. Butler (London, Heineman; New York, Putnam, 1920), 4 vols. Cf. condensed summary of this chapter by Charles Edgar Little, *Institutio Oratoria of Marcus Fabius Quintilianus*, 2 vols. (printed for George Peabody College for Teachers, Nashville, Tenn. 1951).

Furthermore rhetoric, according to Aristotle, unfolds the broad per-spective of the case to be decided—surveys all sides of the issue and refutes sufficiently the weak side. "Things that are true and things that are better, are by their very nature easier to prove and to believe in." [3]

Finally, according to Aristotle, rhetoric or communication is a neces-sary defense against artful but sham criticisms that otherwise would pre-vail. To Aristotle it is absurd to hold that a man will be ashamed of his inability to defend himself physically and yet offer no apology for his inability to do so in the realm of reason and rhetoric. The fact that speech may do great harm is no argument for abandoning such resistance to false propaganda. To condemn speech as harmful is similar to the charge that all things useful—health, strength, wealth—are attended by practices that are not always useful or defensible. [4]

To discover the genuine and the spurious means of persuasion is the office of one and the same art. Both genuine and sham rhetoricians will continue to exist.

Such is the Aristotelian exposition of the practical use of oral commu-nication. The Stagirite's concept of the communicative role is confirmed by the subsequent history of rhetoric in national and world affairs.

Meaning of Rhetoric

Our concern here is with the philosophy of rhetoric. Rhetoric is oral and written communication, especially the instrumental type as against literary expression. In popular meaning, "public speaking," "rhetoric," and "communication" are often used interchangeably. [5]

The original and historical interpretation and application of the term "rhetoric" give it breadth and authenticity for continued use in these later decades of the twentieth century.

Originally, rhetoric was the practical art of public speaking in the Athenian Assembly, where the citizens addressed themselves to legisla-tive, administrative, and judicial subjects. The *rhetor* (alternately known as a "sophist") was the speaker, or the teacher of public speaking; such were Corax, Tisias, Gorgias. The rhetorician was also the philosopher-teacher of rhetoric, one who formulated principles and philosophy of that art, as did Plato and Aristotle.

Although rhetoric was chiefly oral, the rhetoricians also conceived of it as written composition. Sometimes rhetorical performances were writ-

[3] Aristotle, *Rhetoric*, 1355a, tr. W. Rhys Roberts, in *The Works of Aristotle Trans-lated into English*, ed. W. D. Ross (Oxford, Clarendon Press, 1924), XI, 1354a–1420b.

[4] *Ibid.*, 1355b.

[5] *Ibid.*, 1413b. Cf. George Pierce Baker, *Forms of Public Address* (New York, Holt, 1904). The latter includes editorials or letters as examples of public address.

ten in full for silent reading. Isocrates, that eminent teacher of rhetoric after 392 B.C. in Athens, called his written works "orations," as he did his *Panegyrics, Archidamus,* and *Areopagiticus.* Whether he delivered public speeches is problematical. Few of his discourses were composed for spoken presentation. Aristotle also included in his *Rhetoric* suggestions for compositions not primarily intended for delivery. "It should be observed that each kind of rhetoric has its own appropriate style. That of written prose is not the same as that of spoken oratory." [6]

Through the later centuries with the increasing aid of printing, the preachers, politicians, educators, agitators of every sort, resorted to broadsides or pamphlets as well as to speeches. Rhetoric thus applies to all types of practical discourse. Milton's *Areopagitica,* although in form an oration as if to be delivered by an Athenian orator, was a pamphlet, strongly logical and persuasive. It proclaimed for Britain freedom of speech and press. It is a great example both of English prose and of rhetoric.

Chauncey Goodrich, first professor of rhetoric at Yale (1817–1838), conceived of communication as both oral and written. He was under the influence of the later eighteenth and early nineteenth century British rhetoricians, who were heavily concerned with literature. The belleslettres movement exemplified by Hugh Blair gave increased attention to rhetorical and literary criticism. Goodrich, like Aristotle, Bacon, and especially Blair, whose text was used at Yale, assumes that all persuasive communication has oral qualities whether or not the document is delivered. To this American critic, British "eloquence" included the letters of Junius, an excerpt from Burke's *Reflections on the French Revolution,* and Sir James Mackintosh's essay on the *Character of Charles J. Fox.* Goodrich stated of Junius:

The letters of Junius have taken a permanent place in the eloquence of our language. Though often false in statement and malignant in spirit, they will never cease to be read as specimens of powerful composition: For union of brilliancy and force, there is nothing superior to them in our literature. Nor is it for his style alone that Junius deserves to be studied. He shows great rhetorical skill in his mode of developing a subject.

Goodrich calls Junius an "orator." "It is therefore only as an orator—for such he undoubtedly was in public life and such he truly is in these letters —that we now consider him." [7]

---

[6] Hoyt Hudson, "The Field of Rhetoric" (3–15), and "Rhetoric and Poetry" (369–382), in Raymond F. Howes (ed.), *Historical Studies of Rhetoric and Rhetoricians* (Ithaca, N.Y., Cornell University Press, 1961).

[7] Chauncey Allen Goodrich, "Essays," in A. Craig Baird (ed.), *Select British Eloquence* (Carbondale, Ill., Southern Illinois University Press, 1963), 80.

Many of the letters of Lincoln, Theodore Roosevelt, and Franklin D. Roosevelt are excellent rhetoric, as have been certain editorials in the *New York Times, New York Herald Tribune, The Nation,* and the *New Republic.* Other examples of rhetorical prose are the syndicated columns by Walter Lippmann and other journalists, and the dissenting opinions of the United States Supreme Court justices, such as those by Justice Oliver Wendell Holmes, Jr.

Oral rhetoric, as expounded and applied by the Greek rhetoricians, aimed especially at persuasion. Rhetoric, to Aristotle, was "the faculty of observing in a given case the available means of persuasion." [8] Such practical aim, to him, was the study of the modes of persuasion—logical, pathetic, ethical, with a view to influencing the audience. However, he went further in his concept of rhetoric: it both surveyed the means and applied them. Not only was it the examination of the available means of this art of developing the logical and motivative elements, but it meant also to him the implementation of these means in the political, ceremonial, and legal speaking situations.

Rhetoric to Aristotle existed to affect the decisions of judges or legislative bodies. The speaker should make his argument decisive, his personality appealing, and his audience receptive.

Aristotle would not only examine the foundational principles, but would translate or incorporate them into modes of effective communication. [9]

Quintilian would add to Aristotle's definition of persuasion, as "the power of speaking," the idea that the orator should be a "good" man. Quintilian concludes that "rhetoric is the science of speaking well." [10] To him the orator must be a "good" man. Cicero, he reminds us, thinks of rhetoric as identified with politics, Isocrates, with philosophy. But, to Quintilian, the term must include also the idea of the speaker's character. To him no one can speak well unless he is a good man. To him, the definition of rhetoric as the power of persuading is insufficient. "Money, dignity, and other elements may persuade." The character and motives of the speaker must be the test of genuine rhetoric. Quintilian cites Plato and Socrates as supporting his view of this art. Plato, in the *Phaedrus,* requires the master of rhetoric to know justice; and the teachers and practitioners of rhetoric, according to Plato, must identify rhetoric with justice. "The style is the man" represents accurately Quintilian's position. The orator, to him, reveals his character—be it good or bad. The true orator or rhetorician must speak with clearness of language and thought, but also with "the power of truth." States he, "For a man's character is

---

[8] Aristotle, *op. cit.,* 1355b.
[9] *Ibid.,* 1355a.
[10] Quintilian, *op. cit.,* II, xv.

generally revealed and the secrets of his heart are laid bare by his manner of speaking, and there is good ground for the Greek aphorism that 'as a man lives, so will he speak.' " [11]

Among recent writers, Donald Bryant undertakes to clarify further this Aristotelian-Quintilian definition. To Bryant, "Rhetoric is the rationale of informative and suasory discourse." [12] All other meanings of rhetoric derive from this view of this art as primarily persuasive. But its informational character must also be recognized. Aristotle, it is true, treated rhetoric as the practical art of the law court and legislative assembly. He was in the tradition of Corax of Syracuse, "the founder of organized rhetoric," who used rhetoric as an argumentative means of grappling with the mass of litigation on claims of property by exiles. Speaking was argumentative and forensic. Aristotle, by implication, also included exposition. Aristotle's discussions of epideictic discourses and his assumptions of definitional and analytical treatment in discourse in general suggest that his rhetoric should also embrace informational materials.

Bryant also seems to support Quintilian's view of rhetoric as demanding ethical quality. Bryant concludes:

> The resolving of such problems [the deciding of "undecidable questions"] is the province of the "good man skilled in speaking." It always has been so, and it still is. Of that there can be little question. And the comprehensive rationale of the functioning of that good man, so far as he is skilled in speaking, so far as he is a wielder of public opinion, is rhetoric.[13]

Within this general area of both spoken and written composition, the theory and practice of rhetoric have received widely varying emphasis. As Bishop Whately put it in his *Elements of Rhetoric*, "different writers seem not so much to have disagreed in their conception of the same things as to have different things in view when they employed the same term." [14] Some rhetoricians, for example, have been concerned with the function of language. R. C. Jebb defines rhetoric as "the art of using language in such a way as to produce a desired impression on the hearer or reader." [15] According to Kenneth Burke, interpreter of the "new rhetoric," "the basic function of rhetoric" is the "use of words by human agents to form atti-

---

[11] *Ibid.*, XI, 1.

[12] Donald Bryant, "Rhetoric: Its Functions and Its Scope," *Quarterly Journal of Speech*, XXXIX (December, 1953), 404 ff.

[13] *Ibid.*, 407.

[14] Richard Whately, *Elements of Rhetoric*, ed. Douglas Ehninger (Carbondale, Ill., Southern Illinois University Press, 1963).

[15] Richard C. Jebb, article "Rhetoric," in *Encyclopaedia Britannica*, Vol. 19, 246 ff.

tudes or to induce actions on other human agents." It is "rooted in an essential function of language itself, a function that is wholly realistic, and is continually born anew; the use of language as a symbolic means of inducing cooperation in beings that by nature respond to symbols."[16]

Thus a good deal of rhetoric of the later Middle Ages and Renaissance identified the subject with language. In the period of the *trivium*, grammar concerned itself with correctness; logic, with the intellectual content; and rhetoric, with the language of the composition. Tropes and figures and the other ancient details of *eloquentia* became the rhetorical fashion. Artificiality and extravagance of word usages prevailed. Hence *Webster's New World Dictionary* defines rhetoric as "The art or science of using words effectively in speaking or writing, so as to influence or persuade; especially, now, the art or science of literary composition, particularly in prose, including the use of figures of speech." Secondary meanings are: "artificial eloquence; showiness and elaboration of language and literary style."[17]

Rhetoric became Elizabethan affectation of style as illustrated by John Lyly's *Eupheus*. Today to many the term continues to connote bombast and tawdry language.

Other rhetoricians became engrossed in the art as comprising almost exclusively the externals of voice, gesture, and other bodily expression. To them rhetoric was "elocution," which "emphasized" the external graces of delivery, especially voice, sometimes gesture.[18] Prominent writers on elocution were Gilbert Austin with his *Chironomia* and John Bulwer with his *Chirologia*.[19]

Still other rhetoricians have concentrated on written composition, while retaining the title, "rhetoric." George R. Carpenter's *Rhetoric and English Composition* contains seventeen chapters, with only the sixteenth treating oral forms.[20] Bernard Jefferson, Harry Houston Peckham, and Hiram Roy Wilson's *Freshman Rhetoric and Practice Book* is typical of

[16] From Kenneth Burke, *A Rhetoric of Motives*, 36–41; copyright 1950 by Prentice-Hall, Inc., Englewood Cliffs, N.J. Quoted by Marie Hochmuth in "Kenneth Burke and the New Philosophy," *Quarterly Journal of Speech*, XXXVIII (April, 1952), 135.

[17] *Webster's New World Dictionary, College Edition* (Cleveland and New York, World Publishing, 1953). See also Wilbur Samuel Howell, "Renaissance Rhetoric and Modern Rhetoric: A Study in Change," in Donald C. Bryant (ed.), *The Rhetorical Idiom* (Ithaca, N.Y., Cornell University Press, 1958), 53–70.

[18] *Webster's Collegiate Dictionary* (5th ed.; Springfield, Mass., G. & C. Merriam, 1943).

[19] See for example, Frederick W. Haberman, "English Sources of American Elocution," in Karl R. Wallace (ed.), *History of Speech Education in America* (New York, Appleton-Century-Crofts, 1954), 105–129.

[20] George R. Carpenter, *Rhetoric and English Composition* (New York, Macmillan, 1906).

composition texts of the first quarter of the twentieth century. The Jefferson-Peckham-Wilson book ignores *oral* rhetoric.[21]

The later tendency, as Donald Bryant reminds us, is to prefer "composition" or "basic writing," or some similar course description or title that indicates written prose.[22] In recent years departments of speech have largely taken over courses and writings in "rhetoric," and have renewed emphasis on the more historical, classical usage of the word. The required course in "communicative skills" at the State University of Iowa was not long ago relabelled "rhetoric" to describe its instruction in both written and oral communication.

Purposes of Rhetoric

What is the goal to which the teacher, the practitioner of rhetoric, and the philosopher and critic of the subject are committed? That aim has been and still is chiefly to influence an audience to think, feel, and act in harmony with the communicative purposes of the speaker or writer. Audience response has been central in Aristotle's doctrine and in that of most recent rhetoricians. The measure of communicative effectiveness lies in audience behavior, the extent to which the auditor-hearers or readers may be said to:

1. Gain new insight into the theme.
2. Quicken their imagination and emotion through increased understanding of what is already known to them.
3. Move to greater or lesser conviction relating to the topic.
4. Move to covert or overt action.

Such an aim is heavily persuasive, as Aristotle and his students, both contemporary and modern, decided.

But this speaking influence and reaction might result not only through full-fledged argumentative-motivative discourse, but through other communicative aims with results not always reflected in direct action.

These rhetorical purposes as usually listed in treatises of today deal with:

1. Information
2. Ceremony
3. Conviction
4. Persuasion
5. Discussion

[21] Bernard Jefferson, Harry Houston Peckham, and Hiram Roy Wilson, *Freshman Rhetoric and Practice Book* (New York, Doubleday, Doran, 1928). Cf. texts with similar treatment: Adams Sherman Hill, *The Foundations of Rhetoric* (New York, Harper and Bros., 1892); Alphonso G. Newcomer, *Elements of Rhetoric* (New York, Holt, 1906).

[22] Bryant, *op. cit.*, 403. Cf. Arthur K. Moore, "Rhetoric's Wrung Neck," *Western Humanities Review*, XVII (Winter, 1963), 51–62.

6. Criticism
7. Entertainment
8. Some combination of these purposes

The communicator may attempt to convey information and find satisfaction if his audience increases its knowledge. Or he may impress the audience with the virtues of some individual, institution, or event and note the fulfillment of his discourse if the responses indicate a greater appreciation of the person or event. Or the reverse purpose may be to evoke condemnation of an event, individual, or unworthy institution.

He may aim primarily at the intellectual response as effective if conviction is achieved or increased. His materials are primarily those of fact, logic, reasoning, with a minimum of assertion and unrestrained emotionalism.

Or his aim and method may be to actuate through the combination of logical processes with those of balanced persuasion (this concept is here limited to describe motivative factors).[23]

The speaking aim may be that of discussion rather than argumentation and debate. The purpose here is not so much to directly influence others to think and act according to the speaker's beliefs and behavior, as to seek a common sharing in the analysis of a problem, the definition of its terms, the framing of possible outcomes, and the determination of the preferred course of action or belief. Debate and discussion are complementary in that the final or debating positions may end the reflective and social character of genuine discussion—but may later lead again to conditions of inquiry which distinguish discussion. Discussional speaking is similar to that of ancient dialectic—which form Aristotle and other writers failed to feature as a distinct type of address.

Sometimes the purpose may be that of criticism, as distinct from argumentative or persuasive discourse. Criticism, as an intellectual activity, is more closely identified with informative speaking and writing. Such procedure may consist of reports to classes, clubs, committees. It may be a report on a personal experience, a piece of research, a book, the analysis and evaluation of a speaker, a literary production, a play, or on a painting, sculpture, or some other creative work.

Finally, the principal aim of the communication may be that of entertainment. The speaker succeeds if his audience enjoy themselves through his lively recital of events by his vivid descriptions.

Since rhetoric aims at influencing an audience with regard to their beliefs, knowledge, and behavior (overt decisions), the rhetoricians have given little support to entertainment as a significant communicative type. Its more creative elements suggest its alliance with description, narration,

[23] A. Craig Baird and Franklin H. Knower, *General Speech* (New York, McGraw-Hill, 1963), Chap. 18, "Persuasive Speaking."

and other types of literary expression. At its worst it is third-rate dinner speaking. Socrates, for his discussional purposes, would compare such rhetoric with cookery—that is, flattery aiming at gratification and pleasure.

These various rhetorical purposes obviously overlap. Primarily, this art exists to affect the attitudes and conduct of an audience. In developing such outcomes, the discourse usually includes informational details, logical and factual materials, motivative appeals, including those details to interest and even entertain. However these partial aims and techniques are distributed, the aim and end is unitary. The more concrete purposes as suggested by modern rhetoricians may specialize in any one of the processes suggested above. But the over-all governing aim is to influence the individuals and their fellows to adapt to and demonstrate certain standards of conduct.

The audience is thus the key factor in this communicative process. No matter how active and able the communicator, no matter how impressive and convincing his theme and its language, if the audience is unresponsive, the result is failure. Their goals, intelligence, nationality, sex, education, occupations, cultural interests, economic and other attitudes and interests, their needs, wants, and desires, all explain the measure of their individual and combined reactions.[24]

Rhetoric as Measured by Its Influence

The speaker is confronted with the problem of effect. As Herbert Wichelns observed of rhetorical criticism, "It is not concerned with permanence nor yet with beauty. It is concerned with effect. It regards a speech as a communication to a specific audience, and holds its business to be the analysis and appreciation of the orator's method of imparting his ideas to his hearers." [25] Similarly, Lester Thonssen writes, "Orators

[24] For variety of approaches to organization and treatment of speech and public speaking, see, for example: John W. Black and Wilbur E. Moore, Speech: Code, Meaning and Communication (New York, McGraw-Hill, 1955); Waldo Braden and Ernest Brandenberg, Oral Decision Making (New York, Harper, 1955); Winston Brembeck and William S. Howell, Persuasion (Englewood Cliffs, N.J., Prentice-Hall, 1952); W. N. Brigance, Speech (New York, Appleton-Century-Crofts, 1952); Giles H. Gray and Waldo Braden, Public Speaking Principles and Practice (New York, Harper, 1951); Alan Monroe, Principles and Types of Speech (Chicago, Scott Foresman, 1951); James H. McBurney and Ernest Wrage, The Art of Good Speech (Englewood Cliffs, N.J., Prentice-Hall, 1955); G. W. Gray and C. M. Wise, The Bases of Speech (New York, Harper, 1959); Donald Bryant and Karl Wallace, Fundamentals of Public Speaking (New York, Appleton-Century-Crofts, 1953–1960); Loren Reid, First Principles of Public Speaking (Columbia, Mo., Artcraft Press, 1962).

[25] Herbert Wichelns, "The Literary Criticism of Oratory," in Studies in Rhetoric and Public Speaking in Honor of James Albert Winans (New York, Century Co., 1925), 209.

will be judged by what they accomplished, either immediately or in the long run of public affairs." [26]

The judges of communication attempt to estimate the immediate impact of the speaker on his immediate audience. Applause, laughter, impromptu cries or other evidence of approbation (or the reverse), votes, register of immediate opinion through ballots, estimate of audience reaction by recordings by judges or reporters, and other measures attempt to gauge this impact during and at the conclusion of a speech (or series of speeches).[27]

Some commentators have stressed the major aim as perfection of performance rather than effect on the audience. James McBurney and Ernest J. Wrage, for example, observe:

> The Results Theory ignores the very important and easily demonstrable fact that factors other than the speech are always operating along with the speech to influence the outcome. Rather than measuring a speech by its results, and thus falling into this trap which has deluded many speakers, critics and educators with such unfortunate outcomes, the critic who applies the Artistic Theory judges a speech by the principles of the Art.[28]

The critical reply to this "perfection" approach as a measuring of communicative excellence is that the gauging of such results inevitably calls for explanations of *why* the audience seems to behave thus or so. If auditor-observers respond as suggested by their votes, why do they do so? Thus the measure of effect involves the review of the process itself —the focusing on the communicator's personality, the ideas of the discourse, its structure, language, adaptation to situation and audience, the delivery and all else that may explain the outcome.

But the aim of the efficient communicator, as the Greek rhetoricians suggested, was wider than that of developing a highly artistic product. The aim, for example, was broader than that of delivering a well-composed discourse. The purpose was more than that of immediate persuasion of an audience, as Demosthenes did against Philip at Chalcedon. It was more than that of supplying information to the audience, or of developing a logical series of arguments well buttressed by emotional appeals and personal proofs; more than pervading all with stylistic expression that would at once clarify, adapt, and adorn; more than the unfolding of a pattern as well rounded and arranged as in Greek architecture. Aristotle and his fellow philosopher-rhetoricians asked in each case, Why this discourse and these techniques? What were the aims of the communicator? Their answer, still dominant in communication aims today, was

26 Lester Thonssen and A. Craig Baird, *Speech Criticism* (New York, Ronald Press, 1948), 448.

27 *Ibid.*, Chap. 17, "Measures of Effectiveness."

28 From *The Art of Good Speech* by James H. McBurney and Ernest Wrage (pp. 29, 30). Copyright 1953 by Prentice-Hall, Inc., Englewood Cliffs, N.J.

and is that communication is for the purpose of motivating an audience toward the progress of a free society and a good society. What happens to an audience is more significant than the skill or artistry of the technique.

The Rhetorical Medium

Behind this purpose of communication to achieve social coordination or influence lies the concept of directed purpose rather than of aimless discourse. Communicators do so not simply to hear themselves use words, but rather to secure responses.

Every communicative situation, therefore, involves at least five constituents: the agent-communicator; the recipient (audience); the occasion; the speech or document to be transmitted; and the communicative act itself, constituted by the voice, physical expression and the personality of the communicator. The entire process begins with the stimulus or course of stimulation in the agent, and goes on to the formulation of his concepts in specific symbolic forms, the verbalizations for overt expression; the process of transmission through air waves and light waves (voice, articulation, and bodily activity) to stimulate the observer-listener; and the succeeding stages that determine the extent and character of his responses.[29]

According to Wendell Johnson, "To understand speech, or the communicative process in general, is to be aware of the various functions, the modes and degrees of attenuation, the patterns of formulation, and the disorders operating at each stage of the process—and the complex pattern of relationships among the various stages." To Johnson, communication begins with some external "event" that stimulates the organs of the speaker. This stimulation passes from a previsceral state into the framing of ideas and words for overt expression. This communicative process then continues by light waves and sound waves (voice and physical accompaniments) to stimulate the listener. He in turn translates the ideas and words and so "responds" to the original speaker. The entire process is described as "circular response"—completing the circuit from speaker to auditor and again to the speaker. See Chapter 8 for further discussion of Johnson's interpretation of this communicative process.[30]

The Parts of Rhetoric

In the classical tradition, rhetoric consisted of five parts: invention, disposition, elocution, memory, and delivery, or pronunciation. These divi-

[29] Thonssen and Baird, op. cit., 5–8.

[30] Wendell Johnson, "The Spoken Word and the Great Unsaid," Quarterly Journal of Speech, XXXVIII (December, 1951), 425. See also Wendell Johnson, People in Quandaries (New York, Harper, 1946), Chap. 18; and Lyman Bryson (ed.), The Communication of Ideas (New York, Harper, 1948), Chap. 5, "Speech and Personality."

sions, discrete for purposes of analysis and criticism, were an organic unit in their basic purpose, with the "parts" mutually dependent and indistinguishable in their over-all functioning.

These constituents of rhetoric were first expounded in the *Rhetorica ad Herennium* (sometimes attributed to Cicero) published in 86 B.C. "In many respects they constitute the basic pattern of all theoretical and critical investigations into the art and practice of speaking."[31]

Each part had its function. Invention (*inventio*, εὕρεσις) refers to the investigation, analysis, and grasp of subject matter.[32] Content is thus emphasized in Aristotle and in subsequent rhetoricians. It involves status (στάσις), the issues and proofs (πίστεις) —logical, pathetic (emotional) (πάθος), and ethical (ἦθος) —and the topics for development (τόποι).

Disposition (*collocutio*, τάξις) covers the concept of arrangement, of orderly planning, of structure. It deals with both the plan as a whole and the treatment of the specific parts of the speech, including the exordium, proposition, narration, proof, refutation, and peroration. The principles of structure have to do with selection of materials, their order, their relevance, and their proportion or mass.

Style (*elocutio*, λέξις), or composition included the concept of expression in language, both with respect to choice of words (*electio*, ἐκλογή), and their arrangement in larger units of the composition (*compositio*, σύνθεσις).

Cicero (in his *Orator*) and other classical rhetoricians analyzed style also in its broad character as plain, medium, and grand or sublime.[33]

Memory (μνήμη) referred to the speaker's mastery of his composition and his ability to deliver it without notes. Cicero, Quintilian, and other ancients emphasized memory, but such treatment practically disappeared in the rhetorical treatises after the seventeenth century. Present-day rhetoric discusses it as a phase of the problem of delivery in extemporization, memorization, or oral reading.[34]

Delivery (*pronuntiatio*, *actio*, ὑπόκρισις) has to do with vocal utterance and bodily activity, with movements in general, gestures, and posture. It was treated scantily by Aristotle, but in later rhetoric became a major section of the subject.[35]

These ancient designations of the "parts" of discourse have long ago

[31] Thonssen and Baird, *op. cit.*, 77–78. See also Quintilian's *Institutio Oratoria*: III, vi; VI, v; VII; VIII; IX; XI.

[32] Charles Sears Baldwin, *Ancient Rhetoric and Poetic* (New York, Macmillan, 1924), 43.

[33] Cicero, *De Oratore*, III, x, xiv, xxv, xxxviii, *Orator*, 403–444. Cf. Thomas Gibbons, *Rhetoric* (London, J. W. Oliver, 1767).

[34] Cicero, *De Oratore*, II, lxxxvii; Quintilian, *op. cit.*, XI.

[35] Quintilian, *op. cit.*, X, vii; XI, iii. Cf. Thomas Sheridan, *Lectures on Elocution* (London, J. Dodsley, 1781), 6 ff.; Gilbert Austin, *Chironomia* (London, T. Cadell & W. Davies, 1806); Richard Whately, *op. cit.*, 224 ff.; Thonssen and Baird, *op. cit.*, Chap. 3.

lost their labellings and sharp categories. Their classificational interpretations, nevertheless, continue to furnish basic elements for contemporary expositions of speech and rhetoric. Texts of speech have chapters or sections on the subject and materials; definition and analysis; supporting details; audience adaptation through motivative and personal materials; organization; language usages; speaking personality; vocal effectiveness; articulation and pronunciation; gesture, platform poise, and movement; and similar topics. These communicative techniques turn out to be phases of classical invention, disposition, language, and delivery.

Even when a special kind of speaking, as in political debate, business speaking, or radio and television communication, is treated as an exclusive study, the four or five components suggested above continue to form the central core of the subject. These elements, it should be remembered, are the aspects of a single communicative process. In the execution, the ideas, language, and voice act in unison to stimulate the listener-observer. Only for convenience and diagnosis are these "parts" separate entities. Together they compose the communicative movement. No one of them functions without identification with the others, even though the connection may be covert.

Summary and Conclusion

Rhetoric was originally applied chiefly to public address, especially to the deliberative, forensic, and demonstrative types, with the corresponding written forms. The term we have identified with all types of practical (instrumental) communication, oral and written. The possible distinctions between rhetoric and literary expression we have examined in detail in Chapter 10.

The purposes of rhetoric were principally those of persuasion, but have been gradually extended to include the various ends of exposition, entertainment, discussion, and criticism, or combinations of such purposes.

Rhetorical discourse is measured by its influence on an immediate or larger audience. The audience is thus the key factor in the communicative process. But the analysis or explanation of the factors at work in such audience reaction leads to a systematic examination of the components of the entire process: the speaker or agent that evokes the stimulation; the speech or written document itself; the time and place, with their conditioning of the agent and his message; and the audience themselves as readers, hearers, observers.

The "parts" or components of the composition itself are invention, disposition, language, and (if the communication is oral), memory and delivery.

The total functioning of the communicative act is to be related to the social motives of the communicator. Only that discourse is valid which tends to support a more satisfactory social-political climate. Rhetoric is justified only if it contributes to the "good society."

The next chapter will deal in detail with the approaches to rhetoric by way of literature, philosophy, and other avenues.

2

Relationships to Categories of Learning

Rhetoric and Categories of Learning

Rhetoric does not function as an isolated discipline with its own subject matter, but draws on various areas of learning that give it method and substance. The principal categories of experience and learning, all to be related to philosophy, include logic, psychology, ethics, politics, science, literature, language, rhetoric, and metaphysics.

Most of these compose the traditional divisions of philosophy, such as ethics, politics, metaphysics, aesthetics, logic, and theory of knowledge. These divisions, academically conceived and described, obviously overlap. Each, as in formal education, may be treated separately for instruction and institutional administration. Unitedly, they represent the organon of learning.

The diagram opposite illustrates the relation of rhetoric and other categories of experience and learning to philosophy.

Philosophy is the foundational direction toward which each area moves as it penetrates into the basic principles of its own field.

Each area is to be conceived of in terms of its appropriation of data, its framing of techniques in pursuit of its learning aims, its development of principles and a rationale to direct its discipline and, finally, its philosophy.

The divisions of learning and experience are a unit. Each is set off and labelled in discrete segments. Obviously, these categories overlap. Obviously, most of them depend on other divisions for full assimilation of given materials and mutually dependent techniques. These units are reciprocal in their functioning.

In rhetoric, the agent, the audience, the communicative situation, the

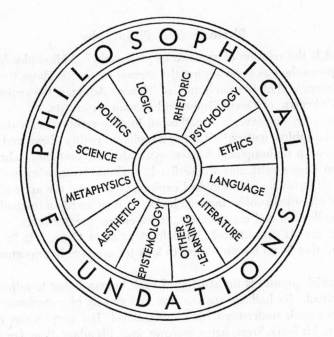

discourse itself, and the process of stimulus and response trace directly or indirectly to these representative subject matter and method areas.

For example, a speech may be a measure of disjointed, haphazard, or conversely of firm logic. The speaker acts through his personality, compounded of intellectual and emotional activities. He is strongly impelled by motives that in the best functioning are keyed to the needs, motives, and sentiments of the respondents. The agent's ethical-moral principles, if he is so conditioned, may pervade the speech and its utterance. The political milieu that characterizes the ideological climate of the day also largely determines the content and appeals of the discourse. Language symbolization by which the ideas and intents are conveyed may take on a clearness and embellishment which impart literary distinction to the style.

Other categories of learning, science, for example, also help to mold the matter and manner of a given discourse. Thus rhetoric is a composite of these contributory subject matter and art disciplines, all shaped, however, to produce a communication at a given time and place.[1]

1 Donald Bryant, "Some Problems in the Scope and Method in Rhetorical Scholarship," *Quarterly Journal of Speech,* XXXIII (April, 1937), 182, 189; Hoyt Hudson, "The Field of Rhetoric," *Quarterly Journal of Speech,* IX (April, 1923), 167–180; Maurice Natanson, "The Limits of Rhetoric," *Quarterly Journal of Speech,* XII (April, 1955), 133–139; Lester Thonssen and A. Craig Baird, *Speech Criticism* (New York, Ronald Press, 1948), Chap. 1.

Rhetoric and Philosophy

What is the relation of rhetoric to philosophy? Philosophy has often been approached as representing the eternal reality of Plato; the seat of First Causes and of Eternal Truth, of Thomas Aquinas; the region of the Great Unknown, of David Hume and of many scientists.

Philosophy, however, is a method of inquiry rather than a depository for special subject matter.[2] It is not a region of reality above and beyond other areas, a philosophical heaven, with absolute certainty, where mysteries no longer exist and where fixed, unalterable answers are spelled out for all fortunate philosophical explorers. It is not the apex of a hierarchy of classified subject matter blocks. It is primarily a method, rather than a collection and classification, of lesser and greater facts.

What are its procedures? Its definition, as in Greece, is "a love of wisdom," that is, an intense desire to look for answers to important problems.

Its initial impulse is the stirring of each human being to adjust to his environment. So baffling are the ups and downs of experience and so little does each understand his surroundings! His perplexities echo or aggravate his fears, loves, hates, sorrows, joys; his adaptations (or failures of adaptation) to survival, health, occupation, recreation, worship, education, family and community, tribal and state relations, war and peace.

Some problems may be trivial, easily solved, endured, or forgotten. The more important ones persist and call for more subtle reflection. These are the issues that evoke the philosopher—a person who reflects systematically in the face of these broader questions.

How does he react? If he is a genuine thinker, he exercises intellectual vigor. He sees clear-eyed his problematic situation. He is in close

[2] Brand Blanshard, *The Nature of Thought*, 2 vols. (London, Allen & Unwin, 1939); John Dewey, *Reconstruction in Philosophy* (New York, Holt, 1920); Durant Drake, *Invitation to Philosophy* (Boston and New York, Houghton Mifflin, 1933); David Hume, *An Enquiry Concerning Human Understanding* (Oxford, Oxford University Press, 1951); C. E. M. Joad, *Guide to Philosophy* (New York, Random House, 1939); William James, *Essays in Pragmatism* (New York, Hafner, 1948); John Locke, *An Essay Concerning Human Understanding* (London, Dent, 1947); Houston Peterson, *Essays in Philosophy* (New York, Pocket Library, 1859); Joseph Ratner (ed.), *Intelligence in the Modern World, John Dewey's Philosophy* (New York, Modern Library, 1939); Bertrand Russell, *The Problems of Philosophy* (New York, Holt, 1943); Bertrand Russell, *A History of Western Philosophy* (New York, Simon & Schuster, 1945); T. V. Smith and Marjorie Greene, *From Descartes to Kant* (Chicago, University of Chicago Press, 1947); E. W. F. Tomlin, *The Great Philosophers* (New York, A. A. Wyn, 1952); Morton White, *The Age of Analysis* (New York, Mentor Books, 1955); Morton White, "New Horizons in Philosophy," *Central State Speech Journal*, XII (Spring, 1961), 188–196; Abraham Wolf, "History of Philosophy," in *Encyclopaedia Britannica*, Vol. 17 (1929); Susanne Langer, *Philosophy in a New Key* (New York, Mentor Books, 1948).

company with the scientists. He is no armchair deductionist, but an observer and a participant.

His mission is not only to face and survey the situation. He is also to label and define it by language symbols that clarify the problem. He also effectively reduces the perplexing factors to a series of questions and definitions to be explored.

His preliminary survey of the problem leads him to inquire "Why?" "With what results?" "By what means?" He becomes a logician in action. He raises tentative questions, even though no answers may be in immediate prospect. He moves in the direction of foundational issues. He refuses to be limited by certified statistics and other specific data. Unlike the scientist, he goes beyond the immediate evidence. He is, however, no more casuist. He does continually refer to antecedent conclusions and available testimony. But he allows no limits to his questions, except that they are tentative, to be constantly reframed; his method calls for wider and wider examination of causes and results. In this pursuit, born of curiosity or expediency, he is following the activities of all men of all ages. As philosopher, he attempts to be systematic. His horizon calls at least for consistent explanation. His roles as historian, psychologist, logician, rhetorician, scientist, and philosopher, all move him to trace causative activities. Edmund Burke, the English parliamentary debater, was described by Chauncey Goodrich as "the great philosophical orator of our language." [3]

What were Burke's marks as a philosopher? According to Goodrich, this eighteenth century British speaker continually raised such questions as "Why?" "Whence?" Burke was attempting to deal with man "in all his multiple relations as the creature of society, to trace out the workings of political institutions, to establish principles of wise legislation, to lay open the sources of national security and advancement."

Another mark of the philosopher is his power of generalization. Here again Goodrich found that Burke had rare philosophical qualities. Burke was one who could "gather all the results of his thinking as by an elective affinity around their appropriate centers; and knowing that truths are valuable just in proportion as they have wider reach, to rise from particulars to generals, and so to shape his statements as to give them the weight and authority of universal propositions." [4] This ability to reason from the simple to the complex, from the concrete to the abstract, through alternate inductive and deductive steps, identifies the philosopher.

Still another characteristic of the philosopher is his comprehensiveness of treatment. He has somewhat the breadth of outlook that Goodrich

[3] Chauncey Goodrich, "Essays," in A. Craig Baird (ed.), *Select British Eloquence* (Carbondale, Ill., Southern Illinois University Press, 1963), 97.
[4] *Ibid.*, 153–154.

attributed to Burke: "He looked upon a subject like a man standing on an eminence taking a large and rounded view of it on every side, contemplating each of its parts under a vast variety of relations, and these relations often extremely complex and remote. There was no subject on which he had not read, no system relating to the interests of man as a social being which he had not thoroughly explored." [5]

Thus the philosopher has amplitude of learning, that amplitude of learning which permits contemplation of any limited area in its complex relations to the wider movements and systems. He, more than most other investigators, relates the separate aspects of knowledge and experience to a common character and end. To the philosopher, economic questions are also political, social, psychological, and even moral and ethical.

One final characteristic of the philosopher is implicit in what we have said. We refer to the relationship of his postulates to moral values and ends. His inquiry is both "What are the responsibilities of the speaker?" and "What are measures of effectiveness?" His answers impel him to examine the structure of society, its attitudes, trends, and goals. Just as he frames a concept of the ideal political institutions against which to judge the worth of the deliberative and forensic speeches, so does he posit behind all communicative situations—political, social, legal, didactic—a design of truth as he understands it. His examination, for example, leads him to psychology, politics, and dialectic; dialectic, to logic; and logic, in turn, to ethics and metaphysics.

As Richard M. Weaver concluded from his analysis of the *Phaedrus* and the nature of rhetoric, "All of the terms in a rhetorical vocabulary are like links in a chain stretching up to some master link which transmits its influence down through the linkage. It is impossible to talk about rhetoric as effective expression without having as a term giving intelligibility to the whole discourse, *the Good*." [6]

Thus philosophy is governed by its direction. It adopts the method of endless exploration, of evolution. It may not have the answers but its practitioners are in eternal quest, to illuminate dark places and minimize the mysteries. Their procedures, from ancient thinkers to those of the present hour, have given leadership, knowledge, and principles to those who would deal with man and his civilization.

What then is the relation of rhetoric to philosophy? Philosophy provides a method by which rhetoric (communication oral and written) selects subject and subject matter of importance; defines terms; develops ideas and their supports with full regard for their logical and psychological validity and significance to an audience; generalizes with due

[5] *Ibid.*, 152.
[6] Richard M. Weaver, *The Ethics of Rhetoric* (Chicago, Henry Regnery, 1953), 23.

account of the details and then moves from the concrete to the abstract, always with due regard for logical consistency in the successive steps; views the subject in its relation to related areas of knowledge; sets up goals that follow through the approaches from the simple to the complex, and that indicate a direction consistent with value judgments.

These approaches are common to the various areas of learning. What stamps them as philosophical is the completeness with which they are applied.

Rhetoric, Art, and Science

Rhetoric is a method of directing and focusing techniques and principles to the specific end of affecting audience attitudes, ideas, and behavior. It is a practical rather than a fine art. It is "the art of adapting discourse in harmony with its subject and occasion to the requirements of the reader or hearer." [7]

As an art, it contrasts with science and other subject matter areas. Science is "systematized knowledge," whereas art utilizes such knowledge to produce skill in the actual execution of discourse. Rhetoric appropriates the disciplines, scientific, logical, ethical, on which this methodology rests. The other representative disciplines confine themselves to an accumulation and interpretation of principles and knowledge. *Communication is the one process that transforms these learnings into creative applications.* Its role is exclusively the transformation of these contingent learnings into materials applied to secure audience responses. Its peculiar function is to stimulate ideas through logical, emotional, and imaginative means of language, organization, and delivery, so that a speaker may "persuade a multitude of persons to renounce their opinions, to change their course of life." [8]

This concept of rhetoric as a practical art and its differentiation from subject matter fields Aristotle had in mind when he observed that persuasion "is not the function of any other art. But rhetoric we look upon as the power of observing the means of persuasion on almost any subject presented to us; and that is why we say that, in its technical character, it is not concerned with any definite class of subjects." [9]

[7] John F. Genung, *Practical Elements of Rhetoric* (Boston and New York, Ginn, 1887), 1.

[8] *The Complete Writings of Ralph Waldo Emerson, Centenary Edition,* 12 vols. (New York, Houghton Mifflin, 1903–31), Vol. 2, 1030.

[9] Aristotle, *Rhetoric,* 1355b, 27–36. Cf. also Donald Bryant, "Rhetoric: Its Functions and Its Scope," *Quarterly Journal of Speech,* XXXIX (December, 1953), 401–424. "To rhetoric and to no other rationale belongs the efficiency—the validity if you will—of the relations in the idea-speaker-audience situation" (p. 413).

Rhetoric, Dialectic, and Logic

The central factor in rhetoric is invention; that is, the area of idea and intellectual content and method.

Aristotle suggested that rhetoric was the "counterpart" of dialectic (logical discussion), which was based on logical principles. He was impelled to write his rhetoric because he felt that his predecessors had neglected to give logical materials their deserved place in speechmaking. Said he, "These writers, however, say nothing about enthymemes [that is, logical arguments], which are the substance of rhetorical persuasion, but deal mainly with non-essentials." [10] Although he gave emotional and ethical proofs full treatment, he held that logical methods were the most important factor and that the communicative act was a rational demonstration. Thus Aristotle would have the public speaker and student of speaking grapple with ideas, political, social, legal, but would make the interpretations and applications in the speaking situation through effective control of the syllogisms (enthymemes). The orator's demonstration is an enthymeme, "and this is in general, the most effective of the modes of persuasion. . . . It follows plainly, therefore, that he who is best able to see how and from what elements a syllogism is produced will also be best skilled in the enthymeme." [11] He would have the student and practitioner skillful in the demonstrative and refutative enthymemes, and in examples. Aristotle's *Rhetoric* was an offshoot of his general writings and lectures as "the founder of rhetoric." His *Categories, Interpretation, Posterior Analytics, The Topics,* and *Sophistical Elenchi* (called by his followers, the *Organon*) comprise his larger view of the area.

Whereas logic is abstract, analytic, a method of study, a "science," rhetoric is concrete, synthetic.[12] Thus rhetoricians then and since have stressed propositions, terms, presumptions, inferences, issues, burden of proofs; have classified arguments and tested them as syllogistic reasoning and as refutation; and have classified and examined fallacies. Francis Bacon contributed inductive patterns; [13] George Campbell, the theory of logical truth; [14] Richard Whately, argumentative composition.[15]

[10] *Rhetoric,* 1354a, 14–15.

[11] *Ibid.,* 1355b, 6–13.

[12] Charles Sears Baldwin, "Aristotle," in Paul Monroe (ed.), *Cyclopedia of Education* (New York, Macmillan, 1919), Vol. 5, 173–179; Charles Sears Baldwin, *Ancient Rhetoric and Poetic* (New York, Macmillan, 1924), 8.

[13] Francis Bacon, *The Advancement of Learning,* ed. W. A. Wright (Oxford, Clarendon Press, 1891). See also Karl R. Wallace, "Bacon's Conception of Rhetoric," *Speech Monographs,* III (1936), 21–48.

[14] George Campbell, *The Philosophy of Rhetoric,* ed. Lloyd F. Bitzer (Carbondale, Ill., Southern Illinois University Press, 1963).

[15] Richard Whately, *Elements of Rhetoric,* ed. Douglas Ehninger (Carbondale, Ill., Southern Illinois University Press, 1963).

Whately, in his preface to his *Elements of Rhetoric,* referred to his own work on *Logic* and stated that "several passages will be found in the following pages which presuppose some acquaintance with Logic. . . . At the same time, it is implied by what I have said of that Science, and indeed by the very circumstance of my having written on it, that I cannot but consider him as undertaking a task of unnecessary difficulty, who endeavors, without studying logic, to become a thoroughly good argumentative writer." [16]

In this section we have suggested the close identification of rhetoric with logic and the primacy of the intellectual quality in discourse. The following chapters analyze in detail the Aristotelian and later interpretations of logic and the relation of that field to psychology and ethics in communication.

Rhetoric and Psychology

The primacy of logic in communicative appeals has nevertheless implied also the important place of emotion in the process.

Aristotle, as we have suggested, saw clearly the role of the audience and the necessity of adaptation to them. To Aristotle, therefore, the speaker must know their character, the motives that govern them, and the pathetic (emotional) proofs that should influence their behavior. Aristotle gives Book I to the speaker, and a considerable part of Book II to the audience. "Proofs," Aristotle reminded his students, may be conveyed through the audience when the speech creates for them an emotional state. "Our judgments when we are pleased and friendly are not the same as when we are pained and hostile." [17] Aristotle, in Book II, analyzes the representative emotions, including calmness, friendship and enmity, fear and confidence, kindness and unkindness, pity, indignation, envy, emulation. Each is treated with respect to "(*a*) the states of mind in which it is felt; (*b*) the people towards whom it is felt; and (*c*) the ground on which it is felt." [18]

This approach to rhetoric in ancient writing and teaching has also permeated representative rhetorical thinking since Cicero; for example, *De Oratore* discusses audience analysis and the technique of pathetic proof with special application to legal situations.

The first modern attempt to provide a systematic treatment of psychological concepts was made by George Campbell in his *Philosophy of Rhetoric:*

When persuasion is the end, passion must also be engaged. . . . To say that it is possible to persuade without speaking to the passions is but, at best,

16 *Ibid.,* p. xvi.
17 *Rhetoric,* 1356a, 14–17.
18 *Ibid.,* 1378a, 22–30.

a kind of specious nonsense. The coolest reasoner always, in persuading, addresseth himself to the passions some way or other. This he cannot avoid doing if he speaks to the purpose. . . . To make me believe, it is enough to show me that things are so; to make me act, it is necessary to show me that the action will answer some end.[19]

Most writers on speech and public speaking, adopting the interpretation of contemporary psychologies, have expounded the techniques of audience analysis and adaptation with emphasis on bodily and social bases of persuasion, attitudes, sentiments, and stereotypes in persuasion, and on such psychological forms as suggestion, "common ground," prestige, and word manipulations.

Charles Woolbert, with a doctorate in psychology at Harvard, discussed at length the adaptation of monistic psychology and urged the necessity of rewriting the theory of rhetoric to fit the new psychological findings. Wrote Woolbert, "To study persuasion intensively is to study human nature minutely. Without a guide to men's action probabilities, without appreciating and understanding their action grooves, a speaker or writer works in a vacuum and so has no possible basis for insuring success."[20]

James Winans, in his *Public Speaking*,[21] also incorporated the applications to public speaking of such psychologists as William James, Gustav Le Bon, William McDougall, John Dewey, E. A. Ross, E. L. Thorndike, and E. B. Titchener. Winans had much to say about attention, emotional attitudes, common ground, characteristics of crowds, derived interest, emotion, motives, imagination, memory, personality, prejudice, and sentiments.

Later Winston L. Brembeck and William Smiley Howell contributed *Persuasion*,[22] a discussion of the means of social control, heavily weighted, as the title indicates, by psychological principles and methods. Similar was Robert Oliver's *The Psychology of Persuasive Speech*,[23] with extensive analysis of motivation in human affairs, principles of attention, suggestion, identification, and modes of appeal, including emotion and imagination.

These rhetoricians, although their chief interest and knowledge are

[19] George Campbell, *op. cit.*, 77.

[20] Charles Henry Woolbert, "Conviction and Persuasion: Some Considerations of Theory," *Quarterly Journal of Public Speaking*, II (July, 1917), 249–264; "Persuasion: Principles and Method, *Quarterly Journal of Speech Education*, V (January, 1919), 12–25; V (March, 1919), 10–19; V (May, 1919), 211–38.

[21] James Winans, *Public Speaking* (2d ed.; New York, Century Co., 1917).

[22] Winston L. Brembeck and William Smiley Howell, *Persuasion* (Englewood Cliffs, N.J., Prentice-Hall, 1952).

[23] Robert Oliver, *The Psychology of Persuasive Speech* (2d ed.); New York, Longmans Green, 1957).

not in the science of psychology, have nevertheless taken over the findings of behavioral science in their applications to speaker-audience-occasion synthesis and to communicative effectiveness.[24] (For further discussion of rhetoric and psychology, see Chapter 7.)

Rhetoric and Politics

"Rhetoric has long been the handmaid of politics." Although politics is not a branch of rhetoric, speechmaking is certainly necessary if the ends of political action are to be realized.[25]

The Athenian demand for forensic and political talks was the incentive for the popularization of rhetorical speaking during that age of Greek democracy. Such application of rhetoric to political speaking and writing is undiminished today. Politics, as used here, embraces more than the concept and operation of the state. It includes also the other aspects of communal life, social, judicial, military, economic. Athenian rhetoric and politics aimed in common at successful society in all representative phases.

The study of government, however, like that of economics, sociology, history, and other social sciences, limits itself to an analysis of principles and problems. Each of these areas of learning constitutes a "science" and in no sense the "art" of persuasion and decision-making rhetoric, as it transforms logic, aesthetics, psychology, and the materials of politics into deliberative, epideictic, and forensic addresses to influence the resulting social-political behavior. As already pointed out, rhetoric has no subject matter of its own, but utilizes the materials "in any given subject." We do not talk talking or write writing, but rather talk and write facts, concepts, and inferences. Our practical purpose is to evoke audience reactions and conduct.

Practically, speechmaking and written rhetoric usually address themselves to ideas and problems that concern the individual and the group in their social nexus. Expediency—the demand for immediate grappling with action on matters of crime and punishment, taxation, national defense, peace or war, the constitution of the governing body, the rights and duties of citizens and their representatives—dictates much of the courtroom and legislative discussion and debate and other public talk. Because the fortunes of the social-political system constantly call for policy determination, the link between politics (as broadly defined) and rhetoric is obvious. The aim of the rhetorician, then, is to voice and support those policies and decisions that help toward the realization of the "good society."

[24] Franklin H. Knower, "Persuasive Speaking," in A. Craig Baird and Franklin H. Knower, *General Speech* (New York, McGraw-Hill, 1963).

[25] Thonssen and Baird, *Speech Criticism*, 466–467.

The rhetorical aim is to foster political structures that make possible such "good society" ends, and to direct such legislative, administrative, and judicial policies as to protect and encourage justice and the well-being of all. Undergirding all is the communicative activity that gives meaning to free assemblies and discussions, popular voting, and the other procedures that create and develop public opinion. (For further discussion of rhetoric and politics, see Chapter 5.)

Rhetoric and Ethics

As the student of rhetoric links it with logic, psychology, and politics, so does he identify rhetoric with ethics. In Aristotelian rhetoric the political, logical, and ethical-moral community were one. As communication was the handmaiden of logic, so was it the offspring of ethics. At the outset of his rhetoric, Aristotle suggests that the first kind of persuasion "depends on the personal character of the speaker. . . . We believe good men more fully and more readily than others. . . . His character may almost be called the most effective means of persuasion he possesses." [26]

Aristotle's studies of ethics, the ultimate problems of human conduct (ἦθος, character; or ἔθος, custom) were contained in his treatises *Eudemian Ethics* (named for one of his students) and *Nicomachean Ethics* (named for his son). His analysis of ethics dealt with the principles of ethics as the highest good of human conduct, its ultimate ideal as the ultimate standard of right conduct, the sources of knowledge of this highest good, the sanctions of moral conduct and motives for such right behavior. His rhetoric was the application of this broad view as a basic means of proof.

What was this ethical factor in persuasion? Aristotle assumed that the measure of communicative effectiveness lay in the *subsequent audience behavior*. The nature of that audience response was determined importantly by the ethos of the speaker. The speaker's moral qualities would in turn *become* those of the audience. In its turn, it would commit itself to programs directed to the happiness of the group and to its highest good.

Quintilian reflected this same philosophy of rhetoric. He stated, "Let the orator, then, whom I propose to form, be such an one as is characterized by the definition of Marcus Cato, a good man skilled in speaking. . . . My judgment carries me further: for I not only say that he who would answer my idea of an orator must be a good man, but that no man, unless he is good, can ever be an orator." [27]

The sponsor of good speaking, therefore asks what useful purpose is

[26] Aristotle, *Rhetoric*, 1356a, 1–12.

[27] Quintilian, *Institutes of Oratory*, tr. and ed. J. S. Watson, 2 vols. (London, H. G. Bohn, 1856), XII, 1, 3, 4.

served by the information or argument, as addressed to a specific audience. Even though most applaud and go forth to act, what guarantee have we that the speech is a "good" one? What is that concept of a "good society" of political writers and speakers—the Augustinian City of God on earth or the Platonic Republic set in some Western urbanized community? Much depends on the immediate and later behavior of the crowd as a result of a specific persuasion or series of persuasions. The rhetorician thus comes face to face with the responsibility for attempting to gauge the worth of a speech by its impact on social change. His method of estimating such worth is both an intellectual and moral judgment. The rhetorician, be he speaker, teacher, writer, or critic, is required to be more than a logician, social psychologist, and rule-of-thumb communicator. He must develop into something of a moral and social philosopher. He must be aware of the societal results of his communication. His assumption is that unless a given public speech on a specific issue influences an audience to make social progress, or at least works against social deterioration, then the speech or writing should never have been produced.

What is this moral force in discourse? It obviously stems from the speaker's personality. He who speaks well, as Quintilian suggested, must be a person of *intellectual consistency, social sensitivity,* and *moral character.*

The modern rhetorician, like the classical ones, endorses sagacity, character, identification of speaker and audience. But our later critics and speakers look to wider tests. *Social utility or usefulness of the appeals in a given speech is the measure of ethical worth.* Survival and improvement potential of the listeners is central in any ethical code. Winston Brembeck, William S. Howell, and other recent writers on persuasion stress ethics as a function of context.[28] (For further discussion of rhetoric and ethics, see Chapter 6.)

Rhetoric and Literature

Rhetoric, aesthetics, and literature have had close association. Rhetoric, however, has been generally categorized as an instrumental or practical art, whereas literary composition is one of the fine arts. Charles Sears Baldwin would divide the compositional types into instrumental art, as argumentation and exposition, and fine art, as narration and description. Aristotle made a similar distinction in his *rhetoric,* as argumentative-expositional prose, and *poetic,* as epic and dramatic poetry, as well as by implication in all other literary forms.

28 Brembeck and Howell, *op. cit.,* Chap. 24. Cf. Vilfredo Pareto, *The Mind and Society,* Arthur Livingston, ed. (New York, Harcourt, Brace, 1935).

Rhetoric and literature have in common imagination, emotion, intellectual patterns, organic structure, and language. Professor C. T. Winchester summarizes these elements of literature:

"1. Emotion, which, if our analysis be correct, is the characteristic and distinguishing element of literature. It is only in the more typical forms of literature, however, that it is the end for which the work is written; in other cases it is incidental or a means to some further end.

"2. Imagination, without which it is impossible in most instances to awaken emotion.

"3. Thought, which must be the basis of all forms of art, except music. In all didactic and persuasive varieties of literature this is the most important element, as it furnishes the purpose for which the book it written.

"4. Form, which is not an end in itself, but the means by which all thought and feeling find expression, and is so important as to deserve separate attention." [29]

Not all writings in prose or verse without regard for their excellence are literature, but only those, whatever their theme or form, that are distinguished by emotion and imagination; by thought (especially important in didactic and persuasive types); and by a certain creativity of form.[30]

Compositions in which such qualities excel have a universal and permanent appeal and so enter into the literary tradition.

Some speeches qualify also as literature and find their way into literary anthologies, for example, some of the addresses by Lincoln, Webster, Burke, Churchill. (For further discussion of rhetoric and literature, see Chapter 10.)

Rhetoric and Language

Under the title of *elocutio*, style and language constituted the third part of rhetoric. Communicative effectiveness is heavily dependent on language skill. These symbols give full scope to the speaker's ideas and to their imaginative and emotional associations. Words and their combinations were and are, with voice and physical activity, the chief conveyor of the ideas.

Language and invention thus mutually interact. The creation of ideas translates itself into the appropriate language. Language, in turn, stimulates the thinking. The interaction pervades the entire communicative process.

Similarly, *elocutio* is closely linked with *dispositio* (structure, organization). Structure is the complement of invention. The order of unfolding,

[29] C. T. Winchester, *Some Principles of Literary Criticism* (New York, Macmillan, 1900), 61.
[30] *Ibid.*, 61.

the relevancy of the materials, the proportion and relative vividness and importance of the ideas, all are expressed through the language. Thus language, the clothing of the discourse, is the essential medium in securing the response. These words, reflecting the total mood, aim, and character of the communicator, become the "style" of given discourse. (For further discussion of style, see Chapter 8.)

Rhetoric and Formal Learning

Rhetoric and the allied subjects were central in medieval education. Rhetoric, grammar, and logic were the *trivium* of the seven liberal arts of the universities. These closely linked strands of classical rhetoric constituted the teaching of communication. Grammar concentrated heavily on the language of communication; rhetoric and logic provided the subject matter, orderly selection, organization, and adaptation of discourse to the audience.

In later educational history, rhetoric lost its central place in the curriculum. The Ramean and other education movements weakened its identification with logic and general learning. The rise of modern science and of industrial civilization and the increase of specialization in the professions also contributed to the decline of rhetoric as a cardinal subject. However, with the upsurge of mass communication, the spread of electronic communication, the rise of social, commercial, and political propaganda, and the significant studies and applications of modern psychology, rhetoric found fresh support for its function of effective communication by invention, organization, language, and delivery.

Rhetoric, both in private arts colleges and public universities, far from being a discredited subject, has been restored to something of its ancient and later educational primacy.[31]

Rhetoric and Types of Oral Communication. Rhetoric, oral communication, and public speaking are synonymous. Rhetoric as written composition is obviously something else. The term, as we have stated above, comprehends the entire process of invention, structure, language adaptation, audience and delivery. Each of these parts is effectively utilized in a well-rounded discourse; in combination, they operate as a unit to affect audience response. Public speaking, in popular usage, often suggests the relative stressing of delivery more than of thought and logical solidity.

The kinds of public address expounded by Aristotle and other classical rhetoricians included those for political, forensic, and epideictic occasions. According to Aristotle, political-deliberative speaking was that chiefly

31 Wilbur S. Howell, "Renaissance Rhetoric and Modern Rhetoric: A Study in Change," in Donald C. Bryant (ed.), *The Rhetorical Idiom* (Ithaca, N.Y., Cornell University Press, 1958), 53–70.

done in parliamentary assemblies. Its purposes were the determination
of future policy and the need was for early action (expediency). The
method would typically be that of persuasion (exhortation and dehorta-
tion). Forensic or legal speaking was that of the law courts. The lawyer
either attacked or defended somebody involved in the case. Such speaking dealt with the past, and the evidence had to do with "things already
done." Epideictic speaking was ceremonial, where the occasion called
for display, speeches of anniversary, dedication, praise, or blame. The
ceremonial oratory was concerned with the present, "since all men praise
or blame in view of the state of things existing at the time." [32]

With the development of preaching in the medieval period, it was
natural that teachers and theorists concern themselves also with sermon-
izing as a fourth type of public address. Saint Augustine, for example, of
the fifth century, wrote of religious rhetoric in his *De Doctrina Christiana*.
George Campbell, Hugh Blair, and other later rhetoricians were themselves preachers and expounders of such speaking in their rhetorical writings and lectures.

Rhetoric as public speaking thus encompasses a variety of speaking
types of the times. Note today's typical forms: speeches on affairs of state
(such as presidential inaugural addresses); political campaign speeches,
acceptance speeches by candidates, keynote convention addresses, stump
speeches, including the many television appeals); legislative debates
(such as Senate and House debates, eulogies); professional lectures (such
as those on the implications of atomic energy, earth satellites); television
discussions (such as those on "great books"); speeches of dedication,
anniversary; sermons (such as television sermons by Fulton J. Sheen,
Ralph Sockman, Harry Emerson Fosdick); educational addresses; military speeches (especially before military personnel); business and labor
speeches; judicial arguments (in criminal and civil trials); judicial decisions and opinions by the members of the U. S. Supreme Court; lunch-
eon and dinner speeches (where they comprise more than a string of
humorous anecdotes).

Rhetoric and Informative Speaking. Contemporary speaking often limits
itself to reporting and other types of informational address. Oral news-
casts, academic lectures, and popular explanations of processes are examples. College speech courses sometimes limit their assignments to
informational speaking. However, in Aristotle's system factual rhetoric
seems to have had little place. His generation was chiefly concerned with
forensic, epideictic, and deliberative speaking, in which speeches of information alone were little regarded. Even in the Aristotelian speaking
situations, however, demonstrations, the outcome of the logical mode,

[32] *Rhetoric*, 1358a, 37; 1358b, 1–28.

necessarily included exposition. Later rhetoric, as Charles Sears Baldwin has written, included expository as well as argumentative-persuasive prose.[33]

Rhetoric and Argumentative Speaking. Traditional rhetoric has much more in common with argumentative composition and delivery. The theory of rhetoric as Richard Whately developed it was heavily concerned with argumentative composition. Argumentation encompassed both written and oral discourse. George Pierce Baker, James M. O'Neill, William T. Foster, and their successors writing on argumentation and debate were in the tradition of Whately and of Aristotle himself. Rhetoric, then, finds itself expounding those logical principles that many teachers and practitioners of general public speaking treat secondarily.

Rhetoric and Debating. Debating is a special kind of argumentation. As taught in schools and colleges and as practiced in court rooms, legislatures, religious conferences, and even in political campaigns, debating usually proceeds by given rules to ensure equal opportunity for both parties to the controversy. Time limits are observed; the argument is conducted under parliamentary rules; prosecution and defense are given equal time for presentation. The subject is framed as a resolution. Rebuttals are an integral part of the program. A decision at the end, that of a judge, jury, or of political or other voting, is "on the merits of the question." [34] In debates, whether in court or elsewhere, the evidence and arguments are central and the emotional appeals are relatively limited, as in argumentative speaking and writing.

Rhetoric and Discussion. Discussion, like debate, is a specialized kind of rhetoric. Discussion, the modern equivalent of dialectic, in theory adheres to a logical attitude and method. Discussion is primarily an occasion for individual and group thinking. It concerns a problem of importance to the group. It defines and analyzes the problem, weighs the possible solutions, and attempts to form a consensus of the group on the "best" solution. Its method is inquiry—investigation rather than advocacy. It has much in common with the inductive method of science. Although it may operate through round tables, committee hearings, panels, symposiums, or forums, its spirit and outcomes are basically intellectual rather than emotional or propagandistic. It thus stands apart from random conversation or full-fledged argumentative or persuasive speaking.

Rhetoric and Persuasive Speaking. Originally rhetoric, as we said, was concerned with persuasive speaking. Aristotle's statement that "rhetoric

[33] C. S. Baldwin, article "Rhetoric," in *Encyclopedia of Education*.
[34] A. Craig Baird, *Argumentation, Discussion and Debate* (New York, McGraw-Hill, 1950), 308–309.

may be defined as the faculty of observing in a given case the available means of persuasion" [35] has been often quoted as the essence of his rhetorical system. Stated he, "The modes of persuasion are the only true constituents of the art. . . ."[36] This is not the function of any other art." [37]

Persuasion, however, was not the whole of Aristotle's method. Exposition by implication was also involved. Nevertheless, the emphasis was strongly in the field of moving an audience by logical, pathetic, and ethical "proofs."

Persuasive speaking, in popular usage today, attempts to influence the auditor-observer or reader not so much by facts, opinions, and inferences, as by suggestion, emotional and imaginative coloring, verbal pictures, and connotative language. Brembeck and Howell describe it as "the conscious attempt to modify thought and action by manipulating the motives of men toward predetermined ends." [38]

Rhetoric and Oratory. Oratory, "impassioned utterance," is persuasive and impressive speaking in which emotion and imagination, characteristic of literature, dominate. However, the adjustment to a specific occasion, audience, and theme usually gives the oration a strongly rhetorical quality different from genuine literature. Occasionally, however, as in Lincoln's Gettysburg Address, oratory becomes also literature.

Typically, the oration (or "eloquence") emerges when the theme is important, as on certain anniversary or memorial occasions; when the language is permeated with high emotional and imaginative appeal; and when the delivery reflects the common mood of the deep feeling of the speaker and his audience. Such concepts Daniel Webster had in mind in his description:

> True eloquence, indeed, does not consist in speech. . . . The clear perception, outrunning the deductions of logic—the high purpose—the firm resolve, the dauntless spirit, speaking on the tongue, beaming from the eye, informing every feature, and urging the whole man onward, right onward to his object—this, this is eloquence; or rather it is something greater and higher than eloquence,—it is action, noble, sublime, godlike action.[39]

Webster no doubt had in mind the ancient concept of oratory as a rare creative performance. Ancient oratory was regarded by its cultivators as a fine art, as "analogous to sculpture, to poetry, to music." [40]

---

[35] *Rhetoric*, 1355b, 26–27.
[36] *Ibid.*, 1354a, 14.
[37] *Ibid.*, 1355b, 26–27.
[38] Brembeck and Howell, *op. cit.*, 24.
[39] Daniel Webster, "Oration on Adams and Jefferson" (August 21, 1826; in many editions).
[40] R. C. Jebb, *The Attic Orators*, 2 vols. (London, Macmillan, 1893), Vol. 1, 16.

Summary

Rhetoric is the functioning of the communicator, audience, occasion, and subject in the oral (sometimes written) transmission of ideas, language, and communicative purposes. It is best understood in its appropriation and application of related arts and subject matters.

It begins with the speaker's purpose; it systematizes its technique of communication by utilizing ideas, organizing them, employing language and delivery; it develops a rationale of this art; and from these specific procedures and more general principles may develop a philosophy of rhetoric. Philosophy is the method by which it moves from immediate data and experience to broader foundational concepts.

Effective rhetoric applies logical methods and principles. The transmission is chiefly that of ideas, to inform, persuade, or otherwise affect audiences. The intellectual quality is primary. Psychology governs the motives and personality of the communicator as he attempts to adjust to the individual and group characteristics of his audience.

Ethics determines the efficacy of the discourse through motives and techniques that aim at the "good society." Ethics is basic to sound communication.

Rhetoric may also have close ties with literature. When the communication is suffused with emotional, imaginative, and logical qualities expressed with beauty and with promise of permanence, the discourse is at once practical rhetoric and a fine literary art.

Language furnishes symbols on which (together with voice and physical manner) the entire transmission depends. Words and their combinations together become the speaker's "style," and so fuse with the other major constituents of the communication to make or break the activity.[41]

These and other disciplines contribute to the heart of rhetoric in action. But the transaction itself is a distinct art—the art of rhetoric.

[41] A. N. Whitehead, *Science and the Modern World* (New York, Macmillan, 1925); *The Function of Reason* (Princeton, N.J., Princeton University Press, 1929); *Alfred North Whitehead: An Anthology*, F. S. C. Northrop and Mason W. Gross (New York, Macmillan, 1953); C. D. Burns, *The Horizon of Experience* (New York, Norton, 1934), 303–304.

3

Analysis, Definition, and Fact

Rhetoric initially is the discovery and selection of essential materials to be incorporated in the development of the discourse—whether the aim is chiefly to explain, persuade, or impress. Such discovery and selection are primarily a process of analysis or division of the subject selected for a given communication.

Exploratory Questions and Analysis

Every subject raises questions to be answered. We use "analysis" here as equivalent to a series of questions. Philosophic inquiry originates in such questions. In exposition the problem is, "What knowledge is to be added to what may already be known to the communicators and to the audience?" Oral lectures or written communications that add nothing to audience information have no justification—or excuse for being. In argumentative and persuasive speaking or writing, types of discourse that aim at solving a problem and framing both policy and action procedures, the questions become basic in guiding the inquiries into channels that both enlighten and move to action, in accordance with the communicator's purposes.

These questions are designated as issues when applied to forensic or deliberative problems. They are fundamental inquiries, the answers to which determine the truth or falsity, the acceptability or unacceptability, of a given proposition, assertion, or tentative question.

Such analysis immediately calls for questions that demand thinking; that are systematic; that relate to the goals assumed or expressed by the communicator in conjunction with his listeners or readers; and that call for diagnosis and solution of problems both of fact and of policy.

In any case, these questions should, first, aim to cover the field; the survey should be comprehensive. Second, the questions should be systematically classified and organized. Overlapping and repetition of sub-divisions is to be avoided. Third, the questions should suggest a genuine division. Unless the analysis brings to light subdivisions and subaspects to be carefully looked into, the process may be without results. Fourth, the questions should reflect those raised by the audience as well as those in the mind of the speaker or writer. Fifth, the questions should have logical connection with each other and, unitedly, should represent a coherent and relevant dealing with the problem. Sixth, clear discrimination should be made between major and minor issues. The communicator must have a sense of balance and apply proportion in his selection. Finally, the questions should be framed clearly and unambiguously. The issues should make possible direct, uncomplicated and fruitful exploration of a given problem.

Patterns of Inquiry

The concept of analysis (Greek στασις, Latin, *status*), of divisions according to basic questions, found its first formal register in the writings of Hermagoras, in the *Rhetorica ad Herrenium,* in Cicero's *De Inventione, Topica,* and *De Oratore,* and in Quintilian's *Institutio Oratoria.*

Rhetoric itself, with its classical concern for forensic speaking, originated in Sicily under Corax, whose rhetoric was especially adapted to forensic speaking.[1]

By providing the speaker with methods by which to find, analyze, and adapt ideas to a given communication, this principle and method had important influence on later theories of rhetoric and in the practice of oral and written communication.

Hermagoras of Temnos (second century B.C.) considered political questions to be those concerning reasoned discourse and those relating to "law and customs." Under reasoned discourse Hermagoras listed four *stases:* conjecture, definition, quality, and objection. Under law and custom he included four types of legal questions.

According to Hermagoras, conjecture deals with whether an act took place; definition, what things were in its essence; quality, the character of the nonessential properties of the thing; objection, the rejection of a charge on technical grounds not directly connected with the act itself. "Arguments pro and con on whether an act took place result in the stasis of conjecture; those about its essential qualities result in definition; those about its non-essential attributes (e.g., extenuating circumstances) result

---

[1] Lester Thonssen and A. Craig Baird, *Speech Criticism* (New York, Ronald Press, 1948), 35. Cf. George Kennedy, *The Art of Persuasion in Greece* (Princeton, N.J., Princeton University Press, 1963), Chap. 1.

in the stasis of quality; and those concerning jurisdiction and similar matters result in the stasis of objection." [2] Cicero commented similarly:

There are in all therefore three sorts of matter, which may possibly fall under doubt and discussion; what is now done, what has been done, or what is to be done; what the nature of a thing is, or how it should be designated; for as to the question which some Greeks add, whether a thing be rightly done, it is wholly included in the inquiry, what the nature of the thing is.[3]

These issues (*stasis*, questions) apply to all types of oratory—forensic, deliberative, and demonstrative.

Quintilian treats at length the status or state of a cause (basis, hypothesis, ground, constitution, question). He comments on the importance of such analysis: "The different names, however, all mean the same thing, nor is it of the least importance to students by what special name things are called, as long as the thing itself is perfectly clear." [4]

Quintilian discusses two general states: the legal and the ratiocinative. Since the legal controversies are complicated—with many laws—the issues are therefore numerous. The ratiocinative division is simpler. It includes questions of conjecture or fact, definition, and quality: Does the thing exist (*an sit*)? If so, what is it? What are its special characteristics (*quid sit*)? What quality or qualification is to be made (*quale sit*)? A courtroom case could thus center about the issue of whether Brown was guilty. Did he commit murder (*fact*)? Was it in self defense (*definition*)? Was it justified (*quality*)? "He committed no crime, for he slew a traitor and betrayer of his country."

These classical suggestions for applying basic issues have been translated into present-day equivalents. Modern American rhetoricians have framed questions (issues) for determining the materials and organization of typical speeches and writings in all fields.

Standard Approaches to Determining Issues

Communicators have turned to methods of classification for framing the basic issues of a subject. These conventional approaches have been called "stock issues" or questions.[5]

---

[2] Ray Nadeau, "Some Aristotelian and Stoic Influences on the Theory of Stases," *Speech Monographs*, XXVI (November, 1959), 248–249. Cf. Otto Alvin Loeb-Dieter, "Stasis," *Speech Monographs*, XXVII (November, 1950), 345–369; Lee S. Hultzen, "Status in Deliberative Analysis," in Donald Bryant (ed.), *The Rhetorical Idiom* (Ithaca, N.Y., Cornell University Press, 1958), 97–124.

[3] Cicero, *De Oratore*, II, xxvi. Cf. Lester Thonssen and Craig Baird, *op. cit.*, 85–93.

[4] Quintilian, *Institutes of Oratory*, III, vi, 3, tr. H. E. Butler, 4 vols. (London, Heinemann; New York, Putnam, 1890).

[5] Cf. Warren Choate Shaw, *Art of Debate* (New York, American Book, 1922).

They are broad questions, which in turn suggest the specific aspects of the topic to be pursued. Typical of these approaches are the chronological, spatial, definitional, topical or classificational, logical, problem-solution, and the indirect or psychological.

The chronological division calls for time sequence. Such division of events leads to the listing and detailed examination of the events within a limited span and to comparison with earlier and later periods and movements. For example, the tracing of the four administrations of Franklin D. Roosevelt are conveniently grouped under the main events and sub-events relating to each period, with its subsections of economic, social, military, and political significance. In any case, the communicator-investigator is confronted with the demands and limitations made by his communicative aim; by the amount of material from which his selections are to be made; by the need for verification of those items to be presented; and by the decisions concerning relative importance. These matters become questions to be explored and modified. They certainly guide the way to further insight into what is to be composed and uttered. Mechanical though this analysis may be at the outset, it contributes to productive and creative thinking.

The topographical or space-order method proceeds from the near to remote (or vice versa). Such resulting speech or article may concern the orbital flight of a space vehicle, the explanation of a mechanism, or the tracing of language to its physical-neurological sources.

A third method of inquiry is definitional. Terms sometimes compose the main question to be grappled with, such as, "What is the theater of the absurd?" Moonlighting? Empiricism?

Attempts to define would stress the various approaches to the meaning of terms, such as the historical or etymological. Operational definitions open a wide field for exploration. "Objectivity," for example, might be interpreted as illustrated by independent verification through capable, interested, and experienced people working independently of each other on an idea or project.

The classificational or topical method of inquiry also offers wide scope for questioning. Ideas may be classified as social, physical, educational, economic, military, religious, logical, philosophical, and so on. Most popular speeches and articles develop their content by such groupings. Scientists, for example, classify their data in complicated subdivisions in which focus is made on some minute part of the field.

These possible categories, framed as questions, should be sufficiently detailed to invite concrete treatment of a given area, and sufficiently restricted to make possible adequate coverage of the field as defined.

Library science, to illustrate further, arranges publications according to the broad fields of knowledge and to the specific subjects within each field. Note how completely the Dewey decimal system or that of the Library of Congress covers all knowledge. Subdivision of the field of communication, for example, would yield public speaking, with its subsections voice, articulation, bodily activity. Voice, in turn, would become quality, pitch, rate, intensity. Each of these would produce a subsection with its restricted field of investigation and interpretation.

Still other questions or issues would use the logical or cause-to-effect method. Interrogations of the causes and results of an event, situation, or condition are listed. What prior facts or events may explain or partly explain a given situation or condition? What details of such alleged causal factors exist, such as economic, political, or otherwise? [6]

In 1964 and later, the relations between Communist Russia and Red China aroused wide speculation. A speech on that topic raised such questions as, Were these nations divided by racial hostilities and memories of old conflicts? Did the Stalin policy of the 1920's sacrifice the Communist movement to Chiang Kai-shek? Was Khrushchev's denunciation of Stalin in 1956 made without consultation with Mao Tse-tung? Did Moscow refuse to support a Chinese invasion of Formosa? Did Moscow refuse to give Red China adequate financial help toward industrialism? Did Moscow oppose China's invasion of India? Did China condemn Moscow's withdrawal of Soviet missiles from Cuba? Thus specific facts and situations that might explain the possible friction of 1964 and later were raised —each phase to be analyzed in detail—with further examination by raising additional questions.

A related series of questions is that of the problem and solution type. Those are the "stock issues" applied by debaters, discussants, and students of controversial speaking and writing to problems of policy and solution.

Queries here are merely an extension of the cause-and-effect approach as outlined above. For such questions of policy, the usual issues are worded in such forms as, What is the cause for the proposal? What principles or goals constitute desirable objectives? What defects, if any, in the present plan or institution are discoverable? Has the present policy or institution outlived its usefulness? Are there objectionable social characteristics or features? Economic characteristics? (Note the classificational method of dealing with alleged economic, social, educational, political, or other disturbing factors.)

Are the results of the present condition or situation, if unchecked, likely to be permanently objectionable? Are the alleged defects inherent in the present system? What proposals are satisfactory in dealing with the problem? Is proposition A preferable to other policies? Is proposition B preferable? Is proposition C preferable? (Each proposition is a

---

[6] See next chapter for full discussion of tests for causal reasoning.

tentative hypothesis to be examined in relationship to the questions raised at the outset of this analysis.)

Are the effects or results of the preferred proposal adequate to meet the alleged needs? Will the preferred proposal be practicable? Sometimes an issue is added: Is the preferred solution morally and legally justified? Note that such questions are merely "stock issues" translated into more specific problems under discussion. The investigator moves into the controversial situation, free to face the data—without the handicap of a mold into which his thinking and analysis may be artificially cast. Note further that the questions all involve comparisons. The matters are logically those of better or worse, of the relative choices for decision making. Note further that the classificational topics illustrate the range of questions. The field of knowledge is without limits.[7]

The problem-solution method here outlined is similar to John Dewey's formula for the solving of problems. Dewey's analysis of reflective thinking proceeds somewhat as follows:

1. What is the "felt difficulty"?
2. What is the location and definition of the problem?
3. What representative hypotheses or solutions are offered?
4. What are the advantages and disadvantages of each solution in comparison with others?
5. What evaluation is developed to justify acceptance or rejection of the preferred solution? [8]

Although Dewey's approach, like that of the other standard "stock issue" methods, is restrictive, formalized, not applicable to some of the "felt difficulties," and does not lend itself directly to some of the perplexing conditions, it does nevertheless provide clues to the thinker's approach to events or situations.

Still other questions are psychological. This method begins with an analysis of the audience attitude toward the theme. If that attitude is neutral (indifferent) or opposed, the materials—and the preliminary questions—should be so phrased and in such order as to adjust to the point of view and temper of the hearers (or readers). Those ideas will be preferred and analyzed which the audiences are most interested in and which will probably be most readily accepted. The method would therefore mean moving from the least controversial ideas to those that are more likely to arouse antagonism.

A variation of this line of inquiry is the so-called motivated-sequence

---

[7] For further illustration and discussion of analysis and issues, see A. Craig Baird, *Argumentation, Discussion and Debate* (New York, McGraw-Hill, 1950), Chap. 6, 61–77.

[8] John Dewey, *How We Think* (New York, Heath, 1933), 71–78, 91–101.

formula advocated by Alan Monroe. (It is also the framework long ago advocated for the sales talk.) The sequence pattern would ask:

1. What materials shall be used to gain attention?
2. What factors suggest the need (or lack of need) for this proposal?
3. What beneficial results (or objectionable results) would follow the adoption of this proposal?
4. What action should be taken to implement the application of this proposal (or to block such application)?

These block questions are not widely different from the Dewey formula. Monroe stressed the "felt need," "visualization," and "satisfaction" steps that suggest psychological appeals and reactions.

Analysis and Status

Related to the concept of *status* and the twentieth century modifications in such terms as "stock issues" is the ancient treatment of topics (Greek (τοπικά), seats or places of issues.

Cicero specified these "places" of argument (*sedes argumentorum*) as those that dealt with definition, contrast, similarity and dissimilarity, conjunction, cause and effect, genus and species, and other categories.[9] Quintilian also gave a full list, including time, place, causes, means, and consequences.[10]

In addition to these common issues (κοινοὶ τόποι commonplaces), the classical rhetoricians recognized the special issues identified with the chief occasions of speaking. In the law courts, justice and equity were important; in epideictic speaking, virtue and vice were main issues; in deliberative speaking, possibility and expediency were the chief lines of inquiry.

John Quincy Adams in his lectures on rhetoric discussed in detail this classical approach, in his "State of the Controversy" (Lecture VIII), and "Topics" (Lecture IX).[11]

Thus the modern conversions of the Greco-Roman method of preliminary analysis of issues and "topics" have persisted and continue to have practical application.

Analysis of Problems of Fact

Thus far we have analyzed questions of general policy or proposed action in the forensic, deliberative, demonstrative, and all other fields. Questions concerning problems of fact also lend themselves to convenient

[9] Cicero, *De Oratore*, 2 vols., tr. E. H. Sutton and H. Rackam (London, Loeb Classical Library, 1942), Vol. 2, 162–173.

[10] Quintilian, *op. cit.*, III, vi.

[11] John Quincy Adams, *Lectures on Rhetoric and Oratory*, 2 vols. (Cambridge, Mass., Hilliard & Metcalf, 1810; reprinted by Russell & Russell, New York, 1962).

listing. Usually they have to do with the method of classification, often with the economic, political, social, or related partitions. "Has the policy of educational integration been detrimental to the best interests of the Southern states?" (a lively question in 1965) might begin with such broad queries as, Has integration been injurious to the economic welfare of these states? Has it been injurious to their social welfare? Has it been detrimental to their political interests? Each of these stock topics would be broken into more definite and meaningful queries.

Where the question hinges primarily on the accurate discovery of fact, it has to do with the issue, "Is so and so true or false?" The statement of issues in such case is usually one of classifying the types of evidence and arguments. To illustrate: Is an attempt to send a space ship to the moon feasible? Do argument and evidence from causal reasoning support such a project? Do argument and evidence from factual details support the project (such details as ability to produce equipment and mechanisms that would withstand the 480,000-mile round trip through outer space)? Do argument and evidence from authority and from previous experiments support such a project?

The various inquiries suggested above are to be answered affirmatively or negatively, without bias. Such preliminary analysis should direct the thinking into productive channels for oral debates, written arguments, editorials, persuasive articles, round table discussions, radio and television talks, and speeches and articles limited to information.

Importance of Facts (or Evidence) in Communication

As indicated above, the basis of all good communication lies in the appropriation of facts, the experience of the communicator with events, situations, "felt difficulties."

What are the facts? They are the concrete or abstract materials out of which we attempt to weave conclusions, from which we try to draw inferences, or between which we attempt to establish relationships. Facts are to be distinguished from theories. The latter are speculative statements, ideas to be tested for truth or falsity. Facts, by contrast, represent concrete items, to be accepted or established as true before further inference or amplification may be attempted. "Facts have to do with the existence of things, the occurrence of events, and the character of phenomena." [12]

They are contrasted with general laws or principles, to which they give rise, and which in turn lead to the investigation of other concrete and related materials. [13]

12 John Dewey, *loc. cit.*
13 Baird, *op. cit.*, 91.

To the scientist, for example, facts are laboratory material experimentally treated. To the historians and biographers, dates of birth, records of careers, and much else are to be verified by every means. So educationalists, psychologists, sociologists, political scientists, microbiologists, and even philosophers delve into facts and rely on them.

To the semanticist, a fact is a description of that which deals with the thought-word-thing relationship. According to Susanne Langer in her *Philosophy in a New Key*, the fact is "that which we conceive to be the source and context of the signs to which we react successfully." [14] The referent, the "thing" itself (*Ding an sich*), we apparently cannot discern, but at least we do assume its reality as the source of stimulation, leading to the "word" and the "thought."

The event, or source of the reaction, provides the original sign or signal and so the consequent emergence in the domain of the sense as a symbol. This symbolic experience or transformation results in the "intellectually formulated event." Thus, the reactive process is that of the observation of the fact as it passes through the spectrum of the individual experience and through the fabric of the total personality, and so constitutes or creates a picture of the original event, real or imagined.

What of definition? It is the method of naming these reactions in an attempt to make them understandable to others. The problem of such defining is that of identifying the symbol with the referent. Although such source may be impossible to clarify completely, the interpreter of the "event" needs to be as explicit as possible. Comprehension of meaning, as I. A. Richards would say, is necessary for the clear expressions of word meanings.[15] Thus confusion between real and merely verbal definitions may be avoided, as well as the limitations of such definitions as have only immediate and local purpose and are not applicable to a wider universe.

The semanticist in dealing with definitions refers to the "abstraction ladder"—from the lowest type of sensory situation to the successively higher levels; as we move upward, more and more characteristics are omitted, until John Smith of West Branch, Iowa, becomes definitionally a member of the universal society. In general, the semanticists are suspicious of definition making, as producing "words about words." [16]

Note that facts may change their character. They are described and accepted only because those who experience them so regard them. Situations, items, and events are so labelled only because observation and

[14] Susanne Langer, *Philosophy in a New Key* (New York, Mentor Books, 1948, 1962), 225.

[15] I. A. Richards, *Speculative Instruments* (Chicago, University of Chicago Press, 1955), 23 ff.

[16] For further discussion of definitions and language usages, see Chapter 8.

opinion so decide. The facts of today may tomorrow be regarded otherwise. Theological, astronomical, and other information of former centuries has now become merely magic and superstition. The practical test
of fact (or evidence) is its approval by competent testimony. (See the
section below for tests of evidence.)

Facts, we should add, range from the specific to the more general.
Minute and concrete details may be grouped into larger categories, which,
in turn, may be "facts." Fact is thus a loose term to refer to a single,
isolated, concrete item, or may cover a much larger grouping. Specific
testing will separate the vague and general use of the word from the
tangible and concrete designations.

What of facts and evidence? Fact, as we stated above, concerns anything that "has really happened," or anything verified by experience,
observation, and testimony as having occurred. In law, fact is "an actual
or alleged physical or mental event or existence," as contrasted with a
"legal effect or consequence." Whether, for example, a statement is made,
is a question of fact. Whether such a statement constitutes a libel is a
question of law ("legal effect"). Evidence, associated in general with
legal situations although also used more widely, refers to the data, as
provided by testimony of witnesses, by documents, or by other objects
as identified by witnesses, "offered to the court or jury in proof of the
facts at issue." More widely, evidence is any data, "facts," situations, or
events that may or may not support a proposition (assertion, hypothesis,
or inference).

What is the relation of evidence (or facts) to proof (conclusions)?
The basis of much speaking and writing is concrete illustration, quotations, instances, figures. This process of advancing from these specific
materials to a generalization or other type of conclusion is inference.[17]

If the discourse is argumentative, the conclusion is "proof," "the sufficient reason for concluding that a given proposition is true or false." [18]
The Declaration of Independence, for example, adopted July 4, 1776,
lists twenty-seven grievances against the British king, as a basis for declar-
ing the formal declaration of independence. "Examined in the candid
light of history, many seem distorted, others inconsequential, some un-
fair." [19]

However inaccurate the "facts" were in this Declaration, they at least
furnished the specific basis for the reasoning that "all men are created
equal" and the other contentions that led to the conclusion advocating
complete separation for Britain.

[17] See next chapter for full discussion of inference.
[18] Francis Wharton, *Treatise on the Law of Evidence in Criminal Cases* (Roch-
ester, N.Y., Lawyers Cooperative Publishing Co., 1932), Vol. 1, 5.
[19] S. E. Morrison and H. S. Commager, *The Growth of the American Republic*
(New York, Oxford University Press, 1930), 76.

Systematization of Evidence

The meaning of "evidence" in the courtroom has restrictions not attached to the general use of the term. Courts of law, for many reasons in the interest of legal justice, limit the application of the term. The orderly conduct of trials, the unreliability of human senses, and similar factors have led the courts to curtail carefully the kinds of evidence allowable. These laws of evidence are established by legislative bodies and also, through a long judicial history, evolve in the common law, and are followed rigidly.

Apart from such forensic occasions these restrictions are ignored, except that the history and application of these legal practices furnish valuable criteria for the appraisal of all "facts."

Evidence is that of the witness himself, or of objects to which his first-hand knowledge applies. Such evidence may be original, that which proceeds from the primary source, or hearsay, that which is transmitted from one person to another and then by this secondary source offered as essential fact. Oral evidence is contrasted with written evidence (but the latter in turn is traced back to the original human being who recorded it). Ordinary evidence is that of the layman, whose function is simply to report the facts as he observed them at first hand. Expert testimony or evidence, on the other hand, is that of an authority whose reputation and training lead others to note carefully his opinion in matters in his special field.

Evidence is further classified as testimonial, or direct, and circumstantial, or indirect, in relation to the conclusion. Direct testimony is that in which the witness testifies to the "principal fact in issue." In circumstantial testimony, the witness testifies only to certain facts which, in turn, are used to support a given conclusion.

Aristotle and his fellow Greeks refused to regard facts and testimonial materials are genuine "proof." He set these concrete bases apart as "inartistic" materials, for forensic and other occasions, as distinguished from the true dialectic-logical methods, or "artistic proofs," of the enthymeme (corresponding to the dialectic syllogism), the apparent enthymeme (corresponding to the apparent syllogism), and the example (corresponding to dialectic induction).

The inartistic or non-technical (extrinsic) means of persuasion "do not strictly belong to the art of rhetoric." These include:

1. Laws
2. Witnesses
3. Contracts

4. Tortures
5. Oaths [20]

Each of these Aristotle discusses and expounds in some detail.[20]

Quintilian states that Aristotle's division is generally accepted. The classification of "inartistic" materials is the same, except that Quintilian substitutes, for laws in general, previous decisions, or precedents, those relating to the case itself and those offered in the case under trial. He also adds "rumor and common report," a matter of taking legal account of public opinion. "Tortures" are materials by which one side will see a sure method of gaining true statements; the other side, a producing only of false confessions and lies, the result of suffering. According to Quintilian, it is important to record who demands torture, who is to suffer, whom the evidence will affect, and whether the evidence is credible or consistent.[21] Unlike Aristotle, Quintilian expounds in detail the handling of these types of artificial proofs in the courtroom. In his explication, the Latin schoolmaster admits that "though they involve no art, all the powers of eloquence are required to disparage or refute them. Consequently, in my opinion, those who would eliminate the whole of this class of proof from their rules of oratory, deserve the strongest condemnation." Thus Quintilian rejects the distinction between the inferential and non-inferential divisions. He is in line with modern treatment of analysis, definition, facts, and types of reasoning as a single reflective process.

Measures of Evaluation

The amount and kind of evidence included will depend on the purpose of the communicator as he attempts to persuade, inform, and convince his readers or listeners.

The evidence should be sufficient in amount to justify the inferences and to satisfy the audience. These materials, again, should be representative. In generalization from instances, for example, the problem is to assure the reading or observing audience that the cases are typical. As we have said above, the items should obviously be accurate. No safeguard of generalization from specific cases, or from analogical reasoning, is more necessary than a thorough knowledge of the underlying facts. The coloring of facts, their partial character, or their downright misrepresentation (usually through ignorance) are the most prevalent fallacies in the use of evidence.

[20] Aristotle, *Rhetoric*, I, xv, tr. W. Rhys Roberts (New York, Modern Library, 1954).
[21] Quintilian, *op. cit.*, V, i, xiv.

Possible negative facts need to be summoned to test the value of the items. Other important checks include that of recency of the evidence, its consistency with the context, and its verification by examination of causal relations and by the principles of analogy.

In addition to the accuracy of the facts themselves, their proper wording, their internal consistency, and the sources of the information will need to be critically examined.

All facts (evidence) trace their origin to observers who have directly experienced the facts and testified to them by utterance or written symbols. In the courtroom these sources are lay witnesses, or experts, where special fitness is recognized. To the rhetorician, the source of evidence refers either to the person who offers oral testimony, or to the printed or otherwise recorded document.

Much of the evidence to support ideas, especially by speakers, is testimonial. Authority, that is, expert testimony, becomes a major source of evidence. In many cases the speaker or writer, however, relies on his own reputation for his authority. Such method saves much time from detailed inferential support that might be challenged.

Facts and the Philosophy of Rhetoric

What is the value of evidence itself, and of the sources? How is its validity determined? And what logical elements are employed? How do we test the original basis of fact?

1. The sources of evidence need to be clearly and accurately set down. They may be cited in a speech or in the footnotes of an article. In any case, the author will be ready, on cross examination or elsewhere, to repeat fully the sources to which interested questioners may go.
2. The alleged source of data should be authentic. Concrete material often is derived from popular or other sources that may be only secondary. The speaker or writer has the obligation to content himself and his audience with his citation of only original sources. Journalists and others who rush into print under pressure sometimes rely on unchecked sources that are unreliable. Ghost writing illustrates the problem of textual authenticity. Franklin D. Roosevelt had his collaborators. Critics have sometimes suggested that the ghost writers should have the major credit for authorship of certain speeches delivered by Roosevelt, Eisenhower, and John F. Kennedy.
3. The alleged source of evidence should be competent to express dependable opinion or to supply accurate facts. The courtroom procedure illustrates the importance of dependable utterances. What special training and reputation gives the authority his alleged competency? What of his ability to observe and interpret the event or datum that he describes? his ability to recall? his opportunity to observe (if he is a witness)?

    Prominence in a given field, as baseball, is no criterion for authority in a quite different area of knowledge. Powers of observation and judgment differ widely. Many who testify have observed badly, or have relied on hearsay evidence. Physical handicaps interfere. Senility, deafness, blindness, poor education, emotional instability, and a dozen other deficiencies, physical, mental, and emotional, all limit the dependability of a given witness or authority.

4. Still another criterion of satisfactory evidence is the witness's freedom from prejudice. Unfortunately human beings, no matter how well intentioned in reporting, are heavily affected by emotional reactions that distort intellectual judgments. Witnesses are all affected by their inherited, environmental, nationalistic, political, economic, military, religious, or purely personal interests. These factors govern their decisions and utterances. Bishop Whately in his *Elements of Rhetoric* concludes that "a man, strongly influenced by prejudice, to which the weakest men are ever most liable, may even fancy he sees what he does not. . . . The more easy of belief any one is in respect of what falls in with his wishes or preconceived notions, the harder of belief he will be of anything that opposes these." [22]

5. Another test of the validity of the source of evidence is the reliability of the person as measured by his tendency to exaggerations, bombast. His bold and confident assertions of "statistics show" need to be viewed with suspicion and checked.

   Is the authority or source primary rather than secondary? "A primary source is the oldest living record that furnishes that information, either explicitly or implicitly, or an authentic copy of that record." [23] Primary sources are either original documents or copies of original documents. External evidence concerns the origin of the document, its authorship, and the source from which the information comes. Internal evidence concerns the manuscript or other recorded source by every means available to decide whether what it says is really true. All tests of evidence and argument are thus involved.

6. Still another criterion for valid evidence has to do with the number of witnesses and the concurrent testimony. Superficial communicators rely on a single authority. Continued reference to one person or source reveals limited research and poorly balanced treatment.

   Obviously, more witnesses produce additional weight for the evidence. "But it is no uncommon mistake to imagine many witnesses to be bearing concurrent testimony to the same thing, when in truth they are attesting different things." Concurrent testimony, however, "positive or negative of several witnesses, when there can have been no concert, and especially when there is any rivalry or hostility between them, carries a weight independent of that which may belong to each of them considered separately." [24]

7. Does the evidence and source testify contrary to his apparent interests? The strongest testimony is that which obviously moves contrary to the economic, social, or other interests and motives of the speaker or writer. His sincerity, as well as the dependability of his other remarks, is thus supported. He helps to establish the consistency of his discourse.

[22] Richard Whately, *Elements of Rhetoric*, ed. Douglas Ehninger (Carbondale, Ill., Southern Illinois University Press, 1963), 61.

[23] Baird, *op. cit.*, 111.

[24] Whately, *op. cit.*, 66–67.

8. Is the authority supported by specific instances, causal relation, and analogy? Evidence from authority, as we have stated above, needs to be supplemented by other varieties of evidence and argument.

9. Finally, the reaction of the audience must be reckoned with; for at every stage of the presentation, no matter how interesting or attractive is the source, it may not be understood by the readers or listeners. If the data presented appear improbable, even though "true," or if things are not believed by the audience, then the report must be recast and adjusted to these hearers. The speaker or writer needs to prepare the minds of the audience for endorsement of his evidence and the related arguments.

10. Behind these specific techniques for selection and evaluation of evidence is the problem of understanding the sources of "fact" in universal experience; the transformation of the Referent or Thing-Itself into signs and symbols to which the complicated reaction occurs; and finally the framing of these reactions into words and personality accompaniments that call for social reaction and appraisal.

Summary

Communication, initially the discovery and selection of materials that compose a given discourse, is first of all the analysis of a given problem or subject area. This analysis calls for the framing of relevant questions, organizing them, and rejecting irrelevant issues.

Such process may be aided by examination of "topics," such as were suggested in ancient rhetoric and continue to be serviceable in dealing with divisions and subdivisions of knowledge. Hence the logical, chronological, psychological, and other lines of inquiry may suggest directions of fruitful development.

The facts, the foundations of these materials, are best understood by consideration of the sources from which they arise and of the filtering process by which they become "facts," as so designated and reported. These considerations of fact-word-thought relationships are basic to the many tests by which facts or evidence are to be evaluated. Ultimately, facts are to be weighed as part of the inferential pattern and process as an "implicative whole."

The following chapter develops further treatment of fact in inference.

4

Logic and Reason in Discourse

Rhetoric as Logic

Rhetoric, oral and written, is primarily logical, rather than non-intellectual, communication.[1] Although representative techniques such as language complete the communicative process, reason, the intellectual content, is central, the core of the activity.[2]

The priority and dominance of reason emerges in the Greece of Plato and the philosopher-rhetoricians of 600–350 B.C. Greek influence, especially that of Plato and Aristotle, differentiated reason from the prevailing poetic, mystic functioning. Reason was exalted "as the crowning human power."[3]

Plato's exaltation of reason he illustrates in his allegory of the cave in the *Republic*. Men are chained in the darkness of the cave, their backs to the light, and face only the shadows of objects reflected on the wall. One prisoner, however, somehow frees himself, and turns toward the objects previously seen only as shadows. He progresses toward the mouth of the cave and the sunlight. This experience, suggests Plato, is man's emergence from darkness to light, from ignorance to knowledge, from superstition to reason. Plato's philosophy is to view this world as universal and eternal rather than temporal and particular, as reasonable rather than irrational.

Aristotle, as has often been observed, wrote his *Rhetoric* as a protest against some predecessors and contemporaries who had failed to exalt logic and reason in communication. Though Aristotle gave prominence to ethical and pathetic proofs, he expounded rational demonstration as

---

[1] See Chapters 1 and 2.

[2] "Intellectual activity," "reason," "logic," and "thought" are used interchangeably in this and other chapters. We here and there attempt to explain the terms in these more formalized and restrictive interpretations.

[3] William Barrett, *Irrational Man* (New York, Doubleday, 1958), 71. Cf. George Kennedy, *The Art of Persuasion in Greece* (Princeton, N.J., Princeton University Press, 1963), Chap. 1.

basic in all communication. Said he, "It would seem, too, that this [reason] is the true self of every man, since it is the supreme and better part. What is naturally proper to every creature is the highest and pleasantest for him. And so, to man, this will be the life of Reason, since Reason is, in the highest sense, a man's self." [4]

The centrality of reason and logic in demonstrative, deliberative, and forensic discourse has prevailed in classical, medieval, and modern rhetorical theory and speech criticism. George Campbell, in his lectures on the philosophy of rhetoric before his students at Aberdeen, Scotland, stressed the need for logic and substance in discourse. In line with his faculty psychology, he stated that every speech was designed to enlighten the understanding, please the imagination, move the passions, and influence the will. Nevertheless, he recognized the central role of reason. Said he, "As logic therefore forges the arms which eloquence teacheth us to wield, we must first have recourse to the former, that being made acquainted with the materials of which her weapons and armor are severally made, we may know their respective strength and temper, and when and how each is to be used." [5]

Chauncey Allen Goodrich regarded reason as all-important in effective rhetoric. Stated he, "A powerful understanding appealing to the sense of truth is the chief instrument to be relied on. The rest should be subsidiary to this. It is then to the understanding of men that eloquence should be chiefly addressed." [6] Goodrich commends Edmund Burke as superior in communication by reason of his "intellectual independence." Burke had "remarkable comprehensiveness," amplitude of mind, and "subtlety of intellect."

Richard Whately, James Winans, George Pierce Baker, and many other recent theorists on communication adhere to this same philosophy of the close relationship of rhetoric to logic. To Whately, rhetoric was an "off-shoot of logic." [7] Blair declared that reason and argument were the foundations of eloquence. Said he, "In order to persuade a man of sense, you must first convince him, which is only done by satisfying his understanding of the reasonableness of what you propose to him." [8] Norwood

[4] Aristotle, *Nicomachean Ethics*, X, vii, tr. H. Rackam (London, Heinemann, 1926).

[5] George Campbell, *Philosophy of Rhetoric* (7th ed.; London, William Baynes and Son, 1823), 47–48.

[6] John Hoshor, "*The Rhetorical Theory of Chauncey Allen Goodrich*" (Unpublished dissertation, Iowa City, State University of Iowa, 1947), 262. See also Goodrich's "Essays" in A Craig Baird, ed., *Select British Eloquence* (Carbondale, Ill., Southern Illinois University Press, 1963), xxxvi.

[7] Richard Whately, *Elements of Rhetoric*, ed. Douglas Ehninger (Carbondale, Ill., Southern Illinois University Press, 1963), 12.

[8] Hugh Blair, *Lectures on Rhetoric and Belles Lettres*, 3 vols. (8th ed.; London, T. Cadell Jun. and W. Davies and W. Greech, 1801), Vol. 2, Lesture XXV, 161.

Brigance, a foremost American authority on public speaking, reminds his students:

Reason's basic use, then, is to show men how to fulfill their needs and how to solve tough problems. If Reason be man's newest and weakest intellectual achievement, it is also the extremely important one by which he climbed slowly, painfully, and with many backslidings, from slavery to civilization. Let there be no misunderstanding of its importance. Without the effective use of Reason, at least by a creative and dominant minority, no free society can maintain itself.[9]

The assumption of contemporary rhetoricians, then, is that rhetorical speaking and writing involve a logical movement; that this method of development tends to minimize haphazard trial and error, and utilizes deliberation; that communicators with such cognitive perceptions apply sufficient skill to move toward consistent and dependable judgments; and that a given society "progresses" most satisfactorily when their decisions and behavior express deliberative rather than demagogic concepts and appeals.

Patterns of Reflective Thinking

Systematic or reflective thinking is mental activity in which judgments emerge that express self-analysis and appraisal of one's ideas. Such mental marks of the communicator are not those of mere reverie; nor of decision making without antecedent and repeated analysis; nor of rationalization, the so-called framing of selected propositions to justify predetermined wishes. In contrast, the rhetorical mind at work is rational.[10]

Not all rhetoricians accept the priority of reasoning and logic. Some judges of communication challenge rationalism as outmoded. Human motivation, they argue, is essentially irrational. Psychoanalysis, behaviorism, social interactionism, and various experimental studies are cited to support such analysis. William Barrett in his *Irrational Man* utilizes the approach of the existentialists, who view the "whole man" as dominated by anxieties, guilts, and fears as they examine man in general and in particular the brevity of his existence.[11]

Such man, it is contended, is by no means a creature of dominant intellect that registers sense data, makes propositions, weighs inferences, draws judicial conclusions, and seeks the certainty of intellectual knowledge. Rather, he is an organism, governed by drives, learned behavior,

[9] From William Norwood Brigance, *Speech: Its Techniques and Disciplines in a Free Society*, 147. Copyright, 1952, Appleton-Century-Crofts, Inc., New York. Reprinted by permission of Appleton-Century-Crofts.

[10] J. H. Robinson, *The Mind in the Making* (New York, Harper, 1921), 40 ff.

[11] William Barrett, *op. cit.*, 3 ff. Cf. William Barrett, *What is Existentialism?* (New York, Grove Press, 1964).

and motives. He is explained by his impulsiveness, attitudes, sentiments, and stereotypes. His action, it is asserted, is often the result of hidden or subliminal appeals. Woodrow Wilson once said, "Life is essentially illogical. The world is governed by a tumultuous sea of commonalities made up of the passions, and we pray God that the good passions should outvote the bad passions." [12]

Anti-intellectualism is as old as hieroglyphic civilization. Its expression continues with changed labels and leaders. Its votaries, especially after World War II, have been the existentialists. Out of Germany, Denmark, and France came these existentialists. Most of them were true anti-intellectuals, though the obvious demarkations were not sharply defined. These thinkers went to the heart of the theory of knowledge and learning. They were not a closely knit cult, but in recent decades have become a well-defined movement. They do not bypass thinking, but concern themselves with the total man, with his complicated conditioning and behavior. The individual, according to them, is moved by his drives, motives, sentiments, habits. His thought processes are intermittent, inconsistent, impotent. His pseudo-propositions are largely rationalizations. To the existentialist and his kind, man's existence takes precedence over his essence, that is, over his ideas. He is finite, marked by his brief beginning and end. He is a compound of passion and prejudice. He lives first and thinks afterward. According to George Santayana, "Importance springs from the stress of nature, from the cry of life, and not from reason and its pale prescription." [13]

More specifically, how does logical expression differ from dominant emotional development of communicative discourse? We are here referring to prose that is instrumental and practical rather than literary. Compositional movement of pervasive emotionalism is relatively disorganized and diffuse. The content is strewn with assertions. Generalizations are hasty; analogies, extreme; thought, a rotation of ideas that bypass or ignore plausibility. The language is colorful, but often bombastic; sentence structure is loose, cumbersome. The emotional fervor blurs or blots out consistent thought direction.

The more systematic thinker, in his informational, persuasive, or other address, obviously prefers more intellectual means. Although his thought may be saturated with motivation, its expression as well as his approach still indicates, by language and voice, a relatively balanced treatment of the theme.

In essence, his technique is that of examining a situation which confronts him or which he seeks out and attempts to deal with. He may be

[12] Woodrow Wilson, "The Training of the Intellect," in J. M. O'Neill (ed.), *Modern Short Speeches* (New York, Century Co., 1923), 261.

[13] George Santayana, *Soliloquies in England* (New York, Scribner, 1924), 137.

merely attempting to transfer information; or his aim may be to quicken more respect for a tradition, a person, or cause; or he may move directly to influence others to change their minds and behavior. In any case, he views critically the language, hypotheses, beliefs, and assumptions attending his own mind and behavior and those of the others of the communicative scene.

Patterns of Logical Inquiry and Development

What is this pattern of communicative inquiry? It originates in typical modes of reaction to surrounding situations, physical, social, political, economic, and all other. The individual, who is also the typical embodiment of man in general in his reactions, expresses his curiosity or other reactions to the circumstance or phenomena that impinge on him. His reaction may be that of awe, fear, terror, perplexity. In any case, once he has abandoned random reverie or random decisions and activity, he moves to add to his information or to change his mind. The experience of thinking, crude though it may be, represents "this kind of thought that has raised man from his pristine savage ignorance and squalor to the degree of knowledge and comfort which he now possesses." [14]

The stirring of "thinking," whether it directly leads to added knowledge or also to new logical positions, is genuinely creative. It makes things look different from what they seemed to be before and "may indeed work for their reconstruction." [15]

This factor of perplexity, conflict, more than "idle" curiosity, marks the genuine thinker. "Men do not," John Dewey said, "in their natural state, think when they have no troubles to deal with, no difficulties to overcome." [16]

The life of even tenor where fate smoothes the way without the agent's efforts would be a thoughtless life. And when, in difficulties, men (or children) rely entirely on authorities for guidance, the mental alertness is also absent. "Difficulties occasion thinking only when the thinking is the imperative or urgent way out—only when it is the indicated road to a solution. Whenever external authority reigns, thinking is discouraged and is even obnoxious." [17]

The first mark of thinking (or mental reaction), then, is the facing of facts. This observation of the situation, rather than withdrawal from reality, is the stage of uncertainty, perhaps of discordant responses. Are the factors that loom before the thinker mere mirages? Can the thinker

[14] J. H. Robinson, *op. cit.*, 49.
[15] *Ibid.*
[16] John Dewey, *Reconstruction in Philosophy*, ed. Edward C. Lindeman (New York, Mentor Book), 13.
[17] Dewey, *op. cit.*, 118.

be sure of the accuracy or clearness of his own responses? And is he able
to size up the most important events, factors that encroach on his placid-
ity? What antecedent facts or movements explain the phenomena confronting him? What factors threaten to increase his doubts, perplexities,
inward and outward peace? Thus the diagnosis proceeds—another way
of marking the thought.

The second phase of systematic inquiry is the attempt to answer the
questions thus raised. Random suggestions evolve into more systematic
hypotheses, each to be ruminated on for tentative acceptance or rejection. Each is compared with other proposed solutions. If the central
problem is that of adding to facts, the scrutiny turns pretty largely on the
tests of evidence and the sources of evidence.[18]

The "way out," whether focusing on the extension of knowledge or
the framing and answering questions of policy, may be thus established.
The comparative superiority of the preferred choices is re-examined in
detail—with further mustering of data and inference.

Such, in essence, is the reflective process accompanying satisfactory
communication. Essentially, as we have stated above, the "thought" activity operates as a systematic rather than blind reaction to the stimulating phenomena. The "thinker's" curiosity or other sensory-motivative
activity, thus quickened, produces a chain reaction of reflective materials.
The observation and interpretation of what is seen and felt become the
heart of the creative experience. The more authentic reporting is supplemented by the attempt to decipher the relatively unknown. This
movement from direct experience to conclusions is inference.

Genesis and Development of the Reflective Process

Reason and reflection function when the mental exploration moves
into a direction hitherto uncharted. The thought movement is controlled
not by chance, whim, daydreaming, but rather, as we have stated above,
by conscious inspection of the facts and related assumptions or notions.
A cautious examination is made of whatever alleged facts and principles
may be clearly or dimly seen. Inference is the ability to see and describe
the connection between facts and related phenomena the close association of which may be immediately apparent. From this immediate connection, based on the observer's previous experiences, relationships may
be discovered. Experience must obviously continue to govern the view
and reaction. This inferential experience is not random guessing, but a
judicious, even theoretically scientific survey of the probabilities and haz-
ards accompanying a fresh and novel position. We agree with Creighton
that "it is essential in inference that there be a real transition from one

[18] See Chapter 3 for review of evidence.

fact to another—that the conclusion reached shall be different from the starting point." [19]

These inferences have in every case an element of speculation. The world of absolute certainty is no longer applicable. But, with the examination of the relevant facts and the review of their relations and connections, we nevertheless have confidence in our deductions. Independent thinkers in another room or country, without direct consultation but with the same data, arrive at similar conclusions. Thus scientific method illustrates creative thinking and suggests its wider incorporation into the thought operating in social and other areas.

What is the explanation of this procedure by which we may proceed from simple facts and more complicated data to a wider horizon? How was it that Galileo, for example, in 1581, while watching a lamp swing in the cathedral at Pisa, was able to visualize and enunciate the principle of the uniform vibration of all pendulums?

Inference and an Order System

The answer to the question of how political interpreters like Burke, Webster and Lincoln and scientists like Galileo, Darwin, and Fermi reasoned lies in the assumption that inference is a description of the relationships of various facts, groups of facts, and principles. The good reasoner understands these relationships. He notes the events and trends that are causally connected, and that certain phenomena apparently occur in exact harmony with other phenomena.

The Implicative Whole

This factor of the universal is the inferential whole, or implicative system. Inference is the method of progressing from one aspect or phase, "by means of the pervading unity which covers these and all elements of that system." [20]

Immanuel Kant defined inference as "that function of thinking by which one judgment is derived from another." These judgments are grounded on facts and will consist of an immediate description of the relationship of these concrete units. This activity, however, based as it is on facts, may include a larger area of units and their factual judgments. Thus do we explain the process by which knowledge is initiated and then widened by insights that we label inferential. "Only a thought system,

[19] J. E. Creighton, An Introductory Logic (4th ed.; New York, Macmillan, 1920), 325.

[20] D. S. Robinson, The Principles of Reasoning (3d ed.; New York, Appleton-Century-Crofts, 1947), 109.

built up by tracing the actual connections within that portion of the real world with which you are dealing, is entitled to the name of knowledge." [21]

Knowledge is organized into a definite grouping of concrete facts, tiny though the related units may be. But knowledge has no limits. Its wider and wider horizon makes it inseparable from "wisdom" and "thought."

What is this "order system," the basis of overt thinking? The explanation lies in the character of the materials, elements, the minutiae under scrutiny. These "objects" of any kind, whether they be the facts concerning five undergraduates or the student population of a given college, or a purely conceptual group as in a number system, are best viewed and described as an order or array. The qualities and relationships of the specific members of the group determine the classification and identification of this array of knowledge. The thinker, appropriating such a limited organic unit, also gains insight into the characteristics of other units and their members, even though no direct examination is made separately and individually of all members of such category. This principle of order, if carefully framed, makes possible knowledge of the group in general.

Josiah Royce stresses such relation of order to inference. "Order belongs to sets of individuals, to collections, to arrays of things, to persons, deeds, or events." [22]

Inference is possible because the world is orderly. Despite the apparent chaos of neutrons and other phenomena, the scientists, philosophers, and most other interpreters of our day recognize the operation of the law of order. Our little systems become the structural essence of the larger "universe." This universe may be physical, spatial, chronological, or conceptual. In any case, "Order is the first law of heaven." Without order, inference is nothing. Without inference, order is nothing.

What justification have we for exalting reflective thinking as an expression of law, uniformity, and cause-and-effect resemblance? Through experience, common sense, and repeated observation, we recognize and apply this principle of consistency and uniformity. Nature confirms our judgments. Every minute produces its little cycle of reflection that is later verified in our personal history. Sequences follow. If we can see the picture clearly enough, every detail of the circumstances tallies with every other detail. Experience of all races verifies this character of our world. "The uniformity of nature, the conviction that things will continue to occur in the same manner as they have hitherto, is undoubtedly the best founded generalization in the whole range of human experience." [23]

---

[21] *Ibid.*, 8.

[22] Josiah Royce, article "Order," in *Hastings' Encyclopaedia of Religion and Ethics* (New York, Scribner, 1960), Vol. 9, 533 ff.

[23] Columbia Associates in Problems in Philosophy, *Philosophy: An Introduction to Reflective Thinking* (New York and Boston, Houghton Mifflin, 1923), 93.

Representative Modes of Inference

What are the representative methods of inference? As I have stated above, the origin in every case lies in observation, personal experiences, data—having to do with the existence of things, the occurrence of events, the specific character of phenomena. These materials are thus particulars, instances, figures, testimony of witnesses or authorities, incidents.

The inferential activity of the speaker-writer is his interpretation of and reaction to such materials. His mental activity may lead to generalization based upon the array of cases or examples; or to comparison between specific objects or relationships; or to the effective (causal) connection that apparently exists between events or particulars; or upon the statements of others who speak with surety and experience concerning events or theories; or upon conclusions relatively specific, but derived from general statements which in turn have been framed from preceding generalizations or hypotheses.

These representative methods of inference are not all the ways of orderly thinking. Aristotelian logicians start with deductive assumptions. Some logicians have approached inferential descriptions according to the form in which they are stated, such as syllogisms, and refer to enthymemes, prosyllogisms, and sorites. Others stress scientific causality, agreements, differences, concomitant variations, or residues. Some treat statistics as a distinct category; some refer to argument from circumstantial detail as a separate concept. Still others would limit "reasoning" to strictly controlled experimental data, to be exhibited as inductive judgments.

The logical modes, however in details they are classified, are the practical substance of discourse. They are not academic forms to be viewed as accessories. Rather, they compose the texture of the unfolding discourse. They are not forms rigidly following each other, but are flexibly utilized in ways and at points that invite their application. Later these typical modes will be examined in detail and their limitations and exceptions noted. The diagram on the next page suggests the relationships of these modes of inference as conventionally labelled. (The classification here is merely suggestive.)

Problems of Generalization

Logicians and rhetoricians have from the Aristotelian period distinguished two general modes of inference: from the specific to the general, and from the general to the more concrete conclusions. The ambiguous use of these terms has led to much confusion in the discussion of logical application. Aristotle stated that "we will first speak of argument by

Representive Modes of Inference

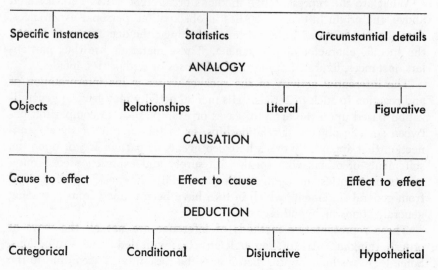

GENERALIZATION

| Specific instances | Statistics | Circumstantial details |

ANALOGY

| Objects | Relationships | Literal | Figurative |

CAUSATION

| Cause to effect | Effect to cause | Effect to effect |

DEDUCTION

| Categorical | Conditional | Disjunctive | Hypothetical |

example, for it is in the nature of induction." But not until Francis Bacon and his contemporaries condemned scholastic reasoning and substituted the chief emphasis on the more experimental concept of the term, did induction take on its modern sense.[24]

Induction begins with concrete facts—phenomena, positive and negative—or "data," a term broad enough to include any fact, event, thing, principle, or law. From them a general law, principle, or proposition may be framed.

Deduction describes a conclusion which in turn is related to premises. It sets up assumptions (hypotheses) that either establish themselves as the outcomes of the inductive method or tentatively become guideposts in the evolution of the problem.

These two methods are not discrete, antagonistic, but are complementary. Deduction is present in all inductive inferences. "Every thought process is really both deductive and inductive and can be exhibited as either a deduction or an induction according to the point of view used in interpreting it." [25] The interpretation of the thinking as deductive and

[24] "The other [new logical approach] constructs its axiom from the senses and particulars, by ascending continually and gradually, till it finally arrives at the most general axioms, which is the true but unattempted way" (Francis Bacon, *Novum Organum*, Bk. 1, Aphorism XIX). The classical category of argument from *sign*, retained by some present-day logicians and rhetoricians, we have excluded. It is probably included under inference by causal relation.

[25] D. S. Robinson, *op. cit.*, 206.

inductive as if these were discrete operations is not dissimilar to the out-moded treatment of the mind as compartmentalized into distinct units of intellect, feeling, and will. The distinctions of these movements as in-ductive and deductive we may conveniently retain as approaches to some analysis of the problem of tracing logical method, but the charting of the mental activity would be done without such sharp demarkations.

Whatever the modes of inference, we are attempting to penetrate into the heart of the order system. Inference, as we have stated, starts with tangible facts and reactions. The thinker-reasoner-rhetorician neverthe-less assumes underlying principles (hypotheses, assertions) into which the items may fit. These "deductive" premises or hypotheses (principles or theories) in turn stem from inductive or specific ways of verification. Induction and deduction are phases of a common process. Analogy and causation, for example, cannot have meaning apart from their function-ing as related to these patterns of generalization or its converse. Logical application and association in communication are central. In contrast to emotional thinking, reflective thinking is directive, deliberative. Its pat-tern is that of a "location" or "situation" of inquiry that emerges as a problematic act of circumstances, which in turn moves toward some answer.

This logical process, through its typical modes of inference, as couched in word symbols, calls for the evaluation of formal definitions and word meanings, of facts and evidence, and of the various forms by which facts are related to judgments (conclusions).

What are the specific modes of inference from induction, and how valid are they?

The reasoning may base itself on specific instances, upon statistics, or upon circumstantial details. Several obvious tests are applied:

1. Are the instances examined "true" or what they appear to be?
2. Are instances examined sufficient in number to warrant the generalization?
3. Are these instances representative?
4. Are negative instances discoverable?
5. Does the method of eliminating alternative hypotheses validate the con-clusion?
6. Does the generalization conform to the laws of probability and causation (scientific analysis)?

1. The approach to such generalization obviously begins with a close examination of the underlying facts (evidence, phenomena, data). The reilability of these details under examination must be established by rais-ing questions of their authenticity through the tests of sensory verifica-tion, including memory, and by support from other witnesses.

2. The second inquiry concerns the observation of the several positive instances. Important though this method of induction is, it is clearly in-

adequate. Though recognized as important by some scholastic logicians, it was condemned by Bacon and later logicians because it ignored negative examples. Bacon called it "puerile, precarious, and exposed to the danger from contradictory instances." The mere accumulation of positive cases cannot ever be satisfactory because it views only a part of its field.

3. Accordingly, the logician and rhetorician look to the character of each specimen as well as to the number of cases. Thus is the resort to the method of sampling. The principle assumes that the use of a considerable number of items, chosen at random from an extensive group would represent the character of the entire field under survey. Random sampling, however, is subject to the prejudices or attitudes of the sampler. Often the samples need to be sampled. To further protect the procedure, the validity of the samples is determined by checking the character of the selections when the statistical units are heterogeneous (different in marked respects). The character of the sample may be more important than its size. Extraordinary measures are taken by reliable statisticians to increase the validity of their sampling usages. The difficulties, nevertheless, of inferring from the character of the samples render this approach open to much question.

4. The full account of negative cases avoids the obvious weakness of the simple enumeration method. Necessary is the inclusion of "contradictory experience." Propositions are not established by long lists of "favorable" cases. Neither is a logical position destroyed by the multiplication of unfavorable instances. The scientific dovetailing of positive and negative data and the addition of any other details with respect to the units under consideration constitute the only sound inferential methods.

5. Still another approach to validating a generalization from instances is the application of the method of residues, the so-called eliminative theory of induction. The method in this case is to examine alternative hypotheses to prove that none will be logically satisfactory. By the method of elimination, the remaining proposition or conclusion is the acceptable one.

The investigator starts with a number of plausible hypotheses, one of which appears to be the preferable explanation of the data. Each tentative generalization is tested by experience in its internal evidence and by its relation to other tests of validation. That conclusion which, relatively, best withstands this critical examination is regarded as the most dependable one.[26]

The difficulty with this mode of justifying a given generalization is that it overemphasizes the negative factors in induction. For example, it assumes that failure to eliminate a hypothesis justifies its validity. Fur-

[26] *Ibid.*, 209.

thermore, the number of alternatives to be eliminated may be too numerous for comprehensive examination. Also, parallel hypotheses may appear
to be equally adequate, equal in scope, in depth. In such cases, another
criterion enters. The principle evoked would be that of systematic simplicity. But here we may be wandering from logical consistency.

Thus the eliminative theory, like that of the simple enumeration, either
by counting positive cases only, or by also including negative cases, is in
itself an insufficient basis for logical pronouncement. Certainly, sum-
moning of the instances is a necessary starting point and logically paves
the way for more basic logical penetration.

6. Does the generalization from instances conform to the requirements
of causal connection? If observation and experience (as we indicated
above) are insufficient as inductive reasoning and if a means of surveying
in detail the entire sphere on the field of objects is not always possible,
what shall be our means in this voyage from the known to the unknown?
Here we need to apply the laws of causation, implied in every generalization. As The Columbia Associates put it:

> Our life is one long course of discovery—of fixed patterns in events. They
> are, in fact, precisely that feature of our universe that makes it an ordered
> cosmos rather than a mere chaos. . . . These patterns which force themselves
> upon our attention and to the analysis of which the scientist devotes his life,
> are causal relations, uniform correlations between causes and effects, such that
> unless some other cause has prevented it, when one part of the pattern is dis-
> covered the rest is sure to follow.[27]

Our method is that of a scientist. He tests the items by complete analysis and experimentation. He calculates results until he recognizes the
principles that explain the cases. He compares and studies results until
the underlying system, to which the instances and their elements belong,
is revealed and framed as a governing principle.

The task of every thinker is to relate the fragments of knowledge concerning, for example, public medicine in the United States. The details
fall into definite patterns. We do not have all the materials to round out
a mosaic, but we do have assembled sufficient bits to describe with confidence the character of the undeveloped area. The jumble of meaning-
less events and objects, as we toil over them, takes on a consistency and
homogeneity that bring to us satisfaction. Ours has been a method of
enumeration, and elimination up to a point, but in so doing we have also
attempted to place the items or fragments into an "order system." The
causal principles have accompanied our insight and so have given our
procedure the stamp of genuine and valid induction.[28]

27 Columbia Associates in Problems of Philosophy, op. cit., 92.
28 A. Craig Baird, Argumentation, Discussion and Debate (New York, McGraw-
Hill, 1950), 123.

Analogical Processes

Inference, as suggested above, often reasons from one particular or instance to another. The logical method is that of comparison, resemblance, or analogy. The inferential method is that of matching two allegedly related objects. If they are alike in observable and verifiable respects, the inference is that they probably resemble each other in certain other respects, known to be true for one but not authenticated in the case of the other.

Analogy and Implied Generalization. Although inference from resemblance concentrates upon specific relationships and aims at a specific conclusion, it nevertheless assumes general principles or propositions that make possible the reasoning. The method starts with the placing of the concrete items, for comparison, in a general field (order system). The reasoner then postulates that all items in that field have certain common characteristics. Thus the development of such reasoning involves both induction and a hypothesis covering the field represented by these cases; then a specific inference concerning the "unknown" elements of the case under examination.

Analogy and Relationships. Analogy may deal with objects or relationships. As John Stuart Mill stated it, "Two things resemble each other in one or more respects; a certain proposition is true of one; therefore it is true of the other." This type is usually labelled logical analogy.[29]

Richard Whately, on the other hand, conceived analogy as dealing with a "resemblance of ratios," or relationships. This type is usually designated as mathematical analogy. According to such reasoners, the relation is that between the captain of a ship and the commander-in-chief and President of the United States in his direction of "the ship of state." ($a{:}b{::}c{:}d$, where a is the captain, b the ship, c the President, and d the government of the United States.) This concept of analogical reasoning is often too tenuous for practical application. Communicators as well as investigators in general limit their conclusions to matching of specific items.

The effort to compare ratios sometimes leads to the distinction between objects in the same field (literal analogy) and between those in a different class (figurative analogy). The figurative associations often become metaphors, similes, and similar usages of literary expression.

These comparisons, simple or complex, follow the law of continuous variation and of continuous similarity. We start with a simple and obvi-

[29] John Stuart Mill, *System of Logic* (New York, Longmans Green, 1872), Book III, Chap. 20, par. 2.

ous comparison and continually widen the categories. No sharp demarkation point is to be indicated. As in all other applications of continuous variation and similarity, we stop where our logical scrutiny limits us. These more immediate resemblances are literal whereas the more remote and intangible relations may be figurative.

The more obviously figurative resemblances are chiefly explanatory, persuasive, or pleasurable. Their function is justified in their stirring of the imagination and their speculative outlook. In any case, the same criteria of validity are to be applied.

Karl Wallace suggests that the validity of the comparison can be made more dependable if each resemblance can be reduced to a proportion. The process of proof then might be made more workable if the rhetorician-logician were to treat the analogy more exactly and at greater length, thus suggesting knowledge it seems to deny if limited to a comparison of the objects or events themselves.[30]

The method of analogy can at best produce only probability. Resemblance, in itself insufficient for satisfactory reasoning, needs to be accompanied by classification, correlation, and other attempts to penetrate into the respective items or ratios under comparison. To many logicians, therefore, inferential analogy is regarded as explanation rather than as genuine inference.

We need not reject analogy as a mode of reasoning, but the criteria for validity are to be carefully applied. Are the facts under observation reliable? Here, as in other types of inference, we ask whether the source of information is competent, free from prejudice, reliable, definite, and supported by other observer-witnesses. Substantiated facts are essential, if the comparison is to have direction.

Are the two objectives or relationships under comparison alike in significant details? Just as any generalization must be based, not merely on many cases or details, but upon those that are representative, so must the comparisons between these objects (events, situations) be made up of significant elements. The very selection of items as a basis of resemblance involves discretion or inferential judgment (inferential discrimination). Obviously, the likenesses are essential when they are necessary to prove the case undertaken. The problem of how to decide what is "representative" or "important" is great.

A related inquiry concerns the number of resemblances. Again, as in inference from generalization, the number of points involved is to be noted. Here, as in generalization, the mere piling up of resemblances will not justify a conclusion. The best we can say of number of resem-

30 Karl R. Wallace, "On Analogies: Redefinition and Some Implications," in *Studies in Speech and Drama in Honor of Alexander M. Drummond* (Ithaca, N.Y., Cornell University Press, 1944), 412–426.

blances is to agree that a relatively large number of favorable items in common would strengthen our confidence in further testing.

A third consideration has to do with the occurrence of significant differences. Highly important, as in generalization, is the need for objective survey to bring to light crucial differences. If we examine Mars and Earth to conclude concerning the possibility of life on Mars, the various differences relating to volume, rotation and revolution in the solar system, and other items are to be clearly listed.

Does review of similar instances confirm the validity of the comparison under examination? The investigation in this case is not so much a scrutiny of the two cases as it is an examination of related ones.

For example, a comparison may be that of the legislative programs for a session just closed in Iowa with those of the corresponding body in Wisconsin, still in session, to predict concerning legislation in the latter state. Further light might be thrown on the predicted character of legislative enactments in Wisconsin by comparing the Minnesota legislative session (just concluded) with that of Iowa and Wisconsin. The approach in such a case is a complex of analogous cases and obviously extends the problem of establishing a valid inference.

Another question, already implied in the tests reviewed above, is whether examination of the underlying generalization confirms or denies the validity of the analogy. Inherent in each analogy, as we have explained, is a generalization. Every comparison is in reality the product of an inference from a particular case to the character of the general field, from which, in turn, we proceed to the related concrete case.

Every case of inference from analogy assumes or implies a general statement. The investigator is committed to defend such an assumed proposition as a further check on the analogy.

Finally, the pattern of inquiry must center in the question, Does inference from causal relation confirm or deny the validity of the analogy?

A definite causal relation should exist between common elements involved in the analogical argument. The general principle or law should be stated and carefully reviewed. A series of propositions should be framed to indicate the causal relationship between the data or phenomena. It is not enough to define, explain, and conclude that certain factors are present in example B because the similarities seem to resemble those of example A. The ultimate question is, Why should this situation allegedly prevail (or not prevail) concerning the unknown solution with respect to factors not directly discernible? [31]

Argument from analogy is similar to the argument from effect to effect, in which a common cause sought to explain the coordinate effect. The very items that we list for comparative purposes are examined in their

[31] Baird, *op. cit.*, 135.

causal effectiveness. Inference from analogy, if valid, reveals itself as typical analysis of causality.[32]

Inference and Causality

Inference from causation is a relation between particulars. As I have suggested above, causal reasoning is more basic and fundamental than any other type, in fact, is the method to which all other tests of reasoning refer. The problem is to determine the relationship of two items or phenomena. In contrast to analogy that seeks to explain certain traits of an "unknown" object or relationship, causation infers concerning both factors. We conclude that "these two phenomena are causally connected; one affects the other, or they mutually affect each other."

Inference from causation assumes that the universe acts consistently and uniformly. What assurance have we that consistent patterns exist in this physical and all other continents of our world?

Our experience would confirm such consistency. "How do we know that these sequences will continue to repeat themselves in the future? Strictly speaking, of course we don't. . . ."[33]

Reasoning by causal relation involves both induction and deduction. Induction occurs in the examination of the instances or details. In every case a generalization is implied. This generalization is framed and assumed as a proposition from which a more specific conclusion is derived. The reasoning, for example, may be that the United States, evolving as it does into great riches and luxurious living (cause), is bound to fall (effect). The initial fact is that the United States is rich and luxurious. Other nations, for example Greece and the Roman Empire, became rich, luxurious. The tentative generalization from these cases would be that such nations had their decline and fall. The concrete case of the United States would fit under these premises. Critics of such reasoning would say that it represents merely reasoning in a circle—assuming the conclusion to be approved. The inferential development, nevertheless, is of this causal character. If the inferences are carefully checked at each stage, something other than circular reasoning occurs.

More significant in the analysis of causal reasoning is the interaction of the relationships. We often describe the phenomena as occurring chronologically. One event succeeds another, and their dates are listed chronologically.

Causality, however, if logically analyzed, cannot be treated so simply. "Action and reaction are equal and opposite" would more obviously describe many examples of causality. "Causation, then, is interaction; cause

[32] See the next section of this chapter for discussion of causality.
[33] Columbia Associates in Philosophy, *op. cit.*

and effect are simultaneous; the effect is not contained in the cause; there is a passive factor." [34]

In addition to the concept of interaction, our modern view of time and space renders obsolete the notion of causation as chronological connection. Here we apply the theory of relativity. Relativity abolishes the idea of unrelated time and space, each absolute in its own sphere. Space-time is substituted. Everything is relative. Theory proceeds "from next to next;" there are no direct relations between "distant" events, such as distance in time or space. "And of course there are no forces acting at a distance; in fact, except as a convenient fiction, there are no forces at all." [35]

In this newer universe, time and space are united in a four-dimensional world made up of "events." If, then, these are relative concepts, it is only for illustrative purposes that we speak of "cause" and "effect" in our limited, earthbound perspective.

What of causation and continuity of events or data? Not only does this modern concept of time and space reject the simple chronological-spatial description of the events or data of our reasoning, but the continuity of these phenomena also makes it impossible to establish a distinction between cause and effect.

The idea of a continuum—or of an organic unity—makes erroneous and naive the concept of simple sequence. Does the murderer's bullet explain the death? Logicians and scientists would mark out many successive events, each one of which could be held as the explanation of the outcome. "Every event, according to the philosopher and logician, may be divided and subdivided into a complete system or series of systems." [36]

Moreover, the problem of fixing causes and results is complicated by the reciprocity of phenomena. Causes and effects are so closely identified, items are so coexistent, that causes and results seem to be the same. Is the flame the cause of the melting wax of the candle? Or is the melting wax the cause of the flame? [37]

This reciprocity of phenomena suggests also the complexity of the items dealt with. The factors at work as causes or results are seldom single and obvious. Any close examination will quickly note the many strands at work to make up the total activity.

The causal event is imbedded in a plurality of other "causes" that need close inspection and "separation" before a dependable inference can be framed. Similarly, the consequences of later events also require methodi-

[34] F. R. Tennant, article "Cause," in *Hastings' Encyclopaedia of Religion and Ethics* (New York, Scribner, 1911), Vol. 3.
[35] Bertrand Russell, *Outlines of Philosophy* (London, Allen & Unwin, 1927), 117.
[36] Baird, *op. cit.*, 142.
[37] Quoted from Robinson, *op. cit.*, 260.

cal and detailed review. If the problem is that of tracing the historical results of Woodrow Wilson's ill-fated Western tour of September, 1919, with his plea for the League of Nations, we conclude that the immediate result was his physical collapse at Pueblo, Colorado. But many other consequences followed. The concentration upon any one of them would depend on what type of inference we would apply. Wilson's paralysis certainly ended any possibility of his re-election, or perhaps the victory of his party, or ratification of the Paris Treaty with membership in the League of Nations. Other historians, however, have suggested that a wider tracing of outcomes would include a long train of political events culminating in the adoption of the United Nations organization in 1945. These, some said, were the reverberations of the ill-fated Wilson tour of September, 1919. Where does historical judgment draw a line, then carefully control, and in many cases frame only qualified conclusions?

In referring to any group of circumstances, we are thus dealing with a system of events; this system moves within a larger system, and the whole constitutes a wider pattern. We single out a unit and designate it as "cause"; another, "effect." Note the usual classification of types of causal reasoning and their tests.

Logicians and rhetoricians usually classify inference by causation as that from cause to effect (a priori), from effect to cause (a posteriori), and from effect to effect. Reasoning from cause to effect points to a known situation or group of circumstances and looks to alleged results. Inferring from effect to cause concentrates on a fact or set of facts and attempts to explain possible causes. In addition, students of logic sometimes classify causal reasoning as that from "effect to effect." This mode infers from one "effect" to another from the same cause. The separate "effects" do not influence each other, but are each presumably outcomes of a common cause. For example, that excellent comedy, *As You Like It* (effect) was produced by Shakespeare's genius (alleged cause). This alleged cause would presumably produce another excellent comedy—say *Love's Labour's Lost*—even though the reasoner had not read it.

What are the tests of causal reasoning? If we assume that the alleged facts (data, phenomena) have been verified, we ask:

1. Can a causal relation be established between the two sets of phenomena?
2. Is the alleged cause important in influencing the alleged result, or the alleged cause adequate to produce the known or assumed effect?
3. Are other factors operating to prevent the alleged cause from producing the alleged effects?
4. Does the application of other methods of scientific induction confirm or reject the inference from causal relations?

The assumed causal connection often vanishes upon close examination. This failure to identify items or phenomena associated only by chance is the fallacy of *post hoc ergo propter hoc* (after this fact, there-fore because of it).

One of the many causes may be wrongly assumed to be the main or adequate one. The communicator, even though the connection is well established, often oversimplifies the problem by ignoring the associated factors. Moreover, other antecedent factors operate to cancel the influ-ence of the alleged cause.

The inference from casual connections needs to be undergirded by application of other logical approaches. Circumstances immediately re-ferred to need to be grouped into a given system. Each event or circum-stance will fit into the general pattern. Such analysis means the employ-ment of generalization from specific instances, the proper view of attendant circumstances, the comparison of items, and the verification from possible authorities.

The investigator is advised to re-examine John Stuart Mill's canons of causality:

1. Phenomena are causally related when they accur in a sequence.
2. They are not so related when an antecedent is invariably absent.
3. They are causally related when any variation in one phenomenon has a corresponding variation in the other.[38]

Note that these criteria assume the law of causation and the resort to an experimental procedure that relies heavily on an enumeration of in-stances and so has the weakness referred to above under "generalization by enumeration."

Assumptions and Hypotheses in Reasoning

Much communication is developed deductively—that is, the general ideas are expounded or claimed, followed by the detailed supports. The method is thus clear—even if not always persuasive. For situations in which the reader or listener would be opposed to the conclusions ad-vanced, the inductive approach would sometimes be preferable. Concrete details and preliminary propositions would be first set up for approval.

The deductive pattern, with its series of assumptions and hypotheses, is rhetorically justified. The assumptions stem from the analysis of the problem and consist of tentative answers to the questions making up the issues. These assumptions may or may not be expressed. Usually they are obvious and are taken for granted.

Role of Hypotheses. The hypothesis is a preliminary suggestion of a conclusion or proposition to be verified by the appropriate evidence and reasoning. The method is usually applied to scientific investigation.

[38] Cf. John Stuart Mill, *Logic*, Book III, Chap. 9; D. S. Robinson, *The Prin-ciples of Reasoning*, Chaps. 20, 21; Bertrand Russell, *op. cit.*, 280–286.

The scientist uses tentative propositions for assembling his data and for securing fruitful records of his observations. For hundreds of years the Ptolemaic theory or hypothesis of planetary motions prevailed, until the more plausible Copernican theory came forth.

Such a hypothesis should be susceptible of "proof." Only expert judges should pass judgment on the relevancy and practical demonstration of such tentative propositions. The hypothesis should harmonize with the known findings of previous research and should square with what is understood by the known "laws of nature." Every hypothesis should also lend itself to modification as penetration into the subject suggests reconstruction to fit new facts and inferences.

Tentative Propositions and Conclusions

What of tentative problems and conclusions in communication where scientific "hypothesis" is not the appropriate term? Communication is preceded by diagnosis of the subject by definition, analysis, and framing of tentative points to cover the case. If the inquiry concerns a fact, the usual procedure calls for a classification of materials and examination of the "facts" under scrutiny. The theory, for example, might raise the question, What is a piece of chalk? The analysis of the particles might reveal that they are limestone, the fossil shells of foraminifers (the substance, for example, of an old sea bottom). Tentative conclusions on a matter of fact thus become procedures of classification or close examinations of each phase to bring to light the essential "truth" of our inquiry.

For social, political, and other problems, the grouping of the inquiries under subpropositions and with a general conclusion is the usual method. The actual analysis and further study of the subject is invariably done by induction. But the completed discourse, or series of discourses, will often assemble these structural guides into organized sequence and so focus finally on the conclusion to which the communicator points. The presentation is the result of his thinking and not that of his step-by-step arrival at his conclusion.

Suppose the discourse deals with the question, Should Congress provide for a federal sales tax? Subpropositions advanced by the speaker or wirter might in turn conclude:

1. The need for raising further federal revenue demands some modification of our present federal tax program.
2. The further increase of our existing sources of federal taxation, exclusive of sales tax, would be an unsatisfactory method of raising the needed revenue.
3. The federal sales tax would be a significant means of meeting the need for federal revenue.
4. Such a sales tax would be practicable.
5. Such a tax would be fair to all income groups.

In general such structural procedure, as mentioned above, is deductive. Each phase of the development becomes a little unit of inference, the validity of which should be fully established before the next unit is added.

Deductive Patterns in Communication

Traditional logic has organized its concepts and treatment of deduction under the syllogistic forms, categorical, hypothetical, and disjunctive.

The categorical form, for example, includes there propositions, with a major premise, minor premise, and conclusion. The categorical syllogisms of the first figure contain the terms arranged as follows:

Middle–major
Minor–middle
Minor–major

These syllogistic forms take for granted the validity of the premises. Formal logic sets up exact tests for establishing the validity of the syllogisms. In general, these rules aim to examine the consistency and structure of the reasoning rather than its validity as measured by evidential and inductive tests.[39]

Students of communication are interested in examining syllogisms not so much as examples of logic, but as living expressions of opinion and reasoning on the problems of our world.

Those interested in syllogistic reasoning and false reasoning resulting from the violation of the rules should review texts in representative texts on logic.[40]

Since Bacon, many logicians have looked askance at the practical value of reasoning by syllogistic construction. George Campbell, representative British rhetorician of the late eighteenth century, had this to say:

It is long since I was convinced, by what Mr. Locke hath said on the subject, that the syllogistic art, with its figures and moods, serves more to display the ingenuity of the inventor, and to exercise the address and fluency of the learner, than to assist the diligent inquirer in his researches after truth. The method of proving by syllogism appears even on a superficial review both unnatural and prolix. The rules laid down for distinguishing the conclusive from the inconclusive forms of argument, the true syllogism from the various kinds of sophism, are at once cumbersome to the memory and unnecessary in prac-

[39] Baird, op. cit., 157.

[40] See Bertrand Russell, op. cit.; Edwin A. Burtt, Right Thinking (New York, Harper, 1946); Daniel Robinson, The Principles of Reasoning (3d rev. ed.; New York, Appleton-Century-Crofts, 1947); John Dewey, Logic (New York, Holt, 1938); F. C. S. Schiller, Logic For Use (London, George Bell, 1929); Max Black, Critical Thinking (Englewood Cliffs, N.J., Prentice-Hall, 1946); Irving Copi, Symbolic Logic (New York, Macmillan, 1954); Stephen Toulmin, The Uses of Argument (Cambridge, Cambridge University Press, 1928).

tice. No person, one may venture to pronounce, will ever be made a reasoner who stands in need of them. In a word, the whole bears the manifest indications of an artful and ostentatious parade of learning, calculated for giving the appearance of great profundity to what is very shallow.[41]

According to F. C. S. Schiller, to a disputant unwilling to make these concessions (acceptance of the verbal integrity of the terms of the syllogisms as sufficient proof of identity of meaning), the syllogistic form is ludicrously impotent. He cannot be coerced because he can refuse to admit the truth of its premises and can demand proof of them. Thus if the truth of a premise is disputed, it has to be proved; but proved it can be only by a further syllogism. "Thus the demand for true premises is doubled at every step backward the inquiry takes."[42]

Agreeing as we do with the general criticism of syllogistic reasoning, what practical application can we make of deduction as framed so as to relate propositions and from them draw conclusions? The syllogism as a demonstration of the logical formula is of little value to students of modern rhetoric. Formal rhetoric, as Campbell and Schiller suggest, assumes that the premises are "either true or false." Schiller's point that adequate support of a major premise, for example, if challenged, would lead the disputants further and further to the rear in framing acceptable propositions, however, is stretching the case. Certainly serious inquirers, rather than quibble, would agree to assumptions long before the analysis moved backward toward Schiller's "infinity."

Syllogistic methodology, nevertheless, puts down conditions under which the conclusions inevitably follow. Given these assumptions, "absolute certainty" and "truth" operate. "Logic in use" in communication, however, is based on the principle of logical probability. We follow the doctrine of the relativity of knowledge. No propositions that constitute human knowledge can be assumed to be "absolutely true." All conclusions, no matter how plausible, need to be accompanied by qualification. We are at least logically consistent. Probability depends on the amount and character of the supporting evidence. Investigators may move from disbelief to doubt, to favorable opinion, and toward more and more credence, but never to the point of unqualified certainty. Testimony, inference from generalizations, analogy, causal relations, and all other modes of reasoning, all end in limited conclusions. Russell states that "at the very best, induction and analogy only give probability. Every inference worthy of the name is inductive, therefore all inferred knowledge is at best probable."[43] This principle would apply to all investigations, ex-

---

41 George Campbell, *The Philosophy of Rhetoric*, Lloyd Bitzer, ed. (Carbondale, Ill., Southern Illinois University Press, 1963), Book I, Chap. 6.
42 F. C. S. Schiller, *op. cit.*, 271.
43 Bertrand Russell, *op. cit.*, 285.

perimental, scientific, and otherwise. Even the law relating to the uniformity of nature, as we suggested above, is largely assumption. "The most we can hope is that the oftener things are found together, the more probable it becomes that they will be found together another time. . . . It can never reach certainty. Thus probability is all that we ought to seek." [44]

Hibben and other logicians attempt to limit the logical meaning of probability to "a comparison of the number of cases when an event occurs with the total number of cases both positive and negative." [45]

Much of our reasoning in communication will continue to be deductive, but not in sharply limited categorical, disjunctive or hypothetical syllogisms. The related propositions will be tested by their reference to experience. We will reject the sharp syllogistic compartmentalization of ideas. The principle of continuous variation in the treatment of concepts, terms, or logical relations will take the place of hard-and-fast definitions and unqualified certainties. The network of surrounding circumstances, the complexity of phenomena, of causal functioning in the "implicative whole" will govern the communicative judgments. The fallacies of "allness" statements will be avoided.

With some such approach to deduction and reasoning in general, the communicator's intelligent framing of general propositions will link together and clarify the inference and will result in genuine effectiveness of thought and expression.

The issue of the character and function of the syllogism continues among contemporary rhetoricians. Some critics retain Aristotle's use of the enthymeme, and the adjustment of the dialectical syllogism to the popular audience. In such situations, according to Aristotle, a long train of argument is to be avoided. Rather, the premises are to be taken for granted since they will probably be admitted.

Lloyd Bitzer has argued that most standard conceptions of the enthymeme have failed—for example, those of Lane Cooper, C. S. Baldwin, and James McBurney. These writers, according to Bitzer, have failed to indicate just how the enthymeme differs from the syllogism. The difference lies not in the probability of the premises, nor in the formal deficiency, nor in the relation of premises to conclusions. The real difference, states Bitzer, lies in joint supplying of the premises by the speaker-audience. "The audience itself helps construct the proofs by which it is persuaded." [46]

[44] Bertrand Russell, *Problems of Philosophy* (London, Oxford University Press, 1946), 101 ff.

[45] Robinson, *op. cit.*, 233. Cf. J. G. Hibben, article "Probability," in *Hastings' Encyclopaedia of Religion and Ethics* (New York, Scribner, 1956), Vol. 10.

[46] Lloyd Bitzer, "Aristotle's Enthymeme Revisited," *Quarterly Journal of Speech*, XXXV (December, 1959), 399–408.

Charles S. Mudd takes a somewhat similar view of the enthymeme. According to him we "create them [the universals of the syllogism], we find them, we invent them, on the basis of what we know about the nature of our audiences as groups of individual men." We need to revise our concept of probability. "If we base our arguments on premises that are probable universals rather than particular absolutes, we avoid the difficulties of formal without violating the requirements of material truth." [47]

Bitzer is interested in an interpretation of the enthymeme that meets the definitions established by Aristotle. His article does not attempt to disprove the older interpretations of these phenomena, but merely to expound them. Bitzer condemns older interpretations as narrow in scope and defends the undistributed middle as an asset. Mudd would thus seem to commit himself to a universal use of probability in his interpretation of the syllogism and enthymeme.

We agree that the Aristotelian vestiges and logic-chopping (that he himself would deplore) still echo in our rhetorical and communicative treatises. We refer here to the misuse of quantity and quality of propositions, several rules of the categorical, disjunctive, and hypothetical types; to immediate inferences, subversion, inversion, and the rest. The canon of probability is to prevail. Nor are syllogisms, dialectical or rhetorical, an isolated or abstract process. Logic is not to be isolated from the setting and audiences in which the thought develops. [48]

Thought, Reasoning, and Emotive Behavior: a Summary

Logical judgment is of the time, place, and experience. It is compounded of tentative propositions; of operational definitions; of relativity and probability in its interpretation of generalizations, causal reasonings, analogies, and general premises; of semantic clearness and consistency; and of the related marks of our twentieth century insights.

The character of the social direction from which the ideas emerge as framed by audience impacts is at the heart of the philosophy of rhetoric.

What is that direction and strength of the movement generated by communicative ideas? Here are standards and goals that incorporate value judgments. Such judgments raise basic questions affecting the good or bad society. What of the consequences that relate to justice and injustice? What are such outcomes as influenced by communication as an intellectual activity?

These turn out to be ethical questions. It is no accident that Aristotle identified reasoning (logic and dialectic) and ethics. Intellectual excel-

[47] Charles S. Mudd, "The Enthymeme and Logical Validity," *Quarterly Journal of Speech*, XXXV (December, 1959), 409–414.

[48] A. Craig Baird, "Speech and the New Philosophies," *Central States Speech Journal*, XIII, No. 5 (Autumn, 1962), 241–246.

lence cannot escape the responsibility for moral excellence. The intellectual quality and development of our discourse is inevitably identified with the social, psychological, and ethical components that together evaluate the communicative enterprise.[49]

[49] See later chapters for the relation of logic to psychological and ethical constituents of discourse.

5

Politics and Public Address

The City-State and Communication

As rhetoric is closely identified with logic and intellectual processes, so is it associated with politics. Politics, in Aristotelian usage, meant the formulation and interpretation of the principles and problems of the state. What was the state? It was the ancient city-state of Greece and had to do with the total life of the community. The Greek *polis*, notably Athens, was a compact unit with its small population and area. Almost all citizens knew their fellows and grappled together with their common civic problems.

Theirs was a natural community, closely knit, "with all the attributes of a living being." [1] The binding force of these citizens and their state was their loyalty to its history and its purposes, past, present, and future. Said Pericles in the famous Funeral Oration, as recorded by the historian Thucydides, "I would have you day by day fix your eyes upon the greatness of Athens, until you become filled with the love of her; and when you are filled with the glory of her; and when you are impressed by the spectacle of her glory, reflect that this empire has been acquired by men who knew their duty and had the courage to do it, who in the hour of conflict had the fear of dishonor always present with them, and who, if they failed an enterprise, would not allow their virtues to be lost to their country, but freely gave their lives to her as the fairest offering which they could present at her feast." [2]

Pericles eloquently boasted that Athens, unique among Greek states, had found the secret of combining the citizen's participation in public life with his attendance to his private affairs. "An Athenian citizen does not neglect the state because he takes care of his own household; and

[1] William Ebenstein, *Great Political Thinkers* (3d ed.; Holt, Rinehart & Winston, 1961), 64, 56.

[2] Thucydides, *History of the Peloponnesian War*, tr. Benjamin Jowett (Oxford University Press, 1900), Book II, 35–46.

even those of us who are engaged in business have a very fair idea of politics. We alone regard the man who takes no interest in public affairs, not as a harmless, but as a useless character; and if few of us are originators, we are all sound judges of policy."

Politics, then, embraced the entire community experience, social, intellectual, economic, military, legal, legislative, and educational. The aim was to establish concepts of social-political theories and influence. What was the essence of Greek political thought? Aristotle and his fellow political thinkers raised such questions as, What is the origin and nature of the state? Is it merely an extension of the family and village to the city-state? Who should direct the ways of living in such community? What would be the qualifications of the citizen? What his specific legislative, judicial, administrative, and military role? What should be the function of slaves and servants? What of quality and inequality in the administration of justice? What should constitute the goal of the "good" community? Is community ethics a separate factor from individual ethics? What should be the character of the government? Should the preferred system be democracy? or monarchy? or oligarchy? or aristocracy? What of the rule of law? Where shall we draw the line between the ideal and the real state? What is the strength and weakness of an ideal republic (utopia)? How are revolutions to be prevented?

Later questions, added to or substituted for these Greek political ponderings, included, Why the failure of the city-state? What of the national state? The world state? The relation of the church and clergy to the state? The nature of society? Republicanism and nationalism? The role of natural law? The influence of scientific materialism on the concept of the state? The economic role of the state? Sociology and liberty? The function of parliamentary government? American constitutional system? Utilitarianism and the state? Dialectic and nationalism? What of liberalism, conservatism, and democratic socialism? Marxian dialectical materialism and the state? Totalitarian Communism?

These and later questions and their tentative answers constitute the field of social-political "science." Note that political philosophy and politics (in the broad sense) are a record of principles and questions that aim at knowledge, but, like the other sciences, comprise no principles and rules of communicative technique.

What is the association of rhetoric with these political principles and philosophies? Whereas the political theorists have framed problems and principles, the communicators have taken these over—or helped devise related ones—and translated them into communication, that is, people talking with people and exchanging writings based on these community experiences and thought. With these speakers of ancient Greece, as

Dobson states, "oratory was instinctive." Skill in speaking was no less highly prized than "valor in battle." [3]

The *polis* state encouraged, or practically required, ability in speaking. The popular assembly at Athens during the fifth century B.C. included most male citizens. It deliberated on questions suggested by the Committee of Five Hundred, which in turn considered legislation. Thus were deliberative sessions and the framing of laws handled.

The organization of the courts too, during the age of Pericles gave opportunity for most Athenians over thirty years of age to act as jurors in the courts. Juries were of considerable size. "Pleaders addressed the jurors as citizens and democrats, and in truth the courts were the stronghold of popular government." [4] These courts were juries without a judge. Every man was his own lawyer; therefore each case gave strong stimulus to effective persuasive speaking.

Rhetoric in the Service of Politics

What close association have rhetoric and communication with politics? Rhetoric, as we have stated above, has long been the handmaiden of politics.[5] Aristotle is concerned that rhetoric should not usurp the province of political science. He warns that the "enumeration and classification of the subjects of public business and polity" belong not to the art of rhetoric, but to political science. "But the more we try to make either dialectic or rhetoric not, what they really are, practical faculties, but sciences, the more we shall be destroying their true nature; for we shall be refashioning them and shall be passing into the region of sciences dealing with definite subjects rather than with words and forms of reasoning." [6]

Little danger was there of Aristotle's fear that communicators would become social, economic, or political scientists. These theories and findings of such investigator-thinkers turn out to be the educational and practical ideas to be applied by the speechmakers and writers. The aim of these communicators is to become highly articulate in deliberative discourse; their aim is that of action on the issues and principles analyzed

[3] Lester Thonssen and A. Craig Baird, *Speech Criticism* (New York, Ronald Press, 1948), 29. For discussion of politics and rhetorics, see Karl Wallace, "Rhetoric and Politics," *The Southern Speech Journal*, XX (Spring, 1955), 195–203; "Rhetoric, Politics, and Education of the Ready Man," in Donald Bryant, ed., *The Rhetorical Idiom* (Ithaca, N.Y., Cornell University Press, 1958), 71–95.

[4] Robert Bonner, *Aspects of Athenian Democracy* (Berkeley, Calif., University of California Press, 1933), 80; G. W. Botsford, *Hellenic History* (4th ed.; New York, Macmillan Co., 1956), 252.

[5] See Chapter 2. See also Thonssen and Baird, *op. cit.*, 465–472.

[6] Aristotle, *Rhetoric*, 1359b, 15 ff. in *The "Rhetoric" and "Poetics,"* ed. Friedrich Solmsen (New York, Random House, 1954).

and interpreted by these theorists or scientists. Thus the speechmaker with his interest in public affairs, finds himself in the local, state, or national legislative chamber, or in the United Nations. He communicates in the city council, the state legislature, in the House of Representatives or Senate, or in the British or continental parliament. He is an active speaker in the United Nations. Or he is a candidate for local, state, or national office. As President of the United States or as a member of the President's cabinet, he engages in defense of his tried or proposed policies. Millions of citizens, without benefit of office or formal deliberative sessions, engage in endless debates and discussions on current questions. School and college debaters, radio and television talkers, popular lecturers, all engage in the nationwide deliberative speaking.

What are the recurrent issues that challenge these moderns as the ancients were also challenged? Aristotle enumerates the areas in which deliberative speaking chiefly takes place, and should take place. "The main matters on which all men deliberate and on which political speakers make speeches are some five in number: finances, ways and means, war and peace, national defense, imports and exports (food supplies) and legislation." [7]

Thus these matters break down into practical problems that demand not simply speculative treatment but realistic formulation of policies to be embodied in law and custom. Specific legislation, some of it trivial, some of it critical for national or even world survival, is at stake.

Politics, Rhetoric, Ethics, and the Good Society

As rhetoric and politics have much in common in their mutual concern about constitutional systems and detailed changes in political continuity, so does rhetoric, again in consort with politics, attempt to achieve the good society. Aristotle assumes the unity of the social-political-ethical aim. He suggests that the three means of achieving persuasion require the persuader to (1) reason logically, (2) understand human character and goodness, and (3) to understand the emotions. States he, "It thus appears that rhetoric is an offshoot of dialectic and also of ethical studies. Ethical studies may fairly be called political and for this reason rhetoric masquerades as political science, and the professors of it as political experts." [8]

Rhetoric and politics both aim at a sound ethical society. To the Greek, no boundaries separated man as a political animal from man as

---

[7] *Ibid.*, 1360a.
[8] Aristotle, *Nicomachean Ethics*, X, ix, 1180–1181. See also *Eudemian Ethics*. See also footnote 14.

an ethical personality, capable of friendships, of virtue, well-being, and goodness. Ethics in the end aims to "decide what type of polity is the best or ideal, how each type must be constructed in order to attain its best, and what laws and customs it must employ to that end." [9]

To Aristotle the supreme practical science is politics (or social science). Of this social science, ethics is an integral part. The science of "politics" falls into two parts, ethics and politics. Aristotle's ethics no doubt, are social, and his politics are ethical; he does not forget that in the *Ethics* "the individual man is essentially a member of society, nor in the *Politics* that the good life of the state exists only in the good lives of its citizens." [10]

The identification of ethics with political life is thus complete. Rhetoric, similarly, has the method and goal of persuasive speaking to develop ethical citizenship. The "good" character of the speaker is essential in persuasiveness. "Persuasion is achieved by the speaker's personal character when the speech is so spoken as to make us think him credible, . . . on the contrary his character may almost be called the most effective means of persuasion he possesses." [11] He is given over extensively to "moral qualities" of virtues, courage, temperance, and other traits that constitute superior ethical personality. These individual qualities in turn permeate and determine the ethical composition of the state. [12]

Not only do rhetoric and politics unite in dealing with largely current problems and in influencing the state toward the "good society," but both are heavily concerned with justice, that is, with what is lawful and what is fair and equal. This justice, in the Greek concept, is conformity to custom and rule and with the entire concept of righteousness. Justice, as obedience to law, is coextensive with virtue. [13]

Justice, however, is more than legal conformity. It concerns the individual relationship of man to man. It involves "justice in the distribution of honour and wealth among the citizens, and remedial justice in the relations of man and man." [14]

Legal justice is concerned with particular laws which the community lays down for the government of its own members: It is partly written and partly custom, but the wider law—universal law—is the law of nature. "For there really is, as every one to some extent divines, a natural justice

[9] Aristotle, *Works,* ed. J. A. Smith and W. D. Ross (Oxford, Clarendon Press, 1908–31).

[10] W. D. Ross, *Aristotle: A Complete Exposition of His Works and Thought* (New York, Meridian Books, 1959), 183.

[11] Aristotle, *Rhetoric,* 1356a. See also Book II.

[12] For detailed discussion of rhetoric and ethics, see Chapter 6.

[13] W. D. Ross, *Aristotle,* 203–204.

[14] *Ethics of Aristotle* (London, Dent; New York, Dutton, 1937). See also W. D. Ross (translator in charge), *Works of Aristotle,* 12 vols. (Oxford, Clarendon Press, 1908–25), Vol. 9, *Ethica Nicomachea,* and *Ethica Eudemia;* Vol. 10, *Politica;* Vol. 11, *Rhetorica.*

and injustice that is binding on all men, even those who have no association or covenant with each other." [15]

Justice, as suggested above, also concerns the extralegal relationship
of man to man. Thus actions relating to justice can be divided into two
classes—those that affect the community and those that affect individuals.

Rhetoric and the Public Philosophy

The principle of individual freedom was eloquently argued by David
Lilienthal, then chairman of the Atomic Energy Commission, in his address of January 16, 1949:

> We believe that the purpose of our society is not primarily to assure the
> safety of the state, but to safeguard human dignity and freedom of the indi-
> vidual. We are a people who have built upon a faith in the spirit of man,
> who conceive that the development and happiness of the individual is the pur-
> pose and goal of American life.[16]

Walter Lippmann went beyond the individual and the state to find his
"public philosophy" in the working of "natural law." In his *The Public
Philosophy* he argues that ideas are important; they are effective when
treated as reality; human nature, which may or may not be affected by
ideas, is plastic. The cultural heritage which contains "the whole structure and fabric of the good life" may be rejected or acquired badly. We
now have an eclipse of the "public philosophy" (liberal democracy).
Mass public opinion has come to have a dominant and dangerous influence on government. Modern democracies are no longer functioning
democracies. We have largely abandoned freedom of speech. The whole
process of democratic government "is fundamentally vitiated." Lippmann
urges the revival of this abandoned philosophy, this "defense of civility."
It means loyalty to the laws of nature. "All agree that whether it is
the commandment of God or the reason of things, it is transcendent. It
is not something it decided on by certain men and then proclaimed by
them. . . . It is there objectively, not subjectively. It can be discovered.
It has to be obeyed." [17]

This ancient political doctrine with its conception of justice that aims
both at equality for the individual and justice for society has been also
a cardinal goal of deliberative and forensic speaking and writing. Many
American forensic speakers, powerful in their equipment of legal history
and procedure, and in their facility to summon major audience approvals,

[15] Aristotle, *Rhetoric*, I, viii, 1373b.

[16] A. Craig Baird, *Representative American Speeches, 1948–1949* (New York,
H. W. Wilson, 1949), 70.

[17] Walter Lippmann, *The Public Philosophy* (Boston and Toronto, Little Brown,
1955), 96, 172, *passim*.

have achieved more than technical impressiveness. Although they have not often agreed with each other or with political scientists in answers, they have nevertheless turned their evidence and logic into the ways of wisdom concerning man and his rights in the state. They have not only interpreted with distinction constitutional and statutory law, but have often, as an accompaniment to their courtroom eloquence, created constructive principles for legal and social justice.

Daniel Webster, for example, argued some one hundred and fifty cases before the higher courts. A thorough student of law, he, even more, was one of America's foremost forensic communicators. Other speakers before the courts who have had unusual ability in discussing law as an instrument of justice in political, industrial, and social affairs would include Alexander Hamilton, William Wirt, John Marshall, Salmon P. Chase, Rufus Choate, Robert G. Ingersoll, Jeremiah Black, William Evarts, John W. Davis, Justice Oliver W. Holmes, Learned Hand, and Clarence Darrow.

Deliberative speaking, too, has challenged with great vigor the rights and wrongs of social justice. In the twentieth century United States, members of the United States Congress, Presidents and their cabinets, candidates for public office, industrialists, union leaders, and other deliberative speakers, important and otherwise, at local and state levels up and down the land, have grappled with the issues of the New Freedom, the Square Deal, the New Deal, and the New Frontier. These speakers have developed pro and con the problems of slums and urban corruption, juvenile delinquency, prohibition, railways, public utility and trust regulation, mining safeguards, agricultural supports, banking and currency reforms, tariff and free trade, minimum wages, the eight-hour day, income, sales, and other taxes, equalization of educational opportunity, and equitable distribution of national wealth.

Speakers who have been impressive on such themes in the United States in this century have been Robert A. Taft, Adlai Stevenson, Wendell Willkie, Norman Thomas, Albert J. Beveridge, Jonathan Dolliver, William J. Bryan, William E. Borah, Robert LaFollette, Herbert Hoover, Harry S. Truman, Henry Wallace, Dwight D. Eisenhower, John F. Kennedy, Paul Douglas, Walter Reuther, Philip Murray, George Meany, John Lewis, and Benjamin Fairless.

Prominent among the issues of social justice have been civil and social rights for Negroes in the United States after the Supreme Court decision of 1955 in its support of integration in American schools. Political scientists have long framed such issues as these:

1. Are all Americans, regardless of race, color, religion, or economic status, to be regarded and treated as of high worth in any progressive society?

This question centers on the Negro more directly than at any time since the tragic era of the 1870's.

2. Do all Americans belong together? Is every social or legal barrier that creates division or undermines this solidarity to be resisted as foreign to our philosophy of equality? This issue, too, produced endless argument as it confronted the white citizens and the restless twenty million Negroes who marched and otherwise protested their status as "second class citizens."

3. Is it the duty of the more fortunate members of the American citizenry to demonstrate more and more the art of ameliorating the lot of the underprivileged? All groups on the surface answered "yes" to this inquiry—but forsook their high principles in their varied proposals for or against fair practices laws, educational integration, and similar programs. Thus the race question occupied much national thought and expression as the ancient and later philosophies of equality and justice dramatically came home to the Americans with the arrival of the atomic age.

Central in political theory has been the problem of the best kind of constitution for a state. The questions that have confronted students of politics from Aristotelian days have been, chiefly: What are the nature and rights of citizenship under a system of public law? How do kingship, aristocracy, and "polity" compare with the constitutional types under tyranny, oligarchy, and democracy? Should states be ruled by the rich, the intelligent elite, or the poor? Who should vote? Is the end of the state to have the common promotion of a good quality of life? How should the powers of the constitution be distributed with respect to the deliberative, executive, and judicial functions? How can changes in government structure be effected without revolution? [18]

Leaders in the twentieth century public address have stoutly defended, with deep, almost religious zeal, their particular governmental brand. Millions who listened in turn preached the same political tenets. Lenin, after the November Revolution, led the way into the camp of Communism (the proletarian socialist state). In Eastern Europe, most of Asia, and elsewhere over the globe, the forgotten hordes followed in this Lenin-Trotsky-Marxian train and, officially at least, declaimed the same principles. Hitler in 1934 accepted full responsibility for the blood purge that helped lead to the Nazi triumph in Germany. Millions of Teutons were spurred on to utter similar declarations for enthronement of an all-powerful Germanic state. Mussolini, too, expounded Fascism with ferocity and dictatorial eloquence. He "applied the torch of civilization" to Ethiopia and so led his nation into World War II until the final stilling of his Fascistic oratory.

In this welter of rival governmental doctrines, the Anglo-Saxon world

[18] Ernest Barker, *The Politics of Aristotle* (Oxford, Clarendon Press, 1946), 92–203.

of Britain and its Commonwealth, the United States, and the other nations where the individual still rated high in constitutionalism continued to interpret their free government systems and to compare them with the closed patterns of the oligarchical, dictatorial absolutism and the eclipse of individualism under Communism, Fascism, and the kindred labellings.

Thus England's foremost orator of the century, Winston Churchill, became the voice of parliamentary survival. In America, Woodrow Wilson stirred this nation and the rest of the free world in deep dedication to these better ways of justice, peace, and good will. So did Franklin D. Roosevelt with his fireside chats and his other more dramatic addresses as in successive crises he expressed anew the principles that embodied the essence of this nation's political ideals.

Many American speakers near the close of the nineteenth century and up through the twentieth differed from each other over how this democratic government structure should be developed. Norman Thomas, for example, was a fearless advocate of socialism. During and in the wake of two world wars, American sentiment heavily strengthened the aims of the American "governmental system," often at the sacrifice of the very principles that these zealous speakers defended as they attempted to suppress them. Nevertheless, the speechmakings by Senator Joseph McCarthy and others of his ilk in the 1950's did not obscure the major contributions to genuine democracy by such speechmakers as Dwight D. Eisenhower, Adlai Stevenson, John F. Kennedy, and the coterie of new leaders whose keynote addresses continued to expound with clarity and some originality the defense of popular government.

Rhetoric, Politics, and Freedom of Thought

One related principle common to politics and rhetoric has to do with freedom of thought, speech, writing, and decision making. Political science is interested in individual opinion and judgment. Communication in turn is committed to unhampered freedom from legislative and other restrictions as these intellectual judgments are embodied in language for audiences. These common goals of politics and rhetoric overlap in the areas discussed above, of analyzing constitutionalism, and of dealing with those policies that will best conserve and develop intellectual freedoms in individual and social development. Democratic government turns out to be the type most favorable to the realization of such liberties.

A free society, to foster such individual emancipation, must minimize the arbitrary power of the top leaders. It must provide unlimited occasions where it is the continual give-and-take of oral exchange. It must have few curbs on speaking and writing. The voting of each must be free from pressures. The elected representatives must also be unshackled in their deliberative decisions. This freedom must be aided by an education for all that will promise dependability of judgment and so of general welfare. Such has been the ideal of the free society, however short it falls in operation.

Freedom of speech and writing has been a central tradition in British political and communicative history. John Milton in his stormy protest to the British parliament in 1644 in his *Areopagitica,* a defense of a free press, stated the case for intellectual liberalism, that truth would prevail over error when these matters might be tested by investigation and discussion:

And though all the winds of doctrine were let loose to play upon the earth, so truth be in the field, we do injuriously by licensing and prohibiting to misdoubt her strength. Let her falsehood grapple; whoever knew truth put to the worse in a free and open encounter? For who knows not that truth is strong next to the Almighty; she needs no policies, nor stratagems, nor licensing to make her victorious, these are the shifts and defense that error uses against her power.[19]

Thomas Erskine, foremost British advocate of the late eighteenth century, repeatedly defended the freedom of speech and press when the critical times seemed to demand restriction of these liberties. In 1781 Erskine successfully pleaded for Lord George Gordon, who had been charged with treason for allegedly leading anti-Catholic riots. In 1783–84 Erskine, in his "On the rights of juries" argument, defended William Shipley, the Dean of Asaph, indicted on a charge of seditious libel for writing a tract on principles of government. Erskine said a little later, at the trial of Warren Hastings:

For minds thus subdued by the terrors of punishment [threats to prohibit a free press] there could issue no works of genius to expand the empire of human reason, nor any masterly compositions on the general nature of government, by which the great commonwealths of mankind have founded their establishments. . . . Under such terrors all the great lights of science and civilization must be extinguished, for men cannot communicate their free thoughts to one another with a free lash over their heads.[20]

Erskine had the power to relate a specific case to broad principles of British life, in his arguments for freedom of the press and trial by jury, against seditious libel law and arbitrary search, seizure and arrest. He

---

[19] John Milton, "Areopagitica" in *Works,* ed. F. A. Patterson, 18 vols. (New York, Columbia University Press, 1931–38), Vol. 4, 347.

[20] Thomas Erskine, "Defense of Stockdale," in *Works,* 4 vols. (London, J. Ridgway, 1812).

also "built ramparts of defense of present-day liberties, still none too secure." [21]

John Stuart Mill, distinguished philosopher, economist, and logician, and member of the British parliament of the nineteenth century, outlined the principles of free speech held then and now by British and American students of communication. According to Mill, the opinion of the side which we ignore or sidestep in discussion may be correct. Therefore it is wise to canvass again and again conclusions or policies that have been for the time determined. Or, continued Mill, the forbidden side or opinion which we ignore or sidestep may be partly true. Or, concluded Mill, even if one hundred per cent of truth is on our side, our opinions become valid and properly significant only if we subject them to examination. In the fire of vigorous opposition, our tenets become securely held. Indeed, as Mill suggested, our beliefs and convictions, unless under continual review, may become enfeebled or lost, and so "inefficacious for good." [22]

The chief problems that communicators and political theorists face concerning freedom of thought involve methods of applying, for example, the principles.

Free Speech and Tolerance

What are the limits of speech in war time? This problem, a constant one during the second world war, Professor Robert Cushman, of the political science department of Cornell University, dealt with in a radio broadcast (March 7, 1942). He concluded:

1. "We must accept without reservation the fact and necessity of wartime leadership with all its implications.
2. "We must also accept as a fact the vital need and value of public criticism and public discussion. . . . Public discussion and criticism are necessary for the safety of the nation.
3. "We must never lose sight of the fact that we are trying to win a war. . . . There are no arbitrary rules to guide the loyal citizen in the use which he makes of his civil liberty in time of war. His freedom of speech comes to him as a citizen of a free government but it is not an outright gift but a trust." [23]

American society in recent years has been indicted because it allegedly forces acceptance of popular standards and goals, imposes majority rule on an unwilling minority, and insists on conformity.

The question concerns not only governmental systems, but the charac-

[21] Houston Peterson, *A Treasury of the World's Great Speeches* (New York, Simon & Schuster, 1954), 185.

[22] John Stuart Mill, *Utilitarianism, Liberty, and Representative Government* (London, Dent, 1910), 78–113.

[23] A. Craig Baird, *Representative American Speeches: 1941–42* (New York, H. W. Wilson, 1942), 91–15.

ter of the public opinion and the forces that determine whether American democracy has vigor to survive and develop.

More specifically, after the first world war a considerable movement was under way to limit freedom of speech in the United States. Internal agencies, regional, municipal, patriotic, some private, some public, were active during the nineteen thirties, even militantly so, to restrict free expression as it was uttered over radio, in the press, on the stage, or platform. The same movement to muzzle free utterance was the inevitable accompaniment of the second world war. The opposition to freedom heightened during the 1950's with the McCarthyites at work up and down the land.

Within this movement to discourage free political give-and-take on soap boxes and behind microphones or loudspeakers was the untoward persistence of intolerance. About 1940 Robert Hutchins, then president of the University of Chicago, said, "We are in for a spree of intolerance." Naturally the second world war confirmed his prophecy—but that "spree" also persisted years later. The second world war made inevitable the rising tide of prejudice, suspicion, and hatred against opposing classes and races. Mill's essay, a hundred years earlier, was a plea, not for the abandonment of political opposition, or for a new political organization, but for a public opinion that would be genuinely tolerant. Tolerance to him meant that opinion would respect different points of view, impose no limits on the amount of agreement required, and would encourage new ideas and positions. A hundred years later liberal Americans have voiced these same sentiments and programs to resist intolerance.

Mill's British contemporary, Walter Bagehot, in his "Basis of Toleration," analyzed intolerance somewhat similarly. Bagehot believed that the tendency to persecute others was inherent in human nature. Persons with strong opinions would wish to perpetuate their ideas. The state has been the instrument for both promoting some ideas and crushing others. The masses are little controlled by theoretical or idealistic notions of free speech and tolerance. The dominant group shows its intolerance everywhere toward those who differ from them in dress, religion, or political views. But discussion, to be profitable, needs an educated citizenry. Intolerance springs from ignorant minds. "The minds of most would-be persecutors are themselves unmixed; their opinions are in a perpetual flux; they would persecute others for tenets which yesterday they had not heard of and which they will not believe tomorrow." To Bagehot, they cling to ideas derived from others and resist the encroachment of new ones. Discussion should thus be free, and it is to be curtailed only if it threatens the government itself.

Here Bagehot seems to be inconsistent. In general, he indicts shallow, emotionalized thinking and attitudes and would battle against intolerance at every point. He is, however, an Aristotlelian opposing "mass" judgments and leadership.[24]

Another common problem of politics and communication has been the mental-emotional immaturity and comparative illiteracy of speakers and their audiences on the matters under dispute. It is axiomatic for free speech and writing that the communicators and their audiences must be well informed.

Talk in America continues to multiply a hundredfold. The output of spoken words, via television, radio, and all other channels linking almost 200,000,000 people, has increased, is increasing, and some of it "ought to be diminished" (to paraphrase the resolution of the British parliament that tried to condemn George the Third). The garrulity and intellectual thinness that Thomas Carlyle deplored too often prevail in these later public talkers. The problem of free speech and the speaker's responsibility raises the ancient question of the kind of education that best fits for citizenship and the best way to develop such education.

How shall political talk and discussion be effective in conserving and promoting the minimum intellectual freedoms and abilities?

Education for effective communication in the political context calls for motivation. Educationally, we must affirm the direct liaison between education and political needs and programs. We do not imply that such training must be directed toward conformity and to some preconceived pattern of orthodoxy for state or nation. It does indicate, however, that every citizen should be well informed in matters economic, social, political, affecting the welfare of himself and his fellows. Citizenship education, though often distorted to mean regimented discipline, is the responsibility of every American school and college. If all are to discuss, debate, and decide, it is obvious that their training should equip them for such a role in the on-going republic. This is not indoctrination. In the United States, the high duty of every elementary and advanced student is to know and to participate in public affairs through free discussion, debate, and policy determination. Every school and college, therefore, is to square its standards to meet such aims. Otherwise, it is without justification for its existence.

Schools have officially announced their goals as including training for citizenship. Colleges have also proclaimed their education "to the nation's service." Nevertheless, the record all too often indicates that these goals are little more than those words. Too little progress is made in knowledge of national issues or in ability to analyze or suggest worthwhile solutions. The ancient and recurrent issues of war and peace, finance, taxation, and tariffs still confront the citizens. Too often the

[24] Emilie Isabel Barrington, *The Works and Life of Walter Bagehot*, 10 vols. (London, New York, Longmans Green, 1915), Vol. 8, 101 ff.

discussants, debaters, and persuasive speakers rattle among ideas and facts without grasp of the propositions or without preliminary research to implement the ideas. Thomas Carlyle, brilliant foe of most things, in his essay on "stump oratory," in 1850, cited above, was especially incensed against the British parliamentary speaking of his day. With tongue in cheek, he was not to be taken literally. But he made his point. Said he, "In these times and for several generations back, there has been strictly considered, no really excellent speech at all, but sham excellent merely." [25]

William G. Carleton, professor of government at the University of Florida, surveyed the communication scene and declared at a southern speech convention in 1947, "There is a decline in the art of delivering a speech. The result is that too often our contemporary speeches are pallid, synthetic hodgepodges, devoid of unity, philosophy, perspective, integrity, personality, and craftsmanship." [26]

Politics, Rhetoric, and Propaganda

In another way free speech and thought are being undermined. Propaganda (and we here refer to *sinister* propaganda) is being directed toward the American public as never before. Governmental political parties, organizations of every shape and sort, are broadcasting to the public, over radio and television, through the press, upon the lecture platform and at many informal gatherings. Or they are stealing upon us in more subtle forms. We are here referring to domestic propaganda. The daily barrage toward us and our fellow free nations out of the Communist world is another aspect of the problem.

Each source, concentrated in public relations agencies often located in New York or Washington, aims at its special economic, political, social, religious, educational, or other propagandistic appeal. And the vigor, skillful techniques, and extent have had a steadily increasing tempo since 1940. The messages sometimes short-circuit fact and dependable inference, visualize and glamorize their product or idea, cleverly or brazenly denounce competing ideas or programs. Suggestion and basic drives and motives supplant meaning throughout.

If we are to carry on the expression of a properly developed public opinion and the preservation of freedom of thought and expression, we must with some objectivity survey these bombardments of beguiling ap-

[25] Thomas Carlyle, "Stump Orator," in *Latter Day Pamphlets* (New York, Harper, 1850), 3–42.
[26] A. Craig Baird, *Representative American Speeches: 1946–47* (New York, H. W. Wilson, 1947), 222–4.

peals. Only thus will the pressure groups and the self-appointed political saviors be properly evaluated.

What contribution can education in communication make for the control of propaganda? Bad propaganda is merely another name for the commission of fallacies in speaking and writing. Instructors in logic, public speaking, and debate have long taught the ways to expose and avoid these illogical and unethical practices. He who has been trained in detecting fallacies, in refutation and rebuttal, is well equipped to reveal, for what they are, these distortions of valid suggestion and persuasion.[27]

One antidote to bad propaganda in the United States is the promotion of debate and discussion courses. Such learning experiences in schools and colleges become an important ally of free speech and thought in their resistance to propaganda.

One other movement works to undermine the influence of these liberties: the assaults on the philosophy and techniques of debate, discussion, and persuasive speaking and writing. Agents of this attack condemn debate as theoretically and practically indefensible. The argumentative technique, we are told, is unscientific and only increases conflict. Debate, it is alleged, is a substitute for investigative fact-finding. It merely sets up conclusions and then proceeds to substantiate them by selected facts and "special pleading"—devices that would not pass muster in any scientific or other discriminating group.[28]

The reply to this indictment is that it ignores a large section of human experience and relationships. Questions of pure science can be decided by laboratory means. But what of many social, political, or philosophical issues of policy? "Shall we go to war, or shall we refuse to fight under any terms?" cannot be decided by statistics or IBM computers. The problem is one of values and concepts. It belongs in a realm in which there is "no body of concepts on which the learned can agree." Hence, as Mill suggests, there should be set forth the rival doctrines, the controversial issues that must be settled if legislative assemblies and their implied free discussion and action are to continue. As former Harvard president James A. Conant put it, "Only from continued debate can new vistas be opened."[29] It is these new vistas which our system of free inquiry must continually glimpse if it is to function. Debate and discus-

---

[27] See Chapters 3 and 4 for treatment of generalization, statistics, authorities, analogies, causal inferences, deductive reasoning, and ignoring and begging the question.

[28] Richard Murphy, "The Forensic Mind," in *Studies in Speech and Drama in Honor of Alexander M. Drummond* (Ithaca, N.Y., Cornell University Press, 1941), 451–472.

[29] James Bryant Conant, "Free Inquiry or Dogma?" *Atlantic Monthly* (April, 1935), CLXV, 436–442.

sion in schools and colleges and in the marketplaces and legislative chambers opens such vistas and applies a technique essential both for valid speaking and for the expression of a mature public opinion.[30]

Richard Murphy voices the opinion that regardless of whether we work with Aristotelian or non-Aristotelian methods, our problem is to strengthen methodologies that encourage fair and thorough investigation, free hearings, and reasoned decisions or solutions. Murphy argues for forensic "minds" that are a combination of traditional virtues, constructive criticism of discussionists and debaters, and for the practical fruits of experimental logic.

Douglas Ehninger concludes similarly, "Debate considered as a generic mode of deliberation is, we must conclude, a cooperative endeavor. Aberrations have been, are today, and undoubtedly always will be committed in its name. But no method, even the one we call 'scientific,' is as flexible and responsive, or as widely applicable or easily mastered as we might like it to be." [31]

Demagogues and untoward propagandists will continue their appeals to our mass society. But powerful leaders of organized thinking and speaking will continue to meet these always recurring crises in our quest for freedom. Men and women, when the future of the state is in doubt, will come forward "to express the aspirations of our people in dignified honest speech." And freedom of thought and communication will prevail.[32]

Summary

Rhetoric will continue to be identified with politics (as that word has been used by Aristotle and since). Communication has been the obvious agency for holding together and directing the fortunes of the community, whether that community is local or national.

The citizenry of leaders and rank and file inevitably deals with the recurring problems of war and peace, finances and taxation, political party policies, and the endless amount of legislation necessary for the changing society.

Thus through small Town meetings and the United States Senate; through endless debates, discussions, informal assemblages; through press releases, journalism of all kinds, columnist and editorial broadcasts;

[30] A. Craig Baird, "The College Debater: 1955," *Southern Speech Journal*, XX (Spring, 1955), 204–211.

[31] Douglas Ehninger, "Decision by Debate: A Re-examination," *Quarterly Journal of Speech*, XLV (October, 1959), 282–287. Cf. A. Craig Baird, *Argumentation, Discussion and Debate* (New York, McGraw-Hill, 1950), 307 ff.

[32] A. Craig Baird, "The College Debater: 1955," *op. cit.*, 211.

through radio and television linkages with the mass audiences the practice of speaking and writing in the interest of public service has proceeded.

In this process full freedom of speech, writing, and thought have been basic. How else can public opinion and the ways of democratic freedom endure and develop? Proper restraint, toleration of dissent are explicit in the utterances and writings.

The goal of the social sciences and of the rhetoricians has been the Good Society, the ideal state, and the direction of the public philosophy toward such goals.

The freedoms of the mass society naturally offer a haven to "bad" as well as "good" propaganda. Rhetoric, with its utilization of logic, politics, and ethics, is importantly concerned with defenses against all forms of loose and deceptive thinking. The aim of rhetoric is to inculcate sound education and intelligent expression.

6

Ethical Responsibilities

Politics, Rhetoric, and Ethics

As rhetoric is closely related to politics, so is it identified with ethics. These four components of philosophy, politics, ethics, logic, and rhetoric, are so closely interwoven and are so mutually dependent as to constitute an entity. Politics largely records the experiences and subjects about which citizens debate. Logic and dialectic help to organize and test these ideas and their specific supports. Ethics provides proper motives and goals in the selection and shaping of the oral or written document. Rhetoric welds together these logical, political and ethical elements into a purposive communicative unit.

In this rhetorical-philosophical synthesis, what is the specific role of ethics? Politics, we noted in the previous chapter, is the theory and practice of establishing knowledge in the social-political-economic realm. Its province is to make clear the principles and supporting details that embody social experience. The description and comparison of the respective types of government, and the politics affecting the political life of each citizen, demand of the investigator logical procedures. Furthermore, since these political analyses deal with justice, individual and social freedoms, and the choices of better and worse, ethical judgments are inevitably involved.

Aristotle, in fact, at the outset of his discussion of politics, apparently viewed ethics as the handmaiden of politics. Said he:

If there is some end to the things we do, which we desire for its own sake, clearly this must be the good and chief end. . . . It would seem to belong to the most authoritative art and that which is truly the master art. And politics appears to be of this nature. For it is this which ordains which of the sciences should be studied in a state. . . . The end of this science must include the others, so that *this end must be the good for man.* (Emphasis added.)[1]

Thus although Aristotle, as Ernest Barker suggests, makes ethics a branch of politics, in the end the Greek philosopher-rhetorician conceded that ethics was dominant. "Ethics and politics are still closely connected; but there is a shifting of values which seems to result in an enthroning of ethics or moral philosophy, with 'nomothetics' or political philosophy serving as its chief minister."[2]

What is this concept of ethics, basic for the successful working of politics, logic, and rhetoric?

Ethics (ἦθος) to the Greek meant "the customs of a race." ("Moral philosophy" was the Latin equivalent, from *mores,* customs.) More specifically, the term meant "the systematic study of the ultimate problems of human conduct" (ἦθος, character, or ἔθος, custom).[3]

These ultimate problems of human conduct to be studied are chiefly, (1) What is the desirable life of the individual? and (2) What is the desirable end of society? Ethical inquiries are not so much a search for facts as they are a dealing with values. Ethics is concerned not so much with behavior as it exists but as it ought to be. This branch of philosophy attempts to describe the ideal individual and the "good" society. It asks, "What is the highest good of human conduct and what is its ultimate aim?"

The *Summum Bonum* and Rhetoric

The classical philosophers, notably Aristotle, and the later ones, pondered the question, What is the highest good? Is it happiness? Is it a form of egoism? utilitarianism? altruism? Is it empirical, rational, intuitional, or another explanation of duty?

What, more specifically, is this *summum bonum?* Aristotle states at the outset of his ethics that "every art and every inquiry, every action and choice, seems to aim at some good; whence the good has been rightly defined as that to which all things aim." He here looks to some end beyond immediate behavior. Activities may not in themselves be good, but become so if their ultimate contribution produces the "good man."

What is this highest good? Aristotle accepts the view that the end of human life is *eudaimonia* (good fortune accompanied by external pros-

[1] *Ethica Nicomachea,* ed. W. D. Ross, in *Works of Aristotle* (Oxford, Clarendon Press, 1925), 1094a, 17 to 1094b, 7. Quoted by Karl Wallace, "Rhetoric and Politics," in Donald Bryant (ed.), *The Rhetorical Idiom* (Ithaca, N.Y., Cornell University Press, 1958), 75.

[2] Ernest Barker, *The Politics of Aristotle* (Oxford, Clarendon Press, 1946), 356.

[3] Abraham Wolf, article "Ethics," in *Encyclopaedia Britannica,* Vol. 8.

perity). The Greek word is inadequately translated as *happiness*. Permanent pleasure is implied. A more comprehensive translation would be "well-being." [4]

This life of "well-being" may be pleasure, or honor, or virtue, or wealth, or contemplation. Aristotle regards virtues as expressions of "feelings," as capacities, or dispositions. These "virtues" become most significant and typical when they conform to Aristotle's doctrine of the mean. The mean is opposed to excesses or deficiency. If, for example, the reaction might be fear, the excess would be cowardice, or rashness, with true courage as the mean. Liberality is the mean of prodigality or frugality. Self-respect is balanced between vanity and humility. Modesty is the mean between bashfulness and shamelessness. Contemplation is the "highest aim." Thus in this hierarchy or continuum from the lesser to the greater "goods," Aristotle places contemplation at the top. To him, however, contemplation is not a passive, expressionless state, but rather one of activity. It embodies the best of several virtues. It deals with those truths already received from mathematics, metaphysics, and perhaps natural philosophy. Such activity at this highest level is consistent, advancing, and permanent.[5]

Hedonism and Communication

What specific happiness or well-being is involved? Is it only that of an individual? or of the group? or both? Is the individual the protagonist or even the sole agent? One philosophical school would identify this satisfaction as personal pleasure. This is the hedonistic doctrine. But such egoistic eudaimonisticism also recognized mental and aesthetic as well as physiological satisfactions. Epicurus expounded the life of pleasure but he also advocated asceticism to minimize the pain and excesses that would accompany and destroy pleasure. To Epicurus and the mature hedonists pleasure alone is good, but they recognized the impossibility of separating pleasure from pain and the impossibility of developing only isolated individual satisfactions through personal activities in a world that at every point affected individual motives and conditions. Thus this policy, as far as it stressed only private happiness and ignored the social mores, gradually lost its appeal.

Cynicism and similar approaches attempted an answer as to what should be done about the pain and adversity that hedonism could not avoid. Diogenes and other cynics attempted to ignore the world—or to practice immunity from its violence or beguilements. Satisfaction and serenity lay in antisociality. The extreme cynic was an ascetic, who re-

[4] W. D. Ross, *Aristotle* (New York, Meridian Books, 1959), 186.
[5] Aristotle, *Topica*, 1097a, 13, to 1098a, 20.

sorted to a monk-cloistered life. Zeno (third century B.C.) was of this school, with his tenets of indifference to the ups and downs of civilized society. The one effective way to combat this confused world with its individual misfortunes and existence was to cultivate invariable indifference, stoicism. Epictetus preached the necessity of resistance to external influences. The only true good lies within one's self.[6]

Good or evil depends on the self. Virtue resides in the will. Only will is good or bad. And the only true good is virtue. Independent virtue in itself is sufficient for happiness or well-being. Such stoic self-control and attitudes assure independence from the world.

Such philosophy led to the assumption of the role of destiny. All happenings were fixed by God. The human soul is nature—but nature is the expression of Deity. Epictetus continually expresses reverence for Deity. Such direction of stoicism allied it with religion. The individual was at the center of the scene, but had responsibility for the successful working of the divine order. And divine order governs the universe.

The Highest Good and Social Consequences

Still another view of the highest good and the testing of it lay in the emphasis on social consequences. This was the doctrine of utilitarianism, the well-being of the community rather than merely that of the individual. Jeremy Bentham (1748–1832) and John Stuart Mill (1806–1873) were prominent expositors of such social ethics. To such philosophers, whether a given action was right or wrong was to be determined by social behavior. A right action is one that produces the greatest happiness to the greatest number. Here was hedonism, but the pleasure or well-being concentrated on the group alone. Any action that produced benefits would be "right." The consequences of the act, not the motives of the agents, would be the determinant. The aims and methods would thus be semiscientific, semiexperimental. Bentham, for example, insisted that the pleasurable results were to be measured solely by "their intensity, duration, certainty, propinquity, fecundity, purity, and extent." He would obviously examine in detail whatever later conditions were to be assigned to these "causes."

Utilitarianism and Rhetoric

The critics of utilitarianism asked, How can we measure with any accuracy the extent of the happiness produced? Can we properly analyze the mental and other reactions of the individuals to decide whether on the whole these people are the happy ones? And do we match them

6 Epictetus, *The Works of Epictetus,* tr. Thomas W. Higginson (Boston, Little Brown, 1866), "Progress," 14–16.

with the other, less fortunate group? But are some people not more important than others? Nietzsche so argued. The statistical "hedonistic calculus" of Bentham, the critics claimed, placed undue weight on the "average" man. The happiness or woe of the genius outweighs that of the low-grade, or rank and file. It is a case of poorly managed statistics. Furthermore, what constitutes "effect"? How many specific "effects" are to be examined? Are they to be isolated by some laboratory methods and each one diagnosed to ascertain its pleasurable or painful characteristics? Also, what is to be said of "results" that are one thing today and different tomorrow? Shall we concentrate on the immediate afterconditions, or shall we attempt to journey long-range "consequences"? The practical problem is to assess all important results and to determine at what point to estimate them.

Furthermore, what degree of certainty is to attend the evaluation? What degree of probability is sufficient to justify the alleged consequences? And is it not also necessary to appraise the motives with which the action is done? Do evil purposes justify an act that apparently produces beneficial results? Critics of utilitarianism were quick to point out that means were not to be separated from ends. The moral worth of the transaction must take account of motives, but the process must be examined in its totality—with no distinction between means and ends. Such, in general, have been the logical and speculative qualifications attached to the utilitarian treatment and validation of ethics.

The disposition of some utilitarian exponents to minimize motives was countered by those who conceived duty as the supreme good. This was the Kantian philosophy of describing right conduct as reflecting the sense of duty accompanying all behavior.

What, according to Kant, distinguished the moral man from the nonmoral one? Answer: A sense of duty. Every man has a moral pulse, a sense of obligation—that which he ought to do, despite his opposing inclinations. The moral man suppresses his random impulses and follows the line his moral nature indicates. Such is Kant's good man.

What, then, is the test of moral action in a given situation? To Kant, every action is weighed in the light of its contribution to a universal code of behavior. "Nothing in the world is good except good will." This is Kant's categorical imperative. It is obedience to the unconditional law of duty. "There is therefore but one categorical imperative, namely this: Act only on that maxim whereby thou canst at the same time will that it should become a universal law." [7]

The critics of Kant have suggested that such an ethical concept fails

[7] Immanuel Kant, *The Philosophy of Kant,* selected and translated by John Watson (New York, Macmillan, 1888), 241.

to account sufficiently for the results. More importantly, the problem of what to do about a conflict of motives or duties cannot be sidestepped. Sentiments and other complicated reactions confuse the "duties" to be obeyed. Moreover, is not duty and moral sensitivity merely a correlative of learning? High ideals are the product of education. Conscience and similar designations have no reality apart from the psychological pattern of personality. And a good many feelings, attitudes, and sentiments represented submission to the force of state, church, or community authority and tradition. Kantian adherents have asked, How can good and evil, duty and dereliction of duty, be distinguished?

One answer has been intuitionism: Every person has inherited this impulse toward the right and needs only to develop it. Such an approach cleaves to faith in human nature and its endowment within immortal stature. As William Faulkner put it in his speech in acceptance of the Nobel Prize, "It is easy enough to say that man is immortal simply because he will endure. . . . I refuse to accept this. I believe that man will not merely endure; he will prevail. He is immortal, not because alone among creatures he has an inexhaustible voice, but because he has a soul, a spirit capable of compassion and sacrifice and endurance. . . ."[8]

These have been the attempts to describe and define the good life as the highest good, as well-being, with its detailed virtues of courage and wisdom, and other attributes; its goals of individual behavior through pleasure seeking, adjustment to environment, or stoic rejection of such relationships; its concentration on individual excellencies, or upon the social values of "right" conduct, or on some combination of individual and social living; and upon ethical progress as judged by man's obligations to duty; the reliance upon reasoning for vindication of ethical values; or resort to experimental or other utilitarian social proofs to estimate the specific moral consequences.

How are these representative ethical concepts, however they are harmonized, qualified, or otherwise interpreted, woven into rhetoric and practical communication?

Aristotelian Ethics and Rhetoric

Aristotle, whose influence on communication has been more important than that of any other classical thinker, believed that successful communication—and he was expounding persuasive communication—depended on "the moral character of the speaker, or in the production of a certain

[8] William Faulkner, address, accepting the Nobel Prize, December 10, 1950. See Houston Peterson (ed.), *A Treasury of the World's Best Speeches* (New York, Simon & Schuster, 1954), 815–16.

disposition in the audience, or in the speech itself by means of real or
apparent demonstration." [9]

Of the means of persuasion, he said, the speech contains three kinds.
"The first kind reside in the character of the speaker [ἦθος]; the second
consist in producing a certain [the right] attitude of the hearer; the third
appertain to the argument proper, in so far as it actually or seemingly
demonstrates." [10]

What, according to Aristotle, marks the character of the speaker?

> The character of the speaker is a cause of persuasion when the speech is
> so uttered as to make him worthy of belief; for as a rule we trust men of probity
> more, and more quickly, about things in general, while on points outside the
> realm of exact knowledge, where opinion is divided, we trust them abso-
> lutely. . . . It is not true, as some writers on the art maintain, that the probity
> of the speaker contributes nothing to his persuasiveness; on the contrary, we
> might almost affirm that his character (ἦθος) is the most potent of all the
> means of persuasion.[11]

Despite Aristotle's view of the efficacy of ethical proof in discourse, he
still assumed the supreme importance of logical argument. Throughout
his rhetoric, however, are suggestions of the ethics as basic in all good
communication.

"What are the sources of credibility in speakers?"he asks and then
explains: "There are three things, apart from demonstrative proofs,
which inspire belief: viz, sagacity, high character and good will." He
continues:

> Speakers are untrustworthy in what they say or advise from one or more
> of the following causes: Either through want of intelligence they form wrong
> opinions; or while they form correct opinions, their rascality leads them to say
> what they do not think; or while intelligent and honest enough, they are not
> well disposed and so perchance will fail to advise the best course—though
> they see it. It necessarily follows that the speaker who is thought to have all
> these qualifications has the confidence of his hearers.[12]

To Aristotle, the ethical proof is thus connected with the speech itself
—one of the three elements of "proof." Ethical character produces belief
in the realm of opinion—as produced in the speech itself. This *ethos* of
the speaker is not an antecedent impression held toward the speaker by

[9] J. E. C. Welldon, The "Rhetoric" of Aristotle (Macmillan, 1886), 1356a.

[10] From Lane Cooper (tr., ed.), The "Rhetoric" of Aristotle, I, ii, p. 8; copyright,
1932, Lane Cooper. Reprinted by permission of Appleton-Century-Crofts, New York.
See also, in The "Rhetoric" and "Poetics," ed. Fred Solmsen, tr. Rhys Roberts
(Modern Library), Aristotle's Rhetoric, I, ii, 1356a.

[11] Lane Cooper, op. cit., I, ii, pp. 9–12; Solmsen, op. cit., 1356b.

[12] Lane Cooper, op. cit., II, i, p. 92.

the audience, but consists of materials and persuasive details of the communication itself.

The speaker, to Aristotle, establishes sagacity in the discourse if he so handles his materials as to demonstrate intellectual integrity and wisdom. He is consistent and logical in his inferences from causal reasoning, specific instances, analogies, and deductive propositions, and in handling of evidence. He develops these ideas with common sense and moderation, and with close intimacy with his subject and its relationship to important events of the day.

How does the audience gauge the intelligence, character, and good will of the speaker? To Aristotle these traits are evidenced by an analysis of what is "virtuous"; the audience must be convinced that the communicator is virtuous. He can create such a quality of virtue either for himself or for those that are associated with him.

The noble is that which is desirable in and for itself, and also wins praise; or is that which is good, and also pleasant because good. If this definition is right, then it must follow that virtue is noble, since virtue is good, and is worthy of praise. Now virtue, in the popular conception, is a faculty tending to provide and preserve "goods" or a faculty tending to confer many great benefits—indeed, "all manner of benefits on all occasions."

The elements of virtue are:

Justice	Magnificence	Gentleness
Courage	Magnanimity	Prudence
Temperance	Liberality	Wisdom [13]

To create an impression of intelligence and character either of himself or some other person, the speaker presents a listener or reader with the following considerations:

1. He is trustworthy.
2. He identifies his actual qualities with qualities acceptable to the audience.
3. "Whatever the quality an audience esteems, the speaker must attribute that quality to the object of his praise." [14]
4. The speaker shows that the object of his praise is one who acts according to deliberate moral choice.
5. He makes a good deed appear better; an evil deed appears of no importance.

In order to impress the good will of the speaker upon an audience, he must understand what kinds of people others love and admire, what kinds of people they hate and despise, and the causes of these feelings.

Good will can be best understood through the emotions. By these

13 *Ibid.*, I, ix, pp. 46–47.
14 *Ibid.*, 51.

—the emotions—are meant those states which are attended by pain and pleasure, and which as they change, make a difference in our judgments, for example, anger, pity, fear, and all the like, and also their opposites.[15]

To create good will in his listeners, the speaker must know his audience so that he can present himself as a friend to what they consider good, an enemy to what they consider evil. He must present himself as one who has done some good service to them or to their friends.

The speaker must create a feeling of identification with his audience and destroy any feelings of animosity they may have toward him. To create this impression of good will, the speaker must prove

. . . that men are enemies or friends; if they are not enemies or friends, to make them appear to be either; if their friendship or enmity is pretended, to refute them; if there be a dispute whether an act was done through anger or through hatred, to refer the act to either emotion as the speaker may choose.[16]

This good will is revealed by the speaker in these fashions:

1. Through his ability to balance his praise to the audience—not too little, not too much.
2. His close identification with his audience.
3. His personal qualities, devoid of exhibitionism, his straightforwardness.
4. His general air and method of self-control, and tact.[17]

The basic elements of Aristotle's concepts of ethical proof may be thus summarized:

1. The speaker is to possess personal qualities of intelligence, character, and good will and their accompanying virtues if he is to be worthy of belief.

2. These qualities will manifest themselves primarily in the speaker's invention, and to a lesser extent in his arrangement and style and delivery.

3. The speech itself is the communicator of ethical proof rather than the prior reputation of the speaker.

4. The choices made by the speaker for his ethical appeals will be determined by the type of speech and nature of the audience.

5. The proper aim of deliberative speaking is the defense of causes which promote the happiness of society, and the arguments are to be selected with such end in mind.

6. Logical, emotional, and ethical modes of persuasion represent a continuum, each supplementing the other. As Edward Pross concluded, "The only consummately accurate judge as to the forms of proof [logical,

---

[15] *Ibid.*, 92.

[16] *Ibid.*, 107. See also William M. Sattler, "Conceptions of *Ethos* in Ancient Rhetoric," *Speech Monographs*, XIV (1947), 55–65, for an authoritative treatment of the subject.

[17] Thonssen and Baird, *Speech Criticism* (New York, Ronald Press, 1948), 387.

ethical, pathetic] employed by a speaker is the individual auditor. Up to a certain point the veteran of the platform and the skilled rhetorician can predict that author's verdict, but their prognostications can never be perfectly reliable." [18]

7. Truth, right and justice would ultimately prevail when given equally competent advocates. Stated Aristotle:

> . . . the art of Rhetoric has its value. It is valuable, first, because truth and justice are by nature more powerful than their opposites; so that when decisions are not made as they should be, the speakers with the right on their side have only themselves to thank for the outcome. Their neglect of the art needs correction. [19]

Cicero, too, reflected strong interest in ethical qualities of discourse. Wrote the Roman orator:

> It contributes much to the success in speaking, that the morals, principles, conduct, and lives of those for whom they plead, should be such as to merit esteem; and that those of their adversaries should be such as to deserve censure and also that the minds of those before whom the cause is pleaded should be moved as well toward the speaker and toward him for whom he speaks. [20]

Cicero discussed various moral qualities, such as good nature, liberality, gentleness, piety, grateful feelings, and freedom from selfishness and avarice. The art of speaking, he suggested, lay in one's ability to produce these characteristics of the speaker. Said he, "Everything that characterizes men of probity, and humility, not acrimonious, not pertinacious, not litigious, nor harsh, very much conciliates benevolence, and alienates the affections from those in whom such qualities are not apparent." [21]

Quintilian, a schoolmaster, and a rhetorician less affected by the methods of Roman forensic speaking, was more positive in his insistence on ethical standards than were the previous rhetoricians. The perfect orator, in his words, "cannot exist unless he is a good man."

According to Quintilian, it is impossible to regard men as intelligent who, confronting two paths to virtue and vice, choose the latter. Lack of prudence would also condemn them; they should fear both severe legal penalties and the torments of their evil consciences. Concluded Quintilian, "There is nothing so preoccupied, so distracted, so rent and torn

[18] Edward Pross, *"A Critical Analysis of Certain Aspects of Ethical Proof"* (Ph.D. dissertation, State University of Iowa, 1942).

[19] Lane Cooper, *op. cit.*, I.

[20] Cicero, *On Orators and Oratory*, tr. J. S. Watson (London, George Bellows Sons, 1875), II.

[21] Cicero, *De Oratore*, II, xliii.

by so many and such varied passions as an evil mind." [22] He sounds
much like an Israelite prophet, or like Daniel Webster in his plea to the
jury in the White murder case, at Salem, Massachusetts, in which Webster dramatically pictured the dominance of conscience.

Quintilian connects excellence, in his presentation, directly with purity
of character. "Can a bad and unjust man speak on such themes as the
dignity of the subject demands?" He answers negatively. "Shall we
then dignify the traitor, the deserter, the turncoat with the sacred name
of orator? The bad man and the perfect orator can never be identical.
For nothing is perfect if there exists something else that is better."

He continues, "Bad men, in their speaking, drop their mask unawares.
Even when they tell the truth they fail to win belief. Audiences can
detect the truth or falsity of their character." Quintilian defends the
character of Cicero. The latter possessed moral courage and loyalty to
conviction, as illustrated by the manner of his death. "In meeting it he
displayed singular fortitude." [23]

For, however one strives to conceal it, insincerity will always betray
itself. According to Quintilian, "There never was in any man so great
eloquence as would not begin to stumble and hesitate so soon as his words
ran counter to his inmost thoughts."

He concludes: "Therefore let those that are young, or rather let all
of us, whatever our age, since it is not too late to resolve to follow what
is right, strive with all our hearts and devote all our efforts to the pursuit
of virtue and eloquence." [24]

Campbell, Blair, Whately, and Ethics

Later rhetorical writers, and medieval, modern English and American
theorists, did not stress ethics in communication as vividly as did Quintilian. Christian education and rhetoric morality reinforced the Greek
and Roman ethical philosophy in discourse, but the moral quality, when
not expounded at length, was invariably assumed. George Campbell,
Hugh Blair, and Richard Whately, leaders in Christian thought in Britain,
followed the Aristotelian-Ciceronian-Quintilian position.

Campbell enlarges the Aristotelian description by giving "reputation"
a "considerable power" in *ethos*, an ethical role denied by Aristotle but
strongly upheld by Quintilian. But Campbell, like Aristotle, stresses the
personal qualifications of character and intelligence. He strongly affirms
Quintilian's "good man" theory:

[22] Quintilian, *Institutes of Oratory*, tr. H. E. Butler (London, Heinemann; New
York, Putnam, 1922), I, xii, 1, 4, 8, 357 ff.

[23] *Ibid.*, XII, i, 16–20.

[24] *Ibid.*, XII, 30–34.

The reputation of the attestor hath a considerable power. Now the speaker's apparent conviction of the truth of what he advanceth, adds to all his other arguments and evidence. . . . Sympathy in the hearers to the speaker may be lessened in several ways, chiefly by these two: by a low opinion of his intellectual abilities, and by a bad opinion of his morals. The latter is the more prejudicial of the two. . . . Hence it hath become a common topic with rhetoricians, that in order to be a successful orator, one must be a good man; for to be good is the only sure way of being long esteemed good, and to be esteemed good is previously necessary to one's being heard with due attention and regard. Consequently, the topic hath a foundation in human nature. There are, indeed, other things in the character of the speaker, which in a less degree will hurt his influence: youth, inexperience of affairs, former want of success, and the like.[25]

Hugh Blair, in his *Lectures on Rhetoric and Belles Lettres,* expounds his view of *ethos* and suggests the importance of this concept in rhetorical theory: "What stands highest in the order of means [of improving in eloquence] is personal character and disposition. In order to be a truly eloquent or persuasive speaker, nothing is more necessary than to be a virtuous man. This was a favorite position among ancient rhetoricians."

To Blair probity, disinterestness, candor, and "other good moral qualities" of the person trying to persuade others "give weight and force to every thing he utters." The reverse the audience views as artifice, trick, "as the play only of speech; and viewed in this light, whom can it persuade?"

Blair goes beyond Campbell and Aristotle in contending that "virtue" assists the speaker in all of his speaking preparation, this assemblage of materials and prior thinking. Indeed, virtue is a prerequisite to *pathos* (in the Greek sense: emotion). Without *ethos,* the audience appeals cannot be effective. "No kind of Language is so generally understood and so powerfully felt, as the native language of worthy and virtuous feelings. It is only a native and unaffected glow of feeling, which can transmit the emotion to others."

Blair mentions all nine of the virtues which Aristotle recommends, and concludes that the speaker equipped with ethical firmness has that which "bespeaks a consciousness of his being thoroughly persuaded of the truth, or justice of what he delivered."

Thus Blair expands the theory of *ethos* into these wider areas, re-emphasizes its prime importance in persuasion, and restates from his eighteenth century British experience the Aristotelian "virtues."

Bishop Richard Whately, in contrast to Campbell and Blair, makes clear that he is discussing the "impression produced in the minds of

[25] George Campbell, *The Philosophy of Rhetoric,* ed. Lloyd Bitzer (Carbondale, Ill., Southern Illinois University Press, 1963), 97.

hearers" rather than "the real character of the speaker." [26] Since he is primarily concerned with argumentative discourse, he gives comparatively little space to ethics. His theological background and leadership, however, move him to follow the classical ethical tradition. Said he, "There is, I conceive, no point in which the idea of dishonest artifice is so intimately associated with that of rhetoric, as the address to the feelings or active principles of our nature." [27] He recognizes that the play upon the emotions often leads to "bad" ethical expression.

He qualifies Quintilian's assumption that a virtuous man automatically carries over such qualities into his speech. "The possession of the building materials is no part of the art of Architecture." [28]

Like Aristotle, Whately contends that for the virtuous man to develop virtue into rhetorical skill, he must do so within the speech itself—by developing an ethical relationship with the audience.[29]

Whately cites Aristotle's distinction between "real" character and that by which the audience is persuaded. Like Aristotle, Whately divides character into intelligence, virtue, and good will, but unlike Aristotle, this nineteenth century English rhetorician blends ethical expression with the pathetic, so that the ethical becomes subsidiary to the pathetic proof.

American Rhetoricians and Ethics

Among early American rhetoricians, John Quincy Adams, first professor of rhetoric at Harvard (1806–1808), in his *Lectures on Rhetoric and Oratory* devoted the Fifteenth to the "intellectual and moral qualities of an orator."

Said this United States Senator and Harvard professor, "The first and most previous quality then which contributes to the success of a public speaker is an honest heart; a sentiment which I wish above all others may be impressed with indelible force on your minds." Such integrity of heart is founded upon an enlarged and enlightened morality. He is to be a person alert to his duty; correct in his estimate of good and evil; of strong moral sense, in all applications in judicial, deliberative, and pulpit discourse. In the speech itself, according to Adams, "no uniform rule may be prescribed. The only advice I can give you for all emergencies is, before you enter upon that profession, to lay the foundation of your conduct in a well digested system of ethics." [30]

[26] Richard Whately, *Elements of Rhetoric,* ed. Douglas Ehninger (Carbondale, Ill., Southern Illinois University Press, 1963).

[27] *Ibid.,* 122.

[28] *Ibid.,* 4–5.

[29] *Ibid.,* 14–15.

[30] John Quincy Adams, *Lectures on Rhetoric and Oratory,* 2 vols. (New York, Cambridge, Hilliard & Metcalf, 1810), 344, 351.

Chauncey Goodrich gave only qualified endorsement of Quintilian's insistence upon ethical qualities. Virtue, he stated in a lecture, "is certainly not necessary to eloquence though it is favorable to its most perfect exercise." [31]

In his essays on British eloquence, however, Goodrich praises those who have ethical power and obviously discounts Sheridan and others for their apparent lack of strong moral qualities in their character and utterances.[32]

American theorists and teachers of rhetoric and public address in the later twentieth century have continued to transmit and endorse the Aristotelian-classical tradition of the moral character of the communicator and his ethical proofs. Norwood Brigance, Waldo Braden, Richard Murphy, Karl Wallace, Robert Oliver, Donald Bryant, William D. Howell, Winston Brembeck, Franklyn Haiman, to name a few contemporary rhetoricians, have each expounded in their texts and studies the principles and methods of ethics in communication.

Dr. Norwood Brigance was strongly motivated by ethical philosophy. He cited Aristotle and Quintilian, and adopted the classical principles of excellence in communication through character and personal integrity. He analyzed the problem, however, from the audience approach. "We believe men of good will more fully and readily than others." [33] He proceeded to frame a "Hippocratic Oath for Public Speakers," would establish a state licensing examination for competence, and would require an "oath of responsibility" of every communicator.[34]

Professor Karl Wallace proposed "four moralities" of communication:

1. Duty of search and inquiry
2. allegiance to accuracy and fairness
3. expression of individual motive
4. toleration of dissent.[35]

Donald Bryant and Karl Wallace, in their *Fundamentals of Public Speaking*, discuss at length "persuasion and the ethics of the speaker." They insist on respect for ends—"social ideals are inherent in public speaking"; honoring the opinion of others; honoring the speaker's own

[31] John P. Hoshor, "Lectures on Rhetoric and Public Speaking by Chauncey Allen Goodrich," *Speech Monographs*, XIV, 1947, 11.

[32] Chauncey Goodrich, "Essays," in A. Craig Baird (ed.), *Select British Eloquence* (Carbondale, Ill., Southern Illinois University Press, 1963).

[33] Norwood Brigance, *Speech: Its Techniques and Disciplines* (New York, Appleton-Century-Crofts, 1952), 432 ff.

[34] William Norwood Brigance, *Speech Communication* (New York, Appleton-Century-Crofts, 1947), 7–8.

[35] Karl Wallace, "An Ethical Basis of Communication," *Speech Teacher*, IV (January, 1955), 9.

opinion; playing fair with the hearers; respect for information; proper speaker motivation; and sound character and trustworthiness.[36]

These two rhetoricians are obviously enlarging upon and illustrating concretely the standard classical approach to the problem of ethical theory and applications.

Professor Richard Murphy summarized the contemporary thinking relating to ethics in discourse. He met effectively the criticism that (1) all rhetoric is immoral, or (2) that it is amoral. He notes that "rhetoric lags in a concern for value"; that members of the speech profession lacked professional standards; that there was no enforcing agency. He pleads for speech organizations to set up standards of ethics and attempt to enforce them. He notes well the current interest in ethics among various professional organizations and their spokesmen, for example, governmental leaders, psychologists, lawyers, advertisers, radio and television directors. Murphy grapples with specific practices that he regarded as ethically bad, such as ghost writing, but he regards his analysis as "prefatory" only, and refuses to detail the principles to be followed in improving ethical theory and practice of public address.[37]

Dr. Giles W. Gray and Waldo Braden, in their text on public speaking, adopt a utilitarian approach to ethics with the proposition that good speaking requires realization of social responsibility. Citing the "Oath of Hippocrates" for the physician, these authors maintain that the speaker, like the physician, has a social responsibility. The speaker needs to examine his own ethical standards, his motives for speaking, and the effect of his utterances on his listeners and on the welfare of those affected." The authors echo Quintilian's *Institutes* (Book XII, Chapter i) and Paul's Letter to the Corinthians—to indicate the common Roman and Christian foundations of ethics.[38]

Dr. Robert Oliver, in his *The Psychology of Persuasive Speech*,[39] in a chapter on "the ethics of persuasion," rejects the absolutist ethics that God ordained certain ethical laws and that human beings have characteristics that make certain kinds of action forever right, and others forever wrong. Oliver accepts the utilitarian principle of social effects. In the long run, according to Oliver, what is good for society as a whole is ethical and what is detrimental to society is unethical. The problem as

[36] Donald C. Bryant and Karl R. Wallace, *Fundamentals of Public Speaking* (3d ed.; New York, Appleton-Century-Crofts, 1960), 287 ff.

[37] Richard Murphy, "Preface to an Ethic of Rhetoric," in Donald C. Bryant (ed.), *The Rhetorical Idiom* (Ithaca, N.Y., Cornell University Press, 1958), 125–143.

[38] Giles W. Gray and Waldo Braden, *Public Speaking: Principles and Practices* (New York, Harper, 1951), 14 ff.

[39] Dr. Robert Oliver, *The Psychology of Persuasive Speech* (2d ed.; New York, Longmans Green, 1957), 20–36.

Oliver views it is to differentiate what is effective and what is ethical. To him the problem of ethics is "inescapably difficult," but it may be approached by application of simple moral principles. These include:

1. Presentation of sound evidence
2. Knowing the subject on which you speak
3. Linking the audience appeals with emotional values with which the subject has actual connection
4. Avoiding "sneak attacks" on leadership of opposing points of view
5. Rejection of the logic that "the end justifies the means"
6. Avoiding concealing self interest in advocating a proposition
7. Advocating only what you believe.

He pleads for honest motive and honest conviction.

Dr. Franklyn S. Haiman questions whether persuasive discourse adheres to the democratic ethic.[40] Haiman believes that persuasive techniques are inherently unethical by democratic standards. Persuasion is analogous to the use of the atomic bomb, which is unethical. Dropping a bomb is a case of the ends' justifying the means. This author apparently believes that *ethos* and *pathos* should not be taught. He denies that these proofs should be used to support "truth, right, and justice." In a free society, non-rational appeals actually harm the cause of "truth" because the citizens are not allowed to make "rational" choices. Haiman is thus so pessimistic about persuasion, as used, that he would label it all "unethical" and revert to a Platonic condemnation of the entire practice.

Winston L. Brembeck and William S. Howell, in their text, *Persuasion: A Means of Social Control*,[41] present a systematic summary of the problems of ethics. Theirs is a detailed endorsement of the social context theory, with suggestions for applying ethical standards to persuasion. Popular approaches, such as avoiding forbidden words, shameful deceptions, the cult of reason, high- and low-motive appeals, the application of the principle that "the end justifies the means," and the ethics of "what you can get away with," are all fragmentary in dealing with the problem. They hardly serve as valid means of reflecting genuine ethical standards and results.

Like Oliver, Gray, Wise, and the utilitarian philosophers Bentham, Mill, and Sedgwick, Brembeck and Howell regard the social context theory as comparatively the most practicable. Their position is to a con-

---

[40] Franklyn S. Haiman, "A Re-examination of the Ethics of Persuasion," *Central States Speech Journal*, III (March, 1952), 4–9.

[41] Winston L. Brembeck and William S. Howell, *Persuasion: A Means of Social Control* (Englewood Cliffs, N.J., Prentice-Hall, 1952), Chap. 24, "The Ethics of Persuasion," 443–466.

siderable degree an adaptation of Vilfredo Pareto, in his *The Mind and Society*.[42]

The test of social influence in communication is determined by the usefulness to the people affected. The term implies survival potential of the group involved. The inquiry should center on the group members and their interests, the ways the persuasion may help or hurt the group, and the favorable or adverse effects upon the individuals.

Like other students and inheritors of the scientific age, these teachers of public address suggest experimental methods for testing ethical behavior and results. "A rigid and unrealistic interpretation of a non-experimental belief for purposes of persuasion is unethical. . . . Ethical standards for persuasion can be formulated through a context analysis using both experimental and non-experimental bases of behavior and the concept of social utility." [43]

Kenneth Anderson and Theodore Clevenger, Jr., summarize the extensive experimental research on *ethos*.[44] They review the studies dealing with the influence of *ethos* upon the intended effect of the communication; studies assuming that *ethos* is fixed; and those assuming that *ethos* is variable. Other studies reviewed include those dealing with extrinsic *ethos* (techniques employed before the message itself begins) and the intrinsic *ethos* (those produced by the speaker during the presentation). These investigators report that "findings are not yet sufficiently numerous and sophisticated to permit definite conclusions about the operation of ethical proof." These reporters conclude that "the utilization of improved designs and measuring devices can create experimental conditions that may lead to more meaningful results than those obtained in the past." [45]

What is the modern view of ethics and its applications in communication? Or rather what is the view of this writer as he emerges from this chapter review of the problem?

Practically all of the self-styled rhetoricians of today continue to follow the underlying concepts of ethics as enunciated by Aristotle, Cicero, Quintilian, and the other classical rhetoricians. We are also heavily influenced by the later Judeo-Christian morality with its sometimes inspiring, but inconsistent, specific guides for conduct.

We have, moreover, inherited modern science. Thus has developed the rejection of ex cathedra propositions and the greater emphasis on evidence and experimentation. Contemporary logic, psychology, politics, anthropology, semantics, and other sciences have all affected heavily the

---

[42] Vilfredo Pareto, *The Mind and Society*, ed. Arthur Livingston, tr. Borgiomo and Livingston (New York, Harcourt Brace, 1935).

[43] Brembeck and Howell, *op. cit.*, 458.

[44] Kenneth Anderson and Theodore Clevenger, Jr., "A Summary of Experimental Research in Ethos," *Speech Monographs*, XXX, No. 2 (June, 1963), 59–78.

[45] *Ibid.*, 78.

interpretations and applications of the Greek-Roman-scholastic precepts for "good" conduct.

Ethics is the science of the conduct of human beings in their collective living. This behavior encompasses the activities of the individual and the group in their entire "reach."

The purpose and method of ethics, different from those of anthropology, psychology, and other "sciences," are not simply to describe but to judge the "goodness, or badness, the right or wrong" of behavior. This conduct or action is to be examined from the point of view of values. The action is to be interpreted from the end which it attempts to realize. Such conduct is more than a collective name for action. It implies, as John Dewey states, more than something taking place. "It implies purpose, motive, intention."

What of the problem of ethical communication? What traits and operations by the speaker mark morality? These include his motives, his speaking goals, the integrity of his ideas, his social appeals, his character, and the consequences of his communication.[46]

Moral effectiveness in this analysis of the speaker is to be estimated not simply by the excellence of his techniques, his ideas, language, and delivery, but by his purposes. If committed to ethical motives, he adopts the individual-social aims comprising the *summum bonum,* the highest good. That objective is not simply happiness, pleasure, a stoical or cynical attitude toward his environment or experience, or even the intuitive impulse to duty. These philosophies he may partly appropriate. His over-all aims nevertheless embrace motives of social amelioration, the good of the society. This better society is his ideal, as he weighs the economic, social, political and other constituents, one or more of these to be set in motion by specific speech. The measure of this attitude is its translation into action. Belief and conduct thus become one. Conduct implies more than an event that takes place. It implies purpose, motive, intention. These sentiments and aims, conversely, also are measured by their execution in action.

This speaker-agent must also account for the divergent needs and interests of the group and the parallel interests of the individual. His commitment to social progress will not lead him to abandon rights and personal growth of the individual. Utilitarian though he is, he still preserves his loyalty to the fulfillment of each individual as a responsible and free thinker, communicator, and doer. His democracy of purpose thus weaves together the strands of private and public morality.

Note more specifically the ideas and intellectual operations of this

46 William Kingdon Clifford, "The Ethics of Belief," in H. S. Reeves and F. H. Ristine, *Representative Essays in Modern Thought* (New York, American Book, 1913), 46–72.

speaker-agent. He adheres to fact, logical inference, and tenable assumptions. His deviations through ignorance may be forgivable until he matures. His superficial treatment, however, and especially his deliberate distortions, half-truths, and similar fallacies, condemn his intellectualism as immoral.

These logical elements in detailed analysis also become emotional and in turn ethical expression. Modern logic, like ethics, minimizes the distinctions between logical, pathetic, and ethical "proofs," just as it eliminates the distinctions between Aristotelian moral goods (virtues) and natural goods (health, economic security, and so forth). Arguments and propositions that deal primarily with human problems also become moral if their content and details help to elevate the human estate.[47]

Thus is the artificial gap between the scientific and the ideal and moral to be lessened.

As the mark of ethical strength is intellectual, so is the social motive and method of the agent. He is a person of good will. He views his audience as akin to each other and to him. He identifies himself with them and they with him. He penetrates the motives, aims, interests, the economic, political, cultural, and other constituents of the group, and adjusts his ideas and appeals accordingly. Conversely, his communicative purposes are to inform, persuade, interest, or inspire, but also he moves these listeners toward a "better" society.

His identifying personality, however, means no surrender to the role of social robot. He retains and develops his individuality, through his development of his insight into human behavior. He is thus better equipped for his own self-diagnosis and for the adjustments of his communication to the people who attend to him. Such "good-will" philosophy will affect the techniques of his communication. He will balance his praise of his audience, will proceed without depreciation of his own candor, will use tact and consideration in his messages, and reveal, without guile or exhibitionism, "his personable qualities as a messenger of the truth."[48]

A third factor in analysis of the morality of the agent is his character. Character, as interpreted here, becomes the sum of the moral feelings as a whole "making up the attitude of the agent toward conduct expressing the kind of whole which impels him to action."[49]

These qualities of character, including the nine virtues described by Aristotle, and those elaborated in many later rhetorical treatises, unitedly convey a profile of the speaker's sincerity as he expresses his intellectual-

[47] John Dewey, *Reconstruction in Philosophy* (Boston, Beacon Press, 1957; original edition, Holt, 1919), 193.
[48] Thonssen and Baird, *op. cit.*, 387.
[49] John Dewey, *op. cit.*, 9.

social motives. The question is, does he really mean what he expresses? Does his technique of good will, benevolence, altruism, virtue genuinely coincide with his innermost being? Difficult though it is to diagnose these idealistic traits and even more difficult though it is to define and prove or disprove "sincerity" in action, this criterion of ethical soundness is at the heart of the problem and must be dealt with in any discussion of ethics.

At least modern theorists of ethics are pretty much agreed, as is this writer, that prior reputation is important in gauging the moral influence of the speaker. Moreover, the traditional admonition to bestow with propriety, praise upon the speaker himself and his associates, does not justify the opposite advice to link the opponent and his cause with what is to be heavily condemned. Cicero and other expounders of forensic procedure urged the unqualified denunciation of the objectionable persons and their causes. The strong pursuit of such rhetorical methods would almost invariably betray the speaker into gross distortion of his "good will" method and message. The good will approach cannot be reconciled with the wholesale denunciation of opposing persons and their programs.

The ethical import of the speech on the audience leads to the contemporary experimentation on audience reaction. What is the audience reaction and what are the specific and larger consequences of the discourse? Scientific and logical inquiry, discovery, and experimentation help to answer such questions. Growth and progress are more significant as indexes of values than are static outcomes. Vague generalities give way to examinations of specific situations. Investigations and experiments, for example, have failed to prove that audiences can detect the difference between the "sincerity" of a speaker and his expert techniques of persuasion.

What of the ethical quality of the message itself? Its logical and other content? As indicated above, we may differentiate logical, pathetic, and ethical aspects of artistic "proofs" as Aristotle would have us do. But our sharp separation and estimate of these differentiations obscure the basic moral factors common to these logical-psychological supports. It is better to treat the communication as a unit rather than as discrete divisions. Ethical appeals attach to every phase of the discourse—the exordium, development, and peroration—contrary to some classical theories of concentration on ethical or pathetic appeals at given points.

Moreover, the moral virtues and their converses crop out not only in invention, but in *dispositio, elocutio,* and delivery. It is experimentally and otherwise difficult to segregate certain aspects of the total communication to estimate the moral effect of a certain technique, as implied in the previous paragraph.

Furthermore, since ethics is a function of the speaker-audience-situation, communication under certain conditions of time and place, it becomes necessary for the critic to examine the moral factors of specific occasions and types of public address. Sermons, for example, would possess, in theory at least, more didactic-moral effectiveness than would straight business communication. Persuasion has long been looked upon as inviting violations of high moral standards. The temptations in politics and law have been great for special pleading and chicanery. Debating, both school and college, has been sharply criticized for its occasional encouragement of sophistry in the handling of evidence, arguments, refutation, and delivery. Some of us, long instructors of this art, have condemned some of the practices, including excessive tournament competition (as amoral or immoral). Bad logic, false appeals, and quasi-demagoguery too often attend these learning exercises.[50]

In contrast to competitive debate, discussion has come in for more educational approval. It presumably encourages inquiry rather than dogmatism, fosters closer interpersonal relations and group experience, and on the whole creates a more favorable climate for ethical realities.

Advertising, political and general propaganda as promoted by public relations, and similar agencies have also affronted what many mature critics have regarded as any reasonable ethical code. The speakers, their messages, wares, and sometimes camouflaged purposes, as presented via radio, television and otherwise, have allegedly beguiled audiences through low-level and bogus appeals. Their devices have been covert, or hidden, suggestive rather than logical.

Their illogical manipulations have been those of name calling, glittering generalities, transfer, card stacking, "plain folks," bandwagon, and other labellings that represent deception.[51]

Conclusion

In conclusion, morality has a practical end. We believe that under freedom and voluntary expression, communication will meet the needs of the expanding environment of the individual in this space age. Maturity of intellect and education, clearer understanding and acceptance of the principles of what is good for neighbors—town, state, nation—is also good for each. From such free choice of good, and not through coercion or

---

[50] Joseph A. Mosher, "Debate and the World We Live In," *Quarterly Journal of Speech Education,* Vol. X (November, 1924), 332–339; Lloyd I. Watkins (ed.), "Ethical Problems in Debating," *Speech Teacher,* VIII (March, 1959), 150–156.

[51] Clyde R. Miller, *Propaganda: Why and How it Works* (Princeton, N.J., Commission on Propaganda Analysis, 1947); Stanley Kelley, Jr., *Profession Public Relations and Political Power* (Baltimore, Johns Hopkins Press, 1956); Vance Packard, *The Hidden Persuaders* (New York, David McKay, 1957).

through Kantian duty alone, will develop virtues and genuine morality. Although no yardstick can be applied indiscriminately to all communicative cases, the principles of social behavior and the analysis of specific appeals in relation to their audiences will, more and more, yield patterns of genuine moral improvement. Our communicators must still be good men skilled in speaking and writing. Our position, however, will continue also to be that of Socrates: "When you strive for noble ends, it is also noble to endure whatever pain the effort may involve." [52]

[52] Plato, *Phaedrus, Ion, Gorgias, and Symposium,* tr. Lane Cooper (New York, Oxford University Press, 1938), 64.

7

Emotional Response

Significance of Emotion in Discourse

Reason and logic, as we suggested in Chapter 4, is, or should be, the strength of worthwhile communication. In its details, this intellectual quality lies in the unfolding of basic ideas; the tentative but well-supported propositions; the operational definitions; the relativity and probability in arguments; appropriate evidence; valid refutation; language that lends clarity and consistency to the discourse.

These intellectual constituents, however, as rhetoricians have long noted, are insufficient to affect markedly the audience. Human beings are still governed by non-intellectual attitudes and behavior. Their prejudices, impulses, motives, and drives seemingly override their more deliberative reactions. As Cicero stated in *De Oratore,* "For mankind make far more determination through hatred, or love, or desire, or anger, or grief, or joy, or hope, or fear, or error, or some other affection of mind, than from regard to truth, or any settled maxim, or principle of right, or judicial form, or adherence to the laws." [1]

Later rhetoricians have also commented on the significance of the emotional appeals. As John Ward stated it: "Bare conviction is not sufficient for many persons, to excite them to action. They will acquiesce in the truth of a thing, which they cannot contradict, or will not give themselves the trouble to examine; and at the same time remain unconcerned to prosecute it." [2]

Role of Emotion in Communication

What is the emotional (or in Greek terms, the pathetic) mode of communication? What is its role in speaker-audience interaction? To Aris-

[1] Cicero, *De Oratore,* II, xiii, tr. and ed. J. S. Watson (London, George Bell, 1876).

[2] John Ward, *A System of Oratory,* 2 vols. (London, J. Ward, 1759), Vol. 2, Book II, 299–300. Cited in Thonssen and Baird, *Speech Criticism* (New York, Ronald Press, 1948), 357.

totle, pathetic proof was one of the three elements of establishing ideas. "Secondly, persuasion is effected through the audience, when they are brought by the speech into a state of emotion; for we give very different decisions under the sway of pain or joy, and liking or hatred." [3]

Although he gave most of his second book to emotion, Aristotle nevertheless warns against its excesses and states that the "true constituents" of rhetoric are logical proofs; all others are "merely accessory." [4]

Concepts of Emotion

What is "emotion"? Psychologists agree that it is a consciousness or awareness of bodily changes. According to Robert Oliver, it is "a state of bodily tension accompanied by an intellectual concept of what the tension means." [5]

The physiological reactions from the stimulus are communicated to the higher centers of the nervous system. "This fused complex of sensory experience is what we call an emotion." [6]

Emotions are not a distinct unity, but are a complex reaction to a specific situation. "Since emotion is a word or name, there is always a tendency to think that emotion is some *thing*, some discrete, distinct definable unity. Experiments have uniformly shown that emotion, like perception, cognition, and attention, *does not exist as a unique entity*, but that there is a variety of perceptive experiences, attendant reactions and cognitive experiences. It is also true that such emotions as anger, fear, pity, disgust do not exist in unique independence, but in relation to concrete situations—in such phenomena as fighting reactions or fearfulness, in the experience of pity or of withdrawal from noxious objects." [7]

These "emotions," whether primary or secondary, become motives for action or satisfaction of needs or wants.

"Emotion" is explained from the derived motive stimulus—the basic wants or needs of all mature human beings, such as food, rest, sexual activities, and the like. These are "physiological imperatives."

These physical reactions in turn produce changes—emotional tensions, such as love, rage, fear, the results of bodily stimulation. These "elementary emotions," as the individual matures, become in turn social drives, or

[3] *The "Rhetoric" of Aristotle*, I, ii, 9, tr. Lane Cooper (New York, Appleton-Century-Crofts, 1932 and 1960).

[4] *Ibid.*, I, i, 1. Quoted in Thonssen and Baird, *op. cit.*, 359. See also Donald Bryant, "Aspects of the Rhetorical Tradition II: Emotion, Style, and Literary Association," *Quarterly Journal of Speech*, XXXVI (October, 1950), 327.

[5] Robert Oliver, *The Psychology of Persuasive Speech* (2d ed.; New York, Longmans Green, 1957), 251.

[6] F. H. Allport, *Social Psychology* (New York, Houghton Mifflin, 1924), 84.

[7] Edwin Garrigues Boring, Herbert Sidney Langfeld, and Harry Porter Weld, *Introduction to Psychology* (New York, Wiley, 1944), 183.

motives, such as mastery, group conformity, or marriage. The physiological is overlaid with social and cultural activities.

Is emotional expression to be set off sharply from logical expression? A frequent error is to assume that they are mutually exclusive, despite long abandonment of the old "faculty psychology," with its departmentalized intellect, feelings, and will. All reaction is the product of complicated nervous, muscular, and glandular activity. Some of these tendencies are predominantly "intellectual" and "logical"; others are largely "emotional." These tendencies are not to be placed upon a single continuum with their extremes at opposite ends. Rather, a more realistic view would be to "place them in two continua which cross at some point between the two extremes." Viewed in this fashion, some communications would be highly illogical or highly motivated—with excess emotional content. Others would be put down as having neither logical nor emotional motivation. Still others would employ the devices of motivation in balanced conjunction.[8]

John Dewey has explained the place of emotion in human behavior:

> The conclusion is not that the emotional, passionate phase of action can be or should be eliminated in behalf of a bloodless reason. More "passions," not fewer, is the answer. To check the influence of hate, there must be sympathy, while to rationalize sympathy there are needed motions of curiosity, caution, respect for the freedom of others—dispositions to which evoke objects which balance those called up by sympathy, and prevent its degeneration into maudlin sentiment and meddling interference. Rationality, once more, is not a force to evoke against impulse and habit. It is the attainment of a working harmony among diverse desires.[9]

Some investigators of communication have suggested that logic strongly permeates all communication. Charles Woolbert, speech leader and writer in the United States before his death in 1929, stated that logic becomes the basis of all persuasive speaking and writing. He expounded such logic as occurring at the "subconscious" level, or at a "partly concealed" level. His application of "logic" fails to coincide with the use of the term, which we usually limit to that discourse in which the listener or reader develops an intellectual reaction, as contrasted with the more extreme, disorganized, subcortical emotional responses.[10]

Philosophers, rhetoricians, scientists have long supported the theory that the growth of civilization has been due to rational rather than emo-

---

[8] A. Craig Baird and Franklin H. Knower, *General Speech* (3d ed.; New York, McGraw-Hill, 1963), 281–283.

[9] John Dewey, *Human Nature and Conduct* (Holt, Rinehart & Winston, 1922), 195–196.

[10] Charles H. Woolbert, "The Place of Logic in a System of Persuasion," *Quarterly Journal of Speech Education*, IV (January, 1918), 19–39.

tional judgments. Human progress has been explained as determined by the processes of rationality.[11]

Though some experimenters have suggested that non-logical communication has influenced audiences more effectively than the logical type, this evidence has not been conclusive. Franklin H. Knower, for example, dealt with the question, "Is an attitude more markedly changed by an argument which is predominantly factual and logical or one which is predominantly emotional?" His conclusion was that: "Although these college students would no doubt have denied that they could be swayed by an emotional appeal, the data show that on the whole approximately as many were swayed by one type of argument as by the other." [12]

William Norwood Brigance, an able philosopher and, until his death, a professor of speech at Wabash College, concerning the intellectual quality of mankind reminds us that man "has lived on this planet for untold thousands of years. To survive during these years he has been forced to adapt himself to biological conditions and to the physical universe. Out of this survival he has acquired wants and culture patterns. These wants and culture patterns are *old*. Through them man has survived. Reason and logic, on the other hand, are *new*." Brigance states: "Most men use reason badly or not at all. Yet by no other means can problems be solved." [13]

Lester Ward, a pioneer American sociologist, put the problem of the intellect in man's progress: "The advent with man, of the thinking, knowing, foreseeing, calculating, designing, inventing, and constructing faculty, repealed the law of nature and enacted in its stead the psychologic law, or the law of the mind." [14]

Conviction and Persuasion: A Duality

In addition to the age-old discussion as to the relative power of the intellectual and emotional appeals, the question as to the dichotomy of the convincing-reasoning and the persuasive-emotional has long confronted rhetorical writers. To Aristotle persuasion, which to him embraced all types of deliberative, forensic, and epideictic communication, meant the combined functioning of emotional (pathetic), ethical, and logical appeals. To him persuasion meant communication that produced action. Despite his concept of "proof" as a single process, he stressed

[11] Winston L. Brembeck and William S. Howell, *Persuasion* (Englewood Cliffs, N.J., Prentice-Hall, 1952), 124.

[12] Franklin H. Knower, "Experimental Studies in Changes of Attitudes," *Journal of Social Psychology*, VI (August, 1935), 315–345.

[13] William Norwood Brigance, *Speech* (New York, Appleton-Century-Crofts, 1952), 102 ff.

[14] Lester Ward, *Dynamics of Sociology*, 2 vols. (New York, D. Appleton Co., 1883), Chaps. 8, 13, and 14.

the logical constituent as the "true" one and disparaged by implication the emotional mode. His analysis does imply a sharp distinction between the materials that satisfy syllogistic-dialectic demonstration and those that otherwise condition audiences and their speakers to accept such propositions with argumentative supports.

Later rhetoricians developed the conviction-persuasion dichotomy. Thomas Hobbes, for example, in his *Leviathan*, referred to "forms of speech by which passions are expressed, as partly the same, and partly different from those, by which we express our thoughts." [15]

George Campbell, under the influence of the "faculty psychology" of the late eighteenth century, approached the problem by stating that every speech is entitled "to enlighten the understanding, to please the imagination, to move the passions, or to influence the will." Each one of these appeals becomes the principal one. Thus is suggested that each functions as a separate movement and technique. In his view, an address to the understanding should in effect reject bold figures of language with their emotional-imaginative reactions. An address to the passions in a speech of information would disturb the operation of the intellectual faculty and so might even be "insidious." [16] To Campbell, "conviction" is argumentative material. "Persuasion" has "marvelous efficacy in arousing the passions."

Richard Whately recognizes the division between the emotive and the rational materials. Conviction he identifies with argument proper, whereas persuasion is the "art of influencing the will." "Conviction of the understanding is an essential part of persuasion. To influence the will the object must be presented as desirable, but must also be established through reasoning. Persuasion thus depends on argument and on the argumentative-emotional appeals." [17]

On the basis of such distinctions, as Lester Thonssen states, controversial dualism has developed. Groupings of the powers of the mind according to its faculties are evident in these separations of basic psychological appeals. The "faculty psychology" in the mental field has led to separation in modes of invention in rhetoric.[18]

Most modern writers on persuasion, speech, and rhetoric have accepted this distinction between conviction and persuasion. The latter

[15] Thomas Hobbes, *The English Works of Thomas Hobbes*, ed. Sir William Molesworth (London, 1839), Vol. 3, 49.

[16] George Campbell, *The Philosophy of Rhetoric*, ed. Lloyd Bitzer (Carbondale, Ill., Southern Illinois University Press, 1963); see also *The Philosophy of Rhetoric* (New York, Harper, 1951), 23–24.

[17] Richard Whately, *Elements of Rhetoric*, ed. Douglas Ehninger (Carbondale, Ill., Southern Illinois University Press, 1963), 175–176.

[18] Thonssen and Baird, *op. cit.*, 375.

term has been largely identified with emotional communication, and "conviction" with severe argumentation. Although later writers qualify these interpretations, the distinctions nevertheless remain in their works. George Pierce Baker's *Principles of Argumentation*, Harry Franklin Covington's *Fundamentals of Debate*, William T. Foster's *Argumentation and Debating*, V. A. Ketcham's *Theory and Practice of Argumentation and Debate*, Egbert Ray Nichols and Joseph Baccus' *Modern Debating*, James M. O'Neill, Craven Laycock, and Robert L. Scale's, *Argumentation and Debate*, and Warren Choate Shaw's *The Art of Debate*, to name a few, have by implication marked off genuine argumentative communication as logical, and persuasive speaking as largely emotional.

Some critics indicted this acceptance of persuasion and conviction as disparate elements. Mary Yost, in her article, "Argument from the Point of View of Sociology" (1917), indicted this approach. She declared that: "the conception of the mind as an organic unit performing a particular function—reasoning, feeling, and willing—as may be demanded by the situation the individual is meeting, has taken the place of the rigid formal idea. Conviction and persuasion were formulated when the belief held sway that the mind was divided into three compartments, the reason, the emotion, the will—roughly the assumptions of the faculty psychology. Today, however, the leading psychologists have found these assumptions inadequate to explain the phenomena of the mind." [19]

Charles Woolbert also condemned such classification. As a behaviorist, he emphasized the process as essentially unitary.[20] He argued that the distinction between conviction and persuasion and similar terms that attempted to mark off overt and non-perceived activity did not exist.

Edward Rowell, professor of philosophy at the University of California, restated the controversy and resolved it by his own findings and philosophical judgment. He stated: "Psychological monism is invalid for at some points in human behavior such distinctions (pluralism and dualism, i.e., reasoning and feeling) become not only legitimate but scientifically inescapable." Taken negatively, psychological monism is no more than

. . . a repudiation of the old faculty psychology which talked of reasoning as the work of a *reason*, of willing as the work of a *will*, and so forth. Taken

---

[19] Mary Yost, "Argument from the Point of View of Sociology," *Quarterly Journal of Public Speaking*, III (April, 1917), 109–124.

[20] Charles H. Woolbert, "Conviction and Persuasion," *Quarterly Journal of Public Speaking*, III (July, 1917), 249–264. See also "Persuasion," *Quarterly Journal of Speech Education*, V (January, 1919), 12–25; V (March, 1919), 110–119; V (May, 1919), 211–238.

positively, it is a recognition of the functional approach to psychological processes, an approach which views men as unified reaction-systems which can
exert the functions called reasoning, feeling, willing, and so forth. Psychological monism makes no denial of the reality of the time-honored distinctions
between reasoning, feeling, and willing. All it denies is the idea that these
forms of behavior are expressions of individual faculties. This monism is as
pluralistic as it is monistic.[21]

Rowell concluded that psychological monism still discusses with as much
ease as did faculty psychology those functions of reasoning, feeling, and
willing, and argued it is less troublesome to modern psychologists than
it is to some rhetoricians.

Winston Brembeck and William Howell, in their *Persuasion,* find no
difficulty in their focusing on motives and analyzing emotional appeals,
and on "a maximum of fact and logical reasoning, or in varying combinations of these employments."[22]

Robert Oliver in his *Psychology of Persuasive Speech* treats the motivative approach similarly and indicates how the emotional and logical aspects of the persuasive process have a common basis.

The analysis of apparent dualism suggests the application of common
sense. Differences in materials become obvious as they seem to guide in
establishing proof or in stirring feelings. What terms we give to these
constituents is secondary. But the recognition and application of such
materials and their application in the understanding of the persuasive
process to support given aims is important.[23]

Drives, Motives, Habits, Attitudes

The discussion above indicates the modern concept of persuasion that
gives it a wider connotation than that which limits it to emotion. Brembeck and Howell define it as the conscious attempt to modify thought
and action by manipulating the motives of men toward predetermined
ends.[24] The dominant basis of belief and action, according to them, is
desire as expressed through a system of motives. Their concept is more
basic than that of James Winans. He was a pioneer in placing the process of persuasion upon a clearly defined psychological foundation. Like
William James, James Winans explained that "what holds attention determines action." To him persuasion was "the process of inducing others to

[21] Edward Z. Rowell, "The Conviction-Persuasion Duality," *Quarterly Journal of
Speech,* XX (November, 1934), 470.
[22] Brembeck and Howell, *op. cit.,* 24.
[23] Thonssen and Baird, *op. cit.,* 372–373.
[24] Brembeck and Howell, *op. cit.,* 24.

give, fair, favorable, or undivided attention to propositions." [25] Ideas which "arouse emotion" hold attention. The best way to fix attention is to awaken desire for the end sought. Desire is a motive.

Norwood Brigance took exception to the assumption of Winans that viewed persuasion as a mental process, and contended that "the generally accepted view today is that persuasion takes place, not on an intellectual, but rather on a motor level." [26] Even though psychologists are divided on many aspects of emotional processes, they are agreed on the fact that the basis for belief and action is desire. According to Brigance, persuasion is the process of "vitalizing old desires, purposes, or ideals, of substituting new desires, purposes, or ideals, for old ones." [27]

More specifically, behavior is to be analyzed with relation to stimuli, tendencies, and responses. The source of behavior, the stimulus, is some form of energy, which affects the sensory receptors of the organism. These stimuli may be largely limited to biological reactions. Man is an organism, whose primary sources of motivation are, in common with those of animals, hunger, sleep, sex, eliminative functions, and self-preservation. These primary reactions—drives—are related both to internal stimuli (such as hunger) and to external stimuli (avoidance of injury). These elemental drives trigger primary emotions, which observers describe as rage, fear, and love.

Since the developing individual moves into social adjustments and faces pressures, the satisfaction of his drives automatically leads to social drives such as conformity, subsistence motives, social approval, status; accumulation of goods becomes convenience, conformity becomes change. Some of these are described as ego drives or motives, such as those for self-respect, assertiveness, pride, dignity. Other motives, sublimated, serve the virtues of trust, integrity, loyalty, fair play, good sportsmanship, justice, and intellectual and aesthetic satisfaction.[28] These social motives, also anticipatory, including responses that reflect earlier experiences, constitute stereotypes, attitudes, sentiments. The stereotyped world, created by each, is a limited one, often largely false. The external world, political, social, moral, economic, deals with the ideas, events, persons, images, values to which we respond favorably or otherwise. Habitual reactions become a set of governing stereotypes, attitudes, sentiments. They are "the chief foundation stones of human behavior." [29]

---

[25] James Winans, *Public Speaking* (rev. ed.; New York, Century Co., 1917), 194 ff.

[26] W. N. Brigance, "Can We Re-define the James Winans Theory of Persuasion?" *Quarterly Journal of Speech*, XXI (February, 1935), 19–26.

[27] W. N. Brigance, *Speech Composition* (New York, Appleton-Century-Crofts, 1939), 19–26.

[28] Baird and Knower, *General Speech*, 281 ff.

[29] Brembeck and Howell, *op. cit.*, 118–119.

Drives and motives, stereotypes, sentiments, attitudes, obviously over-lap. Detailed classifications are difficult.[30]

Thus motivation—drives, motives, stereotypes, habits, sentiments, atti-tudes—embodies the emotional and *intellectual-logical development of the communication.

Emotion and Structure

What relation has emotion to the structure or arrangement of the dis-course? Classical rhetoricians, Cicero and Quintilian, for example, ad-vised that the emotional (pathetic) elements should be concentrated on certain parts of the composition. The introduction and the conclusion were singled out as especially the spots for such extra-logical appeals. Cicero, though he endorses the use of full-measure forensic elements of law and evidence, recognizes also the power of emotional drives. To him, these stimulating passages should occur chiefly in the exordium and peroration.[31]

Quintilian, too, admitting that the appeals to emotion should occur in "the places where they are most often used, argues that they may be employed in other parts of the speech as well." But most of these appeals should be reserved for the opening or close. "But it is in the peroration, if anywhere, that we must let loose the whole torrent of eloquence. . . . It is at the close of our drama that we must really stir the theater." [32]

Pathetic proof (emotion), then, relates not only to invention but to disposition. Which parts of the discourse should be relatively robust with logic and which parts given more to imagination and emotion will obviously depend on the speaker's purpose, the theme, occasion, and the mood of the listeners. Certainly, the emotional current should be genu-ine rather than synthetic. It should grow out of the needs and demands of the occasion rather than out of artificial procedures.[33]

---

[30] For classification and discussion of emotions and drives, see, for example: Kimball Young, *Social Psychology* (New York, F. D. Crofts & Co., 1945), Chap. 4; Robert T. Oliver, *The Psychology of Persuasive Speech* (2d ed., New York, Long-mans Green, 1957), Chap. 3, "Human Motivation"; Walter Lippmann, *Public Opinion* (New York, Macmillan, 1922), Part III, "Stereotypes"; Charles E. Bird, *Social Psy-chology* (New York, Appleton-Century-Crofts, 1940), 78–100; F. H. Allport, *Social Psychology*, 84 ff.; Baird and Knower, *op. cit.*, Chap. 18, "Persuasive Speaking"; Brembeck and Howell, *op. cit.*, Chaps. 4, 5, 6; Boring, Langfeld, and Weld, *Intro-duction to Psychology*, 183–222.

[31] Cicero, *De Oratore*, II, lxxvii.

[32] Quintilian, *Institutio Oratorio*, tr. H. E. Butler (London, William Heinemann; New York, G. P. Putnam's Sons, 1921–22), VI, i, 53.

[33] For full discussion of emotion in relation to disposition, see Thonssen and Baird, *op. cit.*, 363–366.

Emotion and Language

What distinction is to be made between emotion and language? Language, the basic agent in the communicative process, has the dual function of appealing both to the intellectual and emotional human being. The effect of words in a specific communicative situation depends much on the conditions of that occasion, the character of the recipient, and that of the agent. All words have both referential and emotional value.[34]

In a context of dispassionate description, words may suggest largely reactions that convey little quickening of emotion. But it is impossible to classify words or phrases to assure in every case the grouping of words or terms as purely denotative. "Man" may be merely denotative to some sociologists, anthropologists, and psychologists. But to certain persons, the term may convey high connotation. I. A. Richards, like many rhetoricians, comments on this dual influence of words. As he states it, words may be used "for the sake of the references they promote or for the sake of the attitudes and emotions which ensue."[35]

Straightforward summary of data may take on strong emotional overtones. The logical-emotional dichotomony obviously results from the way hearers or readers react to the words and terms, and passages. The degree of evocation will vary much with the insights, experiences, and education of the persuadee. In general, word selection and arrangement have much to do with the results. Adjectives, imagery, and other language applications have much to do with the effective results.[36]

Personality Traits and Emotion

Aristotle conceived rhetoric as comprising a speaker, his message, and the audience. By implication, he also stressed the occasion, with its special demonstrative, forensic, and deliberative types. These constituents would function together to produce the persuasive (action) effect.

The speaker, to effect positive results, should have certain traits. His personality is embodied in the speech itself. "Few if any of the many skills necessary in effective communication are more influential in your final results than the kind of man or woman you are."[37]

The speech is largely molded by the aptitudes, abilities, experiences, emotions, adjustments, and other personality traits of the author.

Personality is a composite of social traits. It reveals itself in the speaker's relations to other individuals and groups.

[34] Thonssen and Baird, *op. cit.*, 368–372.
[35] I. A. Richards, *Principles of Literary Criticism* (5th ed.; New York, Harcourt Brace, 1934), 267.
[36] See next chapter for more detailed discussion of language in communication.
[37] Baird and Knower, *op. cit.*, 211. See Chap. 14, "The Speaker's Personality."

One obvious factor is the purpose or motive of the speaker. Is he merely attempting to attract attention to himself? To satisfy his inner pride? To defend himself from hostile criticism? To deliver a genuine appeal for some cause in which he strongly believes? Is it to share information with others? To persuade them to vote for him or his party? Is it primarily to amuse or entertain? Is it to inspire audiences to a new appreciation of some man or institution? Is it to relieve personal feelings? Obviously, some of these traits possessed and expressed in large measure will facilitate the favorable responses, whereas other attributes (pride, egotism, exhibitionism for instance) are likely to block satisfactory responses.

What underlies these traits that so strongly influence the outcomes of a given communicative situation?

One significant personality trait is that of general intelligence. High intelligence is not essential. Some speakers with such superior mental traits have had serious speaking problems. We assume here, however, that the speaker should know his subject and should avoid quagmires of confused thinking. Audiences will no doubt detect such lapses in what might he called platform common sense. The communicator will fare better if he has knowledge of his subject. Thus all rhetoricians, from Cicero and Quintilian onward, have expounded the necessity of the speaker's broad education, his familiarity not only with his immediate subject but with knowledge in general. We assume that the person with ample education, in school and college, and supplemented by continuation education in professional and general experiences, is better equipped to lecture, argue, or persuade on subjects of his particular choice than are others less well grounded.

A second trait is the speaker's knowledge of audiences—social intelligence. More effective speakers are presumably those who have had relatively more experience in talking to audiences and in understanding the ways of human nature. Their social sensitivity guides them in the selection of the proper ideas for the occasion, the "right" appeals, and the other factors that make for maximum attention and satisfactory response. He who secures relatively better reactions from all kinds of audiences is presumably one who studies people, knows them in detail, and uses his social adaptiveness to good account.[38]

Another personality trait is tact (or lack of it). Tact expresses itself in the ability to impress a listener favorably through appeals and negatively by avoidance of expressing ideas that create inhibitions. Again the success or failure of tact lies in the speaker's understanding of his auditors and in his selection of ideas, words, and stereotypes that secure approval.

[38] *Ibid.*, 216.

In addition to intelligence, knowledge of audiences, and tact, the good communicator will have self-confidence. If he is not sure of his preparation, his ideas, and his right to speak, he may be easily disconcerted or irresolute as audiences react negatively. Confidence without egotism and ability to forget self in the committal to the speaking purpose are more likely to ensure desirable behavior toward the speaker. If the speaker is uncertain of himself, the audience will respond with uncertainty or query.

One other personality trait concerns emotional control. Personality includes both the intellectual and emotional behavior. Rational thinking reflects the well-organized personality. Uncontrolled, disorganized thinking indicates a lack of emotional balance. The emotionality is marked by imagery and language that are extravagant or exaggerated, and by conclusions filled with emotional rationalizations. The production is an expression of wishful thinking and desire.

Other personality traits are earnestness, sincerity, humor, modesty, courtesy, and leadership. These attributes, as mentioned in a classification of emotions, overlap. Their specific application provides important guides to the communicator's effectiveness or lack of it in his audience rapport.

Emotion and Ethical Appeals

Where do we draw the line between pathetic (emotional) appeals and the ethical motivation? The two concepts have much in common. The speaker who enhances his own reputation for good will and moral commitments and simultaneously suggests that the rival speaker may be deficient in knowledge of the subject is using both ethical and pathetic proofs. *Ethos* apparently refers chiefly to what the speaker would do; *pathos*, to what the reaction is doing to the audience.

According to Quintilian, interpreters of his day would explain *pathos* as describing the more violent emotions, and *ethos* as designating those that are calm and gentle. In one case the passions are violent, in the other, subdued. The former command and disturb; "the latter persuade and induce a feeling of good will." [39]

Quintilian refutes this distinction and concludes that the two concepts are "sometimes of the same nature." Like Aristotle, Quintilian insists that "ethos in any of its forms requires the speaker to be a man of good character and courtesy." It occurs whenever the speaker refers to what is honorable and expedient, or "what ought or ought not to be done."

Essentially no difference exists between the motivative appeals in persuasion and the ethical appeals in the same discourse. Only a shad-

[39] Quintilian, *op. cit.*, VI, iii, 9–13.

owy line of demarkation exists. Sincerity, intelligence, good will, and similar patterns fall into either category—according to the results aimed at. If "good will," for example, aims mainly at limited economic or political outcomes, the motivative effect is "pathetic." If the manipulation of these materials attempts to suggest social betterment of the immediate and larger constituency, then the technique may properly be described as "ethical."

Those approaches and details that involve value judgments become moral-ethical motives. Intangible though it is to decide whether personal motives of speakers and communicative results are moral in their tendencies, this differentiation of material and method is to be understood by the communicators and their critics. The appraisal of the logical and emotional materials and the overcasting of moral factors raise the basic questions affecting the good or bad society. On the surface, all emotional categories may be grouped together. Under more deliberate analysis, however, some or all of these pleadings may be associated primarily with ethical drives.

Audience Relationship

What are audiences? They have the same attributes as the speaker —as if the agent were by turns an audience member and platform speaker. Like speakers, audiences have characteristics that largely account for their ability and readiness to react, favorably or otherwise, to the communication. These audience chracteristics include age level, numbers, nationality, sex differences, intelligence, education, occupations, cultural interests, economic status, economic, social, political, religious and other attitudes and interests, representative needs, wants, desires, and audience homogeneity or heterogeneity.

Analysis of an audience notes their attitude toward the subject—knowledge of it, experience with it, stake in it; their attitude toward the speaker —their reaction to his knowledge, reputation, prestige, his social interests, humor, good will, honesty, sincerity, moral responsibility and leadership.

Audience attitudes are also affected by their reaction to the occasion, size, shape, and other elements of the meeting place, the length of speech or speeches, and similar details that make for or interfere with audience morale, polarization.[40]

The audience are to be analyzed both as individuals and as a group. Both as individual and as a group, the audience are affected by emotional responses and desires, as indicated above. They tend to believe what satisfies their primary and secondary needs and wants. They tend

[40] A. Craig Baird, *Argumentation, Discussion and Debate* (New York, McGraw-Hill, 1950), 225–226.

to respond to connotative language, to suggestion, to rationalizing, tend to think and act from prejudice, to accept fallacious arguments.[41]

This analysis of audience characteristics suggests how complicated is the transfer of a message from speaker to listener-observers. Barriers must be surmounted to realize the speaker's aim—even though an audience may be favorably inclined to what is uttered to them. Even though the persons or person addressing them has sympathy, idealism, self-sacrifice, and similar traits of good will and cooperativeness, the appeals will probably fail unless addressed to self-interest and social adaptation. Audiences are both self-centered and socially affected.

Problems of Identification

The basic process of persuasive communication includes four stages or steps:

1. Identification of speaker and audience
2. Creating and maintaining attention
3. Arousing audience desire, for the speaker's proposition
4. Producing the specific response aimed at

These steps or stages obviously overlap. They suggest an orderly progression of analysis and application of techniques which hardly takes place. Their relation to the problem of persuasive and emotive communication, however, is important.

The basic principle of speaker-audience relations is that of identification. Kenneth Burke, original thinker among recent American rhetoricians, makes identification the key to persuasion. In contrasting the "Old" rhetoric with the "New," he said, "The key term for the 'new' rhetoric would be identification, which can include a partially 'unconscious' factor in appeals." [42]

To Burke, identification is identical with consubstantiality. "A doctrine of consubstantiality, either explicit or implicit, may be necessary to any way of life. For substance in the old philosophies was an act; and a way of life is acting—together; and in acting together, men have common sensations, concepts, images, ideas, attitudes that make them consubstantial." [43]

What does "substance" mean to Burke? It involves both identity and separateness, "that which underlies outward manifestations, . . . that which is real; that in which qualities or attributes inhere in things and to which they relate extrinsically. Someone might ask, What is a cell? and

[41] *Ibid.,* 215–221.
[42] Kenneth Burke, "Rhetoric—Old and New," *Journal of General Education,* V (April, 1951), 203.
[43] Kenneth Burke, *A Grammar of Motives* (Englewood Cliffs, N.J., Prentice-Hall, 1945).

receive the answer: Well, it's a mass of protoplasm. The substance thinker would say, No, the substance of a cell is not protoplasmic stuff, but the law according to which the cell divides, reforms, and divides again." [44]

The sensations, concepts, and attitudes by which we identify this substantive relation, Burke calls "property." The relationship "by which ideas, images, or attitudes have a common property, is said to be consubstantial." Properties are goods, services, status, citizenship, home, fraternal associations, and any other attendant constituents of a thing or person. The categories, nevertheless, have close connection with the essential being or thing with which they are associated. Says Burke, "You persuade a man only in as far as you can talk his language, by speech, gesture, tonality, order, image, attitude, idea, *identifying* your ways with him." [45]

Burke's concept of identification turns out to be the classic procedure of close audience adjustment and interpersonal activities in communication. The new insight Burke provides is in the interpretation of the term "persuasion" as linked with identification and this in turn with "substance" (an act or activity) and with social intercourse as "acting together." [46]

As Dennis Day pointed out, James Winans in his discussion of attention in *Public Speaking* (1915), "was actually discussing" identification. Winans stated: "To convince or persuade a man is largely a matter of identifying the opinion or course of action which you wish him to adopt with one or more of his fixed opinions or customary courses of action. When his mind is satisfied of the identity, then doubts vanish." [47]

Winans thus anticipates Burke in analyzing identification. Burke, however, uses the term as practically equivalent to "persuasion." He does suggest that rhetorical analysts use identification with full appreciation of its comprehensive activity, in the social arena of kindred experiences, attitudes, ideas, and so on, that constitute common action and result in consubstantiality. Thus the social institutions and experiences that explain group life become the materials and insights that lead the effective communicator to identify with the group. The reciprocity between communicator and other persons thus yields positive results.

Burke, extremely stimulating, is more of a rhetorician and linguist

[44] Marie Hochmuth, *Rhetoric and Criticism* (Baton Rouge, Louisiana State University Press, 1963), 86.

[45] Kenneth Burke, *A Rhetoric of Motives* (Englewood Cliffs, N.J., Prentice-Hall, 1950), 55.

[46] Dennis Day, "Persuasion and the Concept of Identification," *Quarterly Journal of Speech*, XVI (October, 1960), 270–273.

[47] Winans, *Public Speaking*, 276–277.

than philosopher. Identification, if it fulfills the concept of close correspondence and fairly complete communication, calls for the speaker's
self-analysis with respect to his own intellectual, social, and moral equipment. He is to ensure himself and others of his intellectual control over
his theme and its details; of his selection and interpretation of the logical
framework and order of his discourse; of his direction of the emotional-
imaginative appeals and proofs so as to enforce and not distort the basic
propositions; of his insight into social results, the implications of and
direct reactions to his speech that contribute to the "good" society. He
is thus a qualified "agent," as Burke calls him. He has philosophical
perspective on and direction of his communication.

The audience, too, if genuine identification occurs, is to be examined
with respect to its educational capacities and understanding; its emotional conditioning; its prevailing drives and motives as related to the
economic, social and other problems that deal with their needs, desires,
and policies; its beliefs, imbedded habits, attitudes, including social and
moral outlooks.

On such factors relating to the communicator and the audience, subjective and only partly understood, does the experience of integration or
identification occur. The problem of evolution concerns the conflicts or
differences, which are often major, but may be basic or trivial. The differences involve personality factors, such as audience and/or speaker
intolerance; speaker and/or audience dominance, aggressiveness, social
conformity; and audience and/or speaker commitments to ideologies and
specific political, social, religious, or other programs.

The process of evolving communication that minimizes conflicts, and
establishes rapport and common direction of the thinking and motivation,
must be a reconciliation of the larger areas of mutual satisfactions. The
speaker is affected by the social spirit and judgment of the group. The
group, in turn, may respond to the speaking leadership. In either case,
the problem is one of speaker-audience interaction and polarization.
Basically, if the tide of social judgment flows in one direction and that of
a communicator in another, then only the evaluation of later conditions
and realities will explain properly the cleavage and justify one or the
other line of decisions.

Emotion and Attention

More specifically communication, as illustrated by persuasion, is primarily a process of giving the auditor-observers a "fair, favorable, or undivided attention to propositions," as James Winans observed.[48] Rhetori-

[48] *Ibid.*, 194.

cians and speech theorists are agreed that attention is the initial step in the persuasion process.[49]

What are the psychological and other fundamental forces that create attention and channel it toward a speaker's propositions? Winans quoted William James on what we do and why. James said, "What holds attention determines action." James continues, "When any strong emotional state whatever is upon us, the tendency is for no images but such as are congruous with it to come up. If others by chance offer themselves, they are instantly smothered and crowded out." [50]

How does this psychological activity function? What of its duration? Experimental studies have revealed that the duration of a single act of attention is only a few seconds.[51] Attention by a hearer-auditor in communication thus diminishes or deviates constantly. The speaker who ignores such span and duration of attention may find that his message has been a failure.

Attention may be voluntary, in which case the auditor deliberately attempts to avoid mind wandering, daydreaming, or dozing; or the audience reactions may be involuntary—factors of delivery or other aids will so engross the audience as to make it oblivious of distractions.

What are those procedures which tend to hold attention and translate it toward the involuntary?

One such help is the subject or idea itself. If it is of immediate interest and concern to the audience, if it deals with events that touch them directly, if it has enough novelty or newness of ideas, then the audience attention will be relatively complete.

Another procedure that may secure and retain attention is the inclusion of facts, figures, testimony, significant comparisons, cause-and-effect treatments, and similar supporting details that enrich the framework of thinking, or arouse curiosity. Here again, the materials must have both novelty and familiarity if fixation is to be achieved and retained.

Highly important also in attention-getting are the drives that stimulate favorable audience needs, motives, satisfactions, habits, sentiments, and attitudes. If the speaker, without artifice, will light upon and develop "proofs" that argue for the preservation of health, the acquisition of wealth, the protection of home, family, the opportunity for fair play, for justice, and for duty, honor, loyalty, the results should hold attention to the end.

[49] Andrew Weaver, "Getting or Holding Attention," in *Speech: Forms and Principles* (New York, Longmans Green, 1943), 303–314.

[50] William James, *Principles of Psychology* (New York, Holt, 1896), 451.

[51] We are indebted to Winston Brembeck and William S. Howell's *Persuasion*, for studies cited in their Chap. 14 on "Gaining and Maintaining Attention."

The personality appeals that reflect the speaker's character, intellectual integrity, good will and cooperation, sense of justice, honor, and support of the better social and economic society also may hold hearers who react favorably to these ethical notes. As Harry Overstreet, then professor of philosophy at the College of the City of New York wrote, "What we attend to controls our behavior, and what we can get others to attend to controls their behavior." [52]

Still another attention-getting technique lies in the organization of the address. Each unit of the introduction, main body, and conclusion becomes a miniature speech in itself, with appropriate elements of logical, emotional, or ethical appeals. The general pattern of unfolding the ideas may also enhance audience curiosity and concentration. The inductive method of focusing on successive details and conditional propositions may grip the audience as it looks to the major conclusion; suspense is created. The very continuity, free as it is from ambiguity, should also help maintain attention. Furthermore, the relative strength and importance of a given section, by its very contrast with preceding passages, may capture the thoughts and emotions of the audience.

Attention-getting, we agree, is served directly by the language. Words and combinations that clarify without boring, that select vocabulary best interpreting the ideational, emotional, and ethical import of what is said, will secure and retain interest and approval from start to finish.

Language should enliven and impress if it is native to the audience—or at least is well understood by them. Accurate language, too, free from ambiguity and offensive exaggeration, will help. Attention-getting language is concrete, concise, unhackneyed (and yet familiar). Prominent are illustrative or figurative expressions that gave vividness and impressiveness.

A key factor in attention-getting is certainly delivery. The speaker's personality, appearance, and general conduct during his communication count much for or against him in developing audience polarization. His voice, too, with its quality, rate, pitch, and intensity, will also do much to explain audience behavior during the twenty-minute speech. Articulation, also, if it is unduly local, indistinct, and otherwise disagreeable, may wean away the auditors. The gestures and movements make for animation, enthusiasm. Audiences want movement, variety, if their attention and interest are not to flag.

Note Hugh Blair's suggestions for application of the pathetic mode, in which he warns against "prolonging" unduly the emotional appeals.[53]

[52] Harry A. Overstreet, *Influencing Human Behavior* (New York, Norton, 1925), 9.
[53] Hugh Blair, *Lectures on Rhetoric and Belles Lettres*, 3 vols. (8th ed.; London, T. Cadell Jun. and W. Davies and W. Greech, Edinburgh, 1801), 383 ff.

The Audience and Suggestion

An important though subtle method of moving an audience is through the use of suggestion. Suggestion is the automatic, or uncritical, response to a stimulus, or acceptance of a proposition or idea without deliberation. The approval is direct, immediate, and apparently without conscious motivation. When without reflection the auditor yields to the common urgency, "Support Wintergreen for City Mayor," this persuadee is governed entirely by suggestion. When the listener also endorses Wintergreen after reflection on what he would do for local taxes, improvement of the sewage system, schools, and parking, this listener acts from reason or from clearly expressed motives. Suggestion furnishes the case of an apparently incidental stimulus touching off "responses quite disproportionate to its inherent strength." [54]

Crowds, like individuals, tend to yield to suggestion. The imitative impulse and the lowering of the barriers of individual leadership and direction help to explain the release of emotional controls and the yielding to suggestion. As Bird puts it, "Marked suggestibility and an intensification of emotion have been stressed as outstanding features of crowd behavior." [55]

The methods of suggestion vary widely, as affected by the specific audience, occasion, and leadership of the speaker. General principles of suggestion may be framed, techniques that under certain audience-speaker-occasion conditions have secured definite results, are summarized below.

H. L. Hollingworth, professor of psychology at Barnard College, composed seven laws of suggestion that apply to influencing both audience and individual: [56]

1. The strength of a suggestion depends in part on the degree to which it seems to be of spontaneous origin, an act of the individual's own

[54] Charles Bird, *Social Psychology* (New York, Appleton-Century-Crofts, 1940), 347. See also E. B. Titchener, *A Textbook of Psychology* (New York, Macmillan, 1910), 499; W. D. Scott, *Psychology of Advertising* (New York, Small, Maynard & Co., 1921), 80; William McDougall, *Social Psychology* (New York, John W. Luce Co., 1921), 97; Bird, *op. cit.*, 258–259; Robert Oliver, *op. cit.*, 140–166; Leonard W. Doob, *Propaganda: Its Psychology and Technique* (New York, Holt, 1935), 54; Winston Brembeck and William Howell, *op. cit.*, 164–185; A. Craig Baird, *op. cit.*, 214–221; H. A. Overstreet, *Influencing Human Behavior* (New York, Norton, 1925), 65; H. L. Hollingworth, *The Psychology of the Audience* (New York, American Book, 1935), 141–161; John Eisenson, *Basic Speech* (New York, Macmillan, 1950), 286–289; William Albig, *Modern Public Opinion*, New York, 1956), Chap. 5; Kimball Young, *Social Psychology* (New York, Appleton-Century-Crofts, 1944), 110; Alan Monroe, *Principles and Types of Speech* (3d ed.; Chicago, Scott Foresman, 1949); Donald Bryant and Karl Wallace, *Fundamentals of Public Speaking* (New York, Appleton-Century-Crofts, 1953–1960), 329–345.

[55] Bird, *op. cit.*, 356.

[56] H. L. Hollingworth, *op. cit.*, 142–144.

initiative. Arrogance and domination are at once and instinctively resented and resisted. The more indirect the suggestion, the more it can be made to be an original determination or plan or conclusion on the part of the listener, the greater its dynamic power.

2. Within the limits of the law just indicated, the dynamic power of a suggestion will be the greater, the more forcefully and vividly it is presented. This is especially true when the suggested act is in harmony with the pre-established habits and tendencies. When the suggestion violates lifelong habits and instincts, attempts to be forceful and vigorous usually lapse into arrogance and thereby defeat their own purpose.

3. It is more effective to suggest the desired response directly than it is to argue against a response that is not desired. Suggestion is most active at its positive pole, and the negative suggestion tends to defeat its own purpose. The Old Covenant with its "Thou Shalt Not" was readily displaced by the New Covenant with its simple, positive "Thou Shalt."

4. The action power of a suggestion varies directly with the prestige of its source. The more we revere a speaker, for whatever reason, the greater is the confidence we tend to place in anything he may say, and the more prone we are to imitate him and to adopt his suggestions, even when they are unsupported by sufficient reason.

5. The strength of a suggestion will be determined in part by the degree of internal resistance it encounters. That suggestion will be most effective which can call to its aid or appropriate the dynamic force of some other impulse that is already active or latent. Suggestions to violate lifelong habits, firmly fixed moral feelings, and sacred relationships are without effect, even during the pronounced suggestibility of the hypnotic trance.

6. The strength of a suggestion varies with the frequency with which it is met. But more mechanical repetition avails little unless the repeated suggestion is attended to with interest. Experiment shows that repetition of advertising appeals is twice as effective when the form, style, and expression is varied, with constant theme, as when exact duplication of previous appeals is used. Repetition accompanied by sufficient variety to lend interest, but with sufficient uniformity to acquire a constant meaning, produces a genuine cumulative effect.

7. In appealing over the short circuit for a specific line of action, no interference, substitute, rival idea, or opposing action should be suggested. Such an idea merely impedes the action power of the first suggestion by inviting comparison and thus involves deliberate choice and hesitation.

Our review above, of typical procedures concerned with motivation stimulation and response leading to action, in effect dealt with those that also may promote suggestion (if we assume that the reflective element is practically absent and that the responses are automatic). These applications that create or accompany suggestive behavior are those of emotional and ethical appeals, of language, and even of pseudo-logic.

What are the emotional states of a listener that provide the climate of successful suggestion? "Man is a suggestible animal." [57]

Social cohesion of the group creates a climate more favorable to sug-

[57] Kimball Young, *op. cit.*, 116.

gestion. The assembly needs to be translated into psychological group
rather than remain a crowd (that is, individuals not linked together in
common purposes, attitudes, and emotionality). "Intensity of personality is in inverse proportion to the number of aggregated men." [58] The
sense of social responsibility is less demanding and dominant for the
group than for the individual who confronts alone the need for decision.
The psychological group is more directly affected by basic emotional responses and desires; it is inclined to believe in whatever satisfies its primary and secondary needs and wants. It tends to respond to connotative
language; to rationalize; to react from prejudice; to ignore complicated
arguments and to yield to species or pseudo-arguments. Its thoughts are
less keen; it is credulous. Its habits of restraint are relaxed. Men in
crowds are comparatively primitive.

The moral question is raised of forming a psychological crowd. As
indicated above, the crowd, with its high degree of suggestibility, is more
easily swayed than the deliberative group. On the other hand, a community of feeling and of united action has advantages. Whatever our
reaction to this matter of creating a psychological crowd, we at any rate
need insight into the methods by which group solidarity is achieved.
Certain conditions of the meeting place itself help toward such unity of
the gathering. Hearers, we are advised, need to be seated close together.
Visual symbols such as flags and decorations help. Raised-platform positions for the speakers help to "polarize the audience." Group singing,
much applause, and other unified vocal responses, all increase the common spirit.

Audiences are heavily affected by authority and prestige. Whether
they endorse a brand of soap, political party, or a religious faith, these
authorities have strong appeal. When the context of such a source contains materials that bear out the testimony, the authority is legitimate.
Without logical support and interpretation, however, the favorable response is based purely on invalid suggestion.[59]

Like the respect for authority is the impulse to imitate. According to
A. Wolf, professor of logic and scientific method at the University of
London, "The impulse to imitate is not confined to childhood. There is
among the majority of adults a tendency to assimilate themselves either
to their society or to those they especially admire or respect; this tendency
to shun the eccentric is rooted deeply in human psychology." [60] Even
among highly developed persons the imitative impulse frequently over-

[58] Boris Sidis, *Psychology of Suggestion* (New York, D. Appleton and Co., 1898),
299.
[59] See F. H. Knower on "Valid, Marginal, and Bogus Appeals," in Baird and
Knower, *op. cit.*, 283–284.
[60] *Encyclopaedia Britannica* (1929–44), article on "Imitation."

rides reason, as when an audience, a larger crowd, or even a whole community is carried away by a panic for which no adequate ground has been given. Speakers may evoke vivid imagery, or even through their appealing personality incite their auditor-observers to imitation.

Common ground has been a major method of polarizing the group and creating receptiveness for a proposition and for action. Audiences prefer to be on common ground and respond favorably to speakers who so suggest. The persuader is to be looked upon as one of the group—in speech, ideas, and habits. According to Clyde Miller in his analysis of findings of the Institute for Propaganda Analysis, a prominent "device" is that of the "band wagon." Its theme is "everybody—at least all of us—are doing it." With it the propagandist attempts to convince us that all members of a group to which we belong are accepting this program and that therefore we must follow our crowd and "jump on the band wagon."

Audiences are also rendered suggestible by language manipulation. Repetition, for example, makes it impress through frequency. It takes the form of slogans, such as "No entangling alliances!" "America First!" Such repetitions will determine the psychological-persuasive effect. Monotonous duplication of previous ideas in identical phrasing, obviously, repels auditors. Repeated ideas couched, however, in varied language will effect the desired results.

Such repetition in the service of suggestion is the resort to loaded terms, words, and phrases that, subtly or openly, evoke strong reactions in line with the speaker's purposes. Words that suggest unfavorable reactions would include "flapper," "pedagogue," "atheist," "anarchist," "propagandist," "wishy-washy." Those that are much more pleasing in connotation would be "heroic," "unbiased," "smile," "broadminded," "comrade," "democratic," "logical," "square deal." [61]

The suggestive speaker-writer also utilizes these devices: the imperative mode ("Buy this cigarette," "Vote for Wintergreen,"); questions that imply a positive answer ("Why not contribute your dollar today with your colleagues?" "What is your answer—other than to do your duty in this case?"); the occasional resort to exclamations ("What a travesty of justice is this!" "What a time for victory is this!" "How calm are our hearts as we face these difficulties!").

The thoroughgoing persuader who has gone overboard in the bypassing of logic and fact may nevertheless present a façade of pseudo-logic and seeming plausibility. His generalizations, however, are "glittering," with few or no cases to substantiate them. His testimonials are without contextual supports. His propositions and insinuations stem from bias and his materials and ideas from statements that are badly distorted. He

[61] W. M. Pitkin, "A Study of Loaded Words" (unpublished A.M. thesis, University of Wisconsin, 1931), cited by Brembeck and Howell, op. cit., 116–117.

demonstrates "special pleading" of a pernicious kind and "cardstacking" to eulogize his own case and correspondingly to distort and condemn the opposing idea, person, or product.[62]

Persuasion and Propaganda

The discussion above has occasionally referred to propaganda as one type of persuasion. What marks off such propagandistic communication from persuasion? The essential difference lies in the size of the audiences addressed. Propaganda applies to mass audiences, those of radio-television and the press. The term has attached to itself significant meaning especially since World War I, with the rise of modern, electronic, and other means of influencing large populations. Not all of this barrage has been evil. Franklin D. Roosevelt during World War II directed national energies and loyalties through his continual radio talks. Winston Churchill held Britain together in 1940 and later by the sheer power of his inspired words.

Propaganda has been a highly important means of controlling public opinion, the "mass management of the public mind." It was dramatically applied as psychological warfare to supplement military campaigns in World War II and in lesser wars since. Soviet Russia and her satellites, Red China, Cuba, the Arab Republic, Egypt, and scores of other small or large nations have poured out their propaganda by radio-television and pamphleteering, and before such agencies as the United Nations. In these later times, with newspapers reaching millions and radio or television addressing a single audience of many millions, such appeals have taken on tremendous and sinister proportions.

Propaganda calls for mass audiences. In the United States, for example, the entire nation has been more and more closely knit into a national unit by superhighways, airstrips, electronic communication by telephone, radio, and television. This nation has literally welded itself into one communication family.

The propaganda to this national audience has been heavily directed toward commercial, political, social, and to some extent, cultural and religious ends.

Much of the deluge of talk and printing has been "bad." Whether or not we attempt to disassociate "propaganda" from morality, we do recognize that much that is broadcast or handed out face to face and by documents is communicatively destructive.

The very size and putative homogeneity of the mass audience, and the

[62] C. W. Miller, *The Process of Persuasion* (New York, Crown Publishers, 1946), Part II, "Persuasion Methods," 148–222. Cf. Alfred McClung Lee and Elizabeth Briant Lee (eds.), *The Fine Art of Propaganda* (New York, Harcourt Brace, 1939), 23–24.

comparatively mediocre quality of the mass mind, invite a high degree of devious suggestion. The philosopher surveying the practices raises many questions concerning the validity of the aims and techniques. Although much that is printed for national audiences or released through commercial and educational radio-television channels is rhetorically acceptable, much other material violates rhetorical-logical or ethical validity.

Consider the discourses that fill the air and the daily press. How far from logical thought and factual accuracy have been the mass appeals? What methods were used in ignoring or begging the question? How many common fallacies and tricks of the propagandists have been revealed? What of the hasty generalizations, the false analogies, the questionable premises, the invalid *post hoc* arguments and assumptions? What of the name-calling, the transfer, testimonial, cardstacking and the other objectional devices and techniques listed by the Institute for Propaganda Analysis? [63] What of the unjustified appeals to fear, hate, anger, wishful thinking, rationalization, rumor, distrust? What of the loaded words, and the constant manipulation of ideas to secure at all costs the desired attitude?

The philosopher-rhetorician analyzing such questions of mass communication finds the utterances of the contemporary world far short of acceptable communication standards. He applies the same criteria of judgment that he has always applied. The methods he examines are the same that he has met with in ancient and later rhetoric. The only new aspect of the problem is the size and amorphous weight of the audiences. Thus the rhetorician summons his sociological and psychological understanding as he judges the logical, the political-social, ethical, emotional components of the communications.

Since propaganda will no doubt increase in intensity and extent and in its influence in national and international life, critical judgment on such methods and influences will be necessary for those who would support the objectives of the good society.

Shall the rhetorician join those who would elevate the reasoning and rhetorical sophistication of this national audience? This is his role. Shall the individual lose his personality in the vast chain of social identification? The rhetorician resists such direction and outcome. The equilibrium between the public pressures and private conscience and individuality, he believes, must be retained. With such perspective and goal, he will continue to apply his principles and standards to the oral and written communication of his day.[64]

[63] Miller, *op. cit.*

[64] Everett Hunt, "Ancient Rhetoric and Modern Propaganda," *Quarterly Journal of Speech*, XXXVII (April, 1951), 157–160; Vance Packard, *The Hidden Persuaders* (New York, David McKay, 1957); Stanley Kelley, Jr., *Professional Public Relations and Political Power* (Baltimore, The Johns Hopkins Press, 1956).

Summary

Although, in theory, reason and logic are the heart and soul of worthwhile communication, human beings are still largely non-intellectual, and these latter traits enter heavily into communicative analyses and principles of effective expression. The problem is to include the emotional factors without complete subjugation and destruction of the rationality that gives meaning to the communicative act.

Rhetoric, in company with psychology, examines in detail human behavior—from the aspect of the agent in the process and that of the respondent. The drives, motives, attitudes, and stereotypes are interpreted, classified, and described as, severally or collectively, they express themselves in the communicative situation. Audiences are diagnosed as they behave in typical situations—informative, deliberative, or epideictic, and as they react in specific groups—industrial, economic, educational, religious, and all others.

The overlapping of the emotional labellings and behavior is obvious —but a convenient purpose is served. The old "faculty psychology" with its disparate sources of conviction and persuasion is rejected. But the monistic concept of the reacting personality continues with, however, pluralistic expression, as discussed by Woolbert, Rowell, and others. Persuasion, for example, occurs not on an intellectual but rather on a motor level.

The emotive factor in discourse, highly necessary and contributory, expresses itself in the structure of the discourse; in the patterns of ideas; in the details of language; in the identifications of speaker-agent and the audience; in the ethical factors; in the attention and sustained interest; and in the control and direction of propaganda, as noted in the previous chapter.

8

Language and Style

Language, according to the classical description, was the third of the five communicative elements: invention (*inventio*, εὕρεσις), disposition (*dispositio*, τάξις), language or style (*elocutio*, λέξις), pronunciation (*pronuntiatio*, *actio*, ὑπόκρισις), and memory (*memoria*, μνήμη).

Invention, as interpreted in Chapter 4 above, was central in expression. Disposition as structure comprised orderly selection, cohesion and proportioning of ideas, and their unification in the total discourse. Language became the vehicle by which the ideas and their development were transmitted to audiences through vocal expression or written transcripts.

Language is the instrumentality by which speakers and writers embody their ideas, their logical and emotional supports, and their thematic development. The aim is to produce comprehension and favorable response. Language, it is generally agreed, is necessary for individual and social survival and progress. Cultural cooperation, despite wars and internecine struggles, is the central principle of human existence and progress. Such group association and coordination is of necessity "achieved by language or else it is not achieved at all."[1]

John Ciardi, poet, writer, and teacher at Harvard and elsewhere, stated in a lecture, "A good long time and much wisdom have gone into the development and shaping of any one of the languages the human race uses. . . . Language, greatly used, is important to mankind's own imagination of itself."[2]

Language is the "purposive activity" of human beings who attempt to link themselves with their fellows for mutual support. This activity may be primarily informational, or volitional, or emotional, or may be merely random exchange. Language, "perhaps the chief distinctive mark of humanity," is the seat of practically all political, cultural, aesthetic,

---

[1] S. I. Hayakawa, *Language in Thought and Action* (New York, Harcourt Brace, 1939), 18.
[2] John Ciardi, lecture at the State University of Iowa, October 17, 1963.

economic, social, and religious trends and marks of the small or great community in its common functioning through eye-and-ear language.[3]

Style, Language, and Rhetoric

The significant place that classical and later rhetoricians give language is reflected in the space and value they give to style.

Aristotle treats style or language at length in the first twelve chapters of Book III of his *Rhetoric*.[4] Almost half of *Ad Herennium* is given to style (*elocutio*). Cicero's *Orator* is given entirely to language.[5]

Cicero also devotes at least one third of *De Oratore* to style. Quintilian's *Institutes of Oratory* treats language almost exclusively in Books VIII and IX of his treatise.[6]

Medieval rhetoric, because of the profound changes from Greco-Roman political life, encouraged little deliberative or forensic speaking. Preaching itself was largely epideictic. The medieval tendency was to exalt style, especially the oratory of display.[7] As Donald Clark concluded, "To the late middle ages, rhetoric had come to mean to all intents and purposes nothing more than style."[8]

Thomas Wilson, in his *Arte of Rhetorique*, the first full-length exposition of rhetoric in the English language, gave over the third of the three books to *elocutio* (style).[9] Similarly, John Ward in his *System of Oratory*[10] and John Lawson in his *Lectures Concerning Oratory*[11] continued in the British eighteenth century the classical interest in language as they treated it with invention, disposition, and delivery.

Parallel with this continuation of the Ciceronian tradition in English treatises came the more direct rhetoric of style as inherited from the second sophistic period of the second, third, or fourth centuries A.D., and from the medieval and the renaissance schools. The rhetoric of exorna-

---

[3] Otto Jespersen, article "Language," in *Eycyclopaedia Britannica* (1929–44).

[4] *The "Rhetoric" of Aristotle*, tr. Lane Cooper (New York, Appleton-Century-Crofts, Inc., 1932).

[5] Cicero, *The Orator*, in *The Orations of Marcus Tullius Ciaro*, tr. C. D. Yonge (London, George Bell, 1913), Vol. 4, 384–457.

[6] Quintilian, *The Institutio Oratoria of Quintilian*, tr. H. E. Butler, 4 vols. (London, Heinemann; New York, Putnam, 1921–22).

[7] C. S. Baldwin, *Medieval Rhetoric and Poetic* (New York, Macmillan, 1924); Donald G. Clark, *Rhetoric and Poetry in the Renaissance* (New York, Columbia University Press, 1922); Wilbur Samuel Howell, "Renaissance Rhetoric and Modern Rhetoric: A Study in Change," in Donald C. Bryant, *The Rhetorical Idiom* (Ithaca, N.Y., Cornell University Press, 1958; 53–70; Wilbur Samuel Howell, *Logic and Rhetoric in England: 1500–1700* (Princeton, N.J., Princeton University Press, 1956).

[8] Clark, *op. cit.*, 47.

[9] Thomas Wilson, *Arte of Rhetorique*, ed. G. H. Mair (Oxford, Clarendon Press, 1909).

[10] John Ward, *System of Oratory*, 2 vols. (London, J. Ward, 1759).

[11] John Lawson, *Lectures Concerning Oratory* (Dublin, G. Faulkner, 1760).

tion (1570–1600) reflected the high tide of Elizabethan poetry and drama and popularized among English commentators the rhetoric of ornamentation. Richard Sherry in his *Treatise of Schemes and Tropes* (1550) and his *Figures of Grammar and Rhetoric* (1555) [12] gave first importance to training of educated leaders in ornamental speech. Henry Peacham's *Garden of Eloquence* (1577) [13] continues this stress on figurative discourse.

The movement led by Peter Ramus in France of the sixteenth century, in his analysis of the seven liberal arts, sharply distinguished grammar from the other elements of the *trivium.* Ramistic dialectic (logic) became invention and arrangement. Ramistic rhetoric was limited to style and delivery.[14] Audomarus Talaeus (Omer Talon), a contemporary and associate of Ramus, introduced into England the *Rhetorica* (1577), in which style was limited to tropes and figures.[15] Various other rhetorics in England during the sixteenth and seventeenth centuries and into the eighteenth century continued to enlarge on ornamental style, especially tropes and figures. John Smith, with *The Mysteries of Rhetorique Unveiled* (1657), included "above 130 of the tropes and figures as severally divided from the Greek into the English." [16]

Thomas Gibbons' *Rhetoric* (1767), like those of the Ramean predecessors, systematically classified tropes and figures and cited a considerable number of classical writers to justify and illuminate this examination of embellished prose.[17]

This concentration of rhetoric on connotative language continued, but the classical tradition dominated, with notable contributions by late eighteenth century Scottish thinkers.

George Campbell's *The Philosophy of Rhetoric* (1776) comprised three books, the second and third of which dealt almost entirely with style, or "elocution" as Campbell used the term.[18]

Hugh Blair, in his *Lectures on Rhetoric and Belles Lettres* (1783), thirty-four chapters in all, opened with standards of criticism, and followed with twenty-two lectures on style. Although style to Blair had the

[12] Richard Sherry, *A Treatise of Schemes and Tropes* (London, John Day, 1550); Richard Sherry, *A Treatise of the Figures of Grammar and Rhetoric* (London, Richard Tottell, 1555).

[13] Henry Peacham, *The Garden of Eloquence* (London, H. Jackson, 1577).

[14] Wilbur Samuel Howell, "Ramus and English Rhetoric, 1574–1681," *Quarterly Journal of Speech*, XXXVII (October, 1951), 299–310.

[15] Audomarus Talous, *Rhetorica, 1577*, date of entry for English publication, 1530–1828. See William P. Sandford, *English Theories of Public Address* (Columbus, Ohio, H. Hedrick, 1938).

[16] John Smith, *The Mystery of Rhetorick Unveiled* (London, R. Clavel, 1688).

[17] Thomas Gibbons, *Rhetoric* (London, printed by J. & W. Oliver, for J. Buckland and J. Payne, 1767).

[18] George Campbell, *The Philosophy of Rhetoric*, ed. Lloyd Bitzer (Carbondale, Ill., Southern Illinois University Press, 1963).

greatest prominence, he did dip into criticism, poetry, and the relation of rhetoric to literature. He also restated Quintilian's principles of rhetoric.[19]

Richard Whately developed his *Elements of Rhetoric* (1828), in four parts: Part I, treatment of conviction; Part II, address to the will, or persuasion; Part III, style; Part IV, delivery. The chapters on style comprised about 20 per cent of the volume, even though Whately aimed chiefly to write about the laws of evidence and persuasion and "the rules for argumentative composition and elocution." [20]

John Quincy Adams (at Harvard) included, in the thirty-six lectures of his *Lectures on Rhetoric and Oratory,* ten lectures on style, and of these, four were on figurative language.[21]

Adams Sherman Hill's *Principles of Rhetoric* (1878),[22] is organized in two parts: Part I, composition in general, given almost entirely to language; Part II, kinds of composition-description, narration, exposition, and argument.

John F. Genung, professor of rhetoric at Amherst College, in *The Practical Elements of Rhetoric* (1886), gave Part I to style—or practically half of the total volume, with Part II to invention.[23]

The tendency to restrict rhetoric largely to written composition and to stylistic techniques carried through into schools and colleges during the twentieth century. Scores of texts incorporating the title "rhetoric" dealt almost entirely with written composition, especially with the details and mechanics of syle. The writings and texts on "public speaking," written during the twentieth century, have been Aristotelian-Ciceronian-Quintilian rhetoric, and have invariably included chapters on language.[24]

Thus is maintained the central place of language, through the centuries, in the theory of rhetoric.

What are the purposes of language, oral and written? The varying aims overlap and can be differentiated only by general description. Ordinary conversation, preaching, law, poetry, science, logic, mathematics, philosophy—each has its motives or style. Certain primary types of dis-

---

[19] Hugh Blair, *Lectures on Rhetoric and Belles Lettres,* 3 vols. (8th ed.; London, T. Cadell, Jun., and W. Davies in the Strand, and W. Greech, Edinburgh, 1801).
[20] Richard Whately, *Elements of Rhetoric,* ed. Douglas Ehninger (Carbondale, Ill., Southern Illinois University Press, 1963).
[21] John Quincy Adams, *Lectures on Rhetoric and Oratory,* 2 vols. (Cambridge, Mass., Hilliard & Metcalf, 1810).
[22] Adams Sherman Hill, *Principles of Rhetoric* (New York, American Book, 1878).
[23] John F. Genung, *Practical Elements of Rhetoric* (Boston, The Athenaeum Press, Ginn, 1886).
[24] Hoyt H. Hudson, "The Field of Rhetoric," *Quarterly Journal of Speech Education,* VIII (April, 1923), 167–180. Reprinted in Raymond Howes (ed.), *Historical Studies of Rhetoric and Rhetoricians* (Ithaca, N.Y., Cornell University Press, 1961), 3–15.

course can nevertheless be described and classified for convenience in interpretation by students of rhetoric.

One common use is informational. The speaker or writer hands out knowledge, reports his findings. Such discourse is largely scientific, historical, journalistic (as in good reporting); it is factual and close to the referent level.

A second use is in establishing belief, shaping opinion, the aims of directors of statecraft, and other exponents of high-level policy, to convince.

A third use, stemming chiefly from conviction or belief, is more directly emotive. The aim is chiefly persuasive, with action (behavior) as the goal. Motives are appealed to for the purpose of making sales, securing votes, and accomplishing similar results in audience activity.

One other use of language is aesthetic. The coloring of such discourse creates poetry or appreciative prose. The speaking or writing is chiefly literary or for ends of the emotional creation of beauty. These uses commingle, but usually a dominant motive controls the ideas, language, emotional expression, and delivery (if a speech).[25]

Language as Symbol

What, then, is language? It is the symbol that stands for "other things." Through certain sounds and related physical activities, or their equivalent written characters, the communicator conveys to himself or to others his ideas, attitudes, sentiments, and experiences. From this activity he hits upon and develops certain symbols for ear and eye transmission. As Alfred Korzybski stated, "Man's achievements rest upon the use of symbols."[26] Human beings make certain things "stand for other things. . . . The process by means of which human beings can arbitrarily make certain things *stand* for other things may be called the *symbolic process*."[27]

Symbols are as wide as the experience of a given society. They are the church spires and crosses, the army or navy costumes, the garb of nurses, nuns, and industrial workers; ownership of superior brands of automobiles; association with prestige books, newspapers, celebrities; Santa Clauses; secret order rituals; and an indefinite list of other symbols. They are rich in their suggestion of concrete objects or situations that have given rise to these substitutions.

Language is the most highly developed of multitudinous forms of symbolism. These word coinages grow out of the common experiences and associations of the few or many individuals. As common reactions serve

[25] Joshua Whatmough, *Language* (New York, Mentor Books, 1957), 84–89.
[26] Alfred Korzybski, *Science and Sanity* (New York, Science Press Printing Co., 1933).
[27] S. I. Hayakawa, *op. cit.*, 25.

to convey that which the inventors of these symbols had in mind, these reactions become socially approved and used. The ancient races came to let the sounds issuing from their lungs, throats, tongues, teeth, and lips stand for specific reactions. The translation of these sounds and their accompanying gestures into hieroglyphic or alphabetical combinations gave Hebrew, Greek, Latin, Anglo-Saxon, American, and a thousand other dialects and languages their lineage and direction.

These agreements of organized language are purely arbitrary. There may be no necessary connection between the symbol and the "thing" allegedly duplicated. Onomatopoetic sounds may hark back to their originals in nature, but usually the connection is not so clear. The connection becomes evident, as we have said, only because the people involved agree that it is so.

Furthermore, these designations of sounds and written words are by no means static. The agreements taper off in serving their linguistic purpose. The new and old words mingle, and new generations write off old terms with the dress, social manners, and language of the bygone era. Fresh slang and other innovations become respectable in the dictionaries. Thus language adapts itself to the changing customs. Practicability, rather than grammatical rules and academic edicts, governs.

The symbol may be an isolated sound; or several sounds or written characters may unite in a term, a sentence, a paragraph, or a whole composition. These combinations again are arbitrarily set up for general convenience.

The reaction is to some external agency, as when the nervous system reacts to sounds, sights, smells, temperature, colors, tastes, and other sensory or neurological activities. This symbolization at the sensory level is a recording of experiences that can presumably be verified by others.

Such is the language of "fact"—presumably the reporting of the testimony of witnesses, those who have directly participated in the sensory experience. Facts, however, may be only relative. They may or may not represent reality. "Facts have to do with the existence of things, the occurrence of events, including their causes and results, the classification of data, and the character of phenomena." [28] What is the basis of their possible unreliability?

Despite this fairly specific differentiation of facts or evidence from the general laws or principles that closely relate to speculative statements and theories, "facts" rest on unstable grounds. They are just as "certain" as the testimony that seems to vouch for them. What of the competency of the investigator to validate the "facts"? What of his limited view, his possible distortions through prejudice? Furthermore, "facts" are accept-

[28] A. Craig Baird, *Argumentation, Discussion and Debate* (New York, McGraw-Hill, 1950), 91.

able only because those concerned so categorize them. The alleged information of today, however, may be unacceptable tomorrow. Facts have become myths, and a new set of "truths" created.

Theories of Language Symbols

Note several principles for interpreting these language symbols.

First, the word symbols are to be distinguished from the mental processes from which they spring. Dr. Wendell P. Johnson graphically explains the relationship of symbolization to the mental activities at work.[29] According to Johnson, the communicative process can be comprehended in five stages of its development.

First is the event—source of stimulation—external to the sensory end organs of the speaker or writer. Philosophically and practically it cannot be verified, but it is assumed.

Second is the sensory stimulation within the organism of the speaker or writer. "Once a sensory receptor has been stimulated, nerve currents travel quickly along the spinal cord and normally up through the base of the brain to the higher reaches of the cortex, out again along efferent tracts to the muscles and glands." Their contractions and secretions produce new sensory stimulations which are "fed back" into the cord and brain and effect further changes. This sensory reaction may come from the immediate contact with the object itself, or from analogous experiences—previous contacts with the external world. To illustrate, the map, which the semanticists cite frequently, is not the territory, but may be so identified by actual observation. The word symbolizes a concrete stretch of land that we experience. But the "map" may also represent a fictional country—Jonathan Swift's "Gulliver land." In the latter case, even though it does not possess "reality," it corresponds to the word as pictured. The sensory reactions of the speaker or writer would verify that this imaginary region was clearly put together from genuine experience. Every symbol has at some point a basis in genuine reaction: if it has none, the symbol has no meaning. Through analogy, if not through literal and direct "contact" with the "thing" itself, is such a symbol serviceable.

This stimulus derived from some external event or other source, however we describe this origin, results, as Johnson puts it, in a "preneurophysiological state of activity." This is the third stage, which, according to Johnson, is the "filter stage" because the organism operates as a "kind of filter" through which the sensory impulses must pass before the speaker-

[29] Wendell Johnson, "The Spoken Word and the Great Unsaid," *Quarterly Journal of Speech* (December, 1951), XXXVII, 419–429.

writer becomes conscious of them and before he can "communicate them in some symbolic form." [30]

The fourth stage is that in which the preverbal activities are transformed into words or equivalent symbols. Here the speaker's mind is at work: He subconsciously delves into the latent or active vocabulary accumulated through his learning and retention. Here flash into his consciousness the symbols and series of symbols. Here are the releases of his repressions, wishes, inhibitions, semantic blockages, and all the rest of his mental activity.

The fifth and final stage is that in which this verbal give-and-take becomes limited, selective. The mental flow is reduced to the language of a speech or article addressed to a specific audience, at a given time and place, "a condensed abstract of all that might have been spoken."

Enough is illustrated from these five stages to make clear that symbolization is the product of this inward movement of the communicating organism. The thought frames the symbol. The problem, then, is to secure verbalization that reflects the "thinking." Stage five calls for detailed and faithful reflection of the mental pulsations. The uttered sentiments should correspond to the real thinking, as for example, when a speaker or writer proclaims that "all races should have equality." Are these merely words, or do they duplicate the genuinely inner person?

Second, the symbols of language carry with them both intensional and extensional meaning. Linguists and historians would have done well had they been able to designate one word for one idea. But, as we commented above, proclamations in the language area hardly work. Not only does the literal word or term soon bulge with synonymous, metaphorical meanings, but the specific designation becomes overcast with suggestiveness. Thus we must deal both with extensional (or literal) and intensional meanings in the same word. According to Barrett Wendell:

And here we may see, as distinctly as anywhere, the two functions that every word, every name of an idea, must perform; in the first place, it names something in such way as to identify it, and in the second, it suggests along with it a very subtle and variable set of associated ideas and emotions. . . . A word may be said then, to *denote* the idea it identifies. . . . A word may be said to *connote* the thoughts and emotions that it arouses in the hearer or reader.[31]

The denotative meaning is close to the referent. It originates in the stimulus and accompanying reaction and language that others will accept as designating the "thing" a table, microscope, or whatever else is described.

---

[30] *Ibid.,* 422.
[31] Barrett Wendell, *English Composition* (New York, Scribner, 1891, 1905), 74.

The denotative, or extensional, dimensions of the word or term can be verified by the testimony of other observers and by dictionary definitions. Connotation, on the other hand, represents the subjective, intensional, inward reaction of the speaker-writer, with his purposes and personality. Denotation calls up literal meanings. Denotative language is informational, factual, objective, free from emotional overtones. But this same language may also be freighted with ideas or imaginative and emotional qualities that have little connection with the original extensional image. Connotative language is thus saturated with such figurative elements. Connotative meanings are those of the advocate, the poet, and the fiction writer.

No basic contradiction necessarily exists between these two kinds of meanings. But the denotative must reflect closeness to the referent itself. A statement without extensional implication means that no verification in the external world can be made. Such intensional wordings are purely "inward," "subjective," and personal, and may be confusing. Sufficient denotation must be present to help supply "sense" and comprehension.

This multiplicity of meanings and the varied interpretations of a single word give rise to many semantic wrangles. The special referent that the speaker or writer has in mind and experience should be made clear—as well as his specific communicative aim. Distinction needs to be made between the multiple meanings accompanying almost every word. Dictionaries exist not to give final definitions but to provide a history of the word and to array changing meanings, so that the speaker or writer may choose the one meaning that fits his purpose, and one that can be specifically understood by the audience. "Democracy," "conservatism," "orthodoxy," "freedom," and endless lists of other words have been wrangled over because of no preliminary or later understanding concerning the framework in which the given term is to be viewed.

"Rhetoric," "English composition," "public speaking," "speech fundamentals" are often used synonymously. The word "nice" means (a) fastidious, (b) affecting coy reserve, (c) demanding close discrimination, (d) delicately sensitive, (e) pleasing, kind, considerate, (f) particular, (g) hypercritical, (h) finical, (i) squeamish. To understand the specific referent, we need to know that which the speaker or writer had in mind.

Language symbols, as we implied above, are hardly to be separated from the context. The intent of the speaker or writer becomes necessary for intelligent interpretation. That intent becomes more meaningful if interpreted through the passage. A broadcast announced "When the Earth Stopped . . . a highly successful play. . . ." What the critic had written was, "When the Earth Stopped was far short of a highly successful play." Historic courtroom libel cases have been settled in favor of a defendant by his successful insistence on his intent as determined by the context.

In English forensic history, Thomas Erskine won a celebrated case, "In behalf of Stockdale" (the latter accused of publishing a libelous pamphlet), by convincing the jury that "every composition of this kind is to be taken as a whole, and not judged of by detached passages."

Words become an important agency in producing perception. Perception is the process "by which words, substitute stimuli, cause auditors or readers to respond to the objects, situations, and experiences symbolized by these stimuli." [32]

Theoretically, the symbols uttered by the agent find correspondence in the responses by the hearer or reader. The ideas, sentiments, and attitudes suggested through these symbols should find corresponding ideas, sentiments, and attitudes, in the personalities of those who respond.

In theory, the word symbols enable the listener to construct his own thinking pattern—one that reflects the thinking of the speaker—the referents that presumably moved the latter in his own thinking and expression. Speakers do not automatically transfer meaning. They aim to stimulate another person to develop certain ideas which "when fully assembled will constitute for him the meaning we wish him to have." [33]

In actual experience, this transfer or reconstruction falls far short of the speaker's aim. The listener's many blocks may interfere markedly with the response intended. In fact, counterreactions may develop, strongly opposed to the communicator's intent. This listener, for example, may be ignorant, or prejudiced—mildly or strongly—against what is directed to him. His age, nationality, occupation, religion, experiences in general, and other factors relating to his needs, interests, and desires may explain the wide discrepancy between the message and the appropriation by the receiver.

Aside from the necessary contextual explanation, the definition of the word or "object" (referent) is the starting point in description of the symbols. Definition is a process of selecting certain aspects of the referent or "thing itself" as sufficiently descriptive of the symbol.

Obviously, it is impossible to catalogue and expound every detail of the phenomenon under scrutiny. To do so would require much space and in some cases call for an encyclopedic article. This reporting reflects our point of view and purpose.

This partial description and some good judgment in playing up the selected approach will prevent much confusion. The semanticists, re-

[32] A. Craig Baird and Franklin H. Knower, *General Speech* (3rd ed.; New York, McGraw-Hill, 1963), 153.
[33] Andrew Weaver, *Speech* (New York, Longmans Green, 1943), 319.

minding us of the unexplored aspects of the word or term under definition, suggest the use of "etc." to indicate the additional sections that might be included. Thus, a college is "an institution of higher learning affording a general or liberal education rather than a primarily technical or professional training, etc."

This method of selection ("abstraction," as the semanticists call it) focuses first on the object of the stimulation—that which our nervous system selects from the total situation. This first stage, for example, may be an individual we perceive, or an object of our experience. In any case it is that which our sensory organs react to and which our nervous system selects. This "thing itself," as we report it, omits many of the characteristics of the total possible listing.

At the initial stage, for example, we encounter a human being in Iowa, perhaps a farmer, or typical citizen of Des Moines or some other urban region. We note the distinctive characteristics of the person as we meet him—his features, dress, movements, voice, and age. At the second stage we identify him by a name—any specific name, to translate the primary reaction into an equivalent symbol. In giving a name to this object of our sensory experience, we omit many details. Moving up the scale, from the lower to the more abstract level, we successively identify our individual as an Iowan, a Mid-Westerner, and finally an American. At each higher level we omit traits peculiar to this isolated person. This is the process of moving up the abstraction or selection ladder, from the sensory level where our eyes and ears focus on the individual, to the area where practically all the definite elements are absent.

Why thus exercise such selection from the concrete to the abstract? Obviously, when we attempt to identify this specific object under our observation for others, we cannot carry over every detail. We need some convenient and special telescoping of the word or term. Thus we speak of "people" (rather than a certain down-East, native Maine fisherman), "automobiles" (versus my ancient but still usable Ford or Chevrolet), "college students" (rather than a certain sophomore Harvey Housman, at Swarthman University), "Republicans" (versus H. R. Oneman, a voter), and scores of other abstractions, such as idealism, knowledge, ethics, aesthetics, determinism, love, liberty, art. Such broad usages of language, though they disturb students of precise vocabulary, are necessary. In customary writing or speaking, they help communicative progress. These relatively abstract terms the semanticists would sometimes close in quotation marks, to suggest their remoteness from a referential base.

Definitions are tentative only. Constant changes in word meanings and explanations are necessary. Because we use a limited number of words to describe a vast conglomeration of things, and because our new experiences and reactions call for a fresh view of the symbols, the vocabulary is never the same. Some words quickly drop out of currency; long lists of obsolete words may be found in the *Oxford English Dictionary*. Others change their clothing, take on new meanings, sometimes almost the opposite of their original denotation. *Villain* is often cited as originally designating a simple peasant, but in these days is an archenemy of society. "In sooth," an Elizabethan locution, is today quaintly archaic. *Sad* once meant merely *serious*. *Sentence* meant *thought; abuse* was to *deceive; confuse*, to *destroy*. *Copperhead* and *mugwump*, current after 1860, have little meaning for twentieth century Americans.

The semanticists suggest that we use dates for terms to indicate their changing significance. Dates index the times. Since no two times are identical, so words should be indexed to indicate these chronological changes. "Myself, 1960" is not the same as "myself, 1965." "United States, 1940" is quite different from "United States, 1970." Just as we differentiate specific words from those of the same species by indexing, as in oak ^{1}, oak ^{2}, oak ^{3}, or Hammersmith ^{1}, Hammersmith ^{2}, so do we index these same terms to mark the time changes. We are separating the identity of the moment from the non-identity that immediately follows.[34]

Finally, concerning definitions and interpretations of words, a clearer understanding will result if the concept is seen against a continuous rather than a sharply departmentalized pattern. The principle of locating a term in a general field and then attempting to relate the word to a specific section of the area should not commit the framer to the Aristotelian method of putting the object defined into sharply set-off categories. The error here is that of "two-valued orientation," in which a dichotomy is made in which the terms are separated in two sharp categories. Often, this division simply does not exist. Things are not simply "hot or cold" or "right or wrong."

Events, problems, and word descriptions range along a continuum in which one concept shades into another. Thus, to define *blue, Republican, capitalism*, we construct a scale representing the general character or "property" of the things defined, with the opposite extremes of the concept at the extremes of the scale. Suppose we attempt to locate *intelligence* on such a scale. At one extreme is "idiocy"; at the other, "genius". The unbroken line from "idiocy" to "genius" represents successive but minute changes. The steps from below normal, to normal, and to above normal are imperceptible and arbitrarily designed. This principle of

[34] Wendell Johnson, *People in Quandaries* (New York and London, Harper, 1946), 205–239. Cf. S. I. Hayakawa, *op. cit.*, Chap. 4, "Contexts"; Chap. 13, "Classification"; Chap. 14, "The Two-Valued Orientation."

describing the term by relating it to such a scale and of placing the word at some point in the line is the principle of continuous variation.[35]

Such method stresses relative rather than absolute distinctions. No great gaps occur along the line. *Good* finally becomes *bad; anarchy* becomes *absolutism; atheism* becomes *religious orthodoxy.* Thus we can intelligently differentiate poetry and prose, beauty and ugliness, religion and morality, discussion and debate.

The "property" or character of the broad line is to be clearly set forth, as well as the precision with which the concept is placed in the scale, and the definiteness with which the term is described in its relative position.

This descriptive precision need not result in the error of assuming that the word label implies sharp compartments. On the other hand, the demarking of units should lead to no denial that differences really exist. Certainly, an autocrat is different from a plebian democrat. A bad stutterer is different from the possessor of pure speech. All definitions stem from assumptions that the area of common properties is continuous and yet one in which details differ recognizably from each other.

Thus, by the application of logical principles, placing a term in a class or group, applying a continuous rather than sharply departmentalized pattern, defining terms in relation to the context, regarding all definitions as selective, as governed by the point of view of the speaker or writer, the definitions or explanations may be more intelligently set forth. To assure speakers and audiences of the clarity of such explanations, specific methods, expounded at some length in treatises on rhetoric or composition, are usually given. These stress definition by authority, by history (how the term developed), by function or purpose (what it does), by operational description (how it works), by comparison and contrast, or by an enumeration of details.

Style, Invention, and Mass Communication

What is style? Language and style are often used interchangeably—as in this chapter. Language is obviously the broad term to encompass all communication through words and their combinations that produce artistic and literary effect. Aristotle and his rhetorical successors so discussed it. According to Hugh Blair, style was "the peculiar manner in which a man stresses his conceptions by means of language. It is different from mere Language or words." To Blair, style has to do with a man's thinking and his emotional-imaginative reactions. "It is a picture of the ideas that rise in his mind, and of the manner in which they rise there." [36]

[35] Baird, *op. cit.,* Chap. 5, "Definition."
[36] Blair, *op. cit.,* 212-13.

Blair thus identifies style with thought but he recognizes that, as he puts it, "in many cases it is difficult to separate the style from the sentiment."

John Genung, in the classical tradition, views style similarly. "By style is meant, in general, manner of expressing thought in language; and more particularly of giving such skilled expression as invests the idea with fitting dignity and distinction." [37] Ordinary prose, he goes on to say, is too "rudimentary" to admit the idea of style.

A work characterized by style derives equal importance from the particular manner of saying a thing: there is a force or a felicity in the use of language that adapts the thought to the occasion, and gives it fullness and power. That is, there must be some dignity or distinction in the expression before we can begin to estimate it as style.

Style, as *elocutio* (or λέξις), the third of the five rhetorical constituents, is "inextricably interwoven" with the other parts. It plays an interacting role with invention.

Style, as Genung states, is the embodiment of thought. The speaker or writer's communication aims "not so much at qualities of style in themselves as at the demands of the subject, in order to bring out in its fullness what is essentially there." [38] Style cannot be thought of as something added from the outside. It *is* the thought, "freed from crudeness, and incompleteness, and presented in its intrinsic power and beauty." Prior to style must be thought, knowledge, precise experience and "sanity of reasoning power. The perfect union is that between adequate matter and an adequate form." [39] Style also becomes the agency by which the emotional and elements of the discourse express themselves as in the case of Lincoln's Gettysburg Address. Such language similarly enables the structure of the discourse to give full value to the order and proportion of the movement.

Style is closely influenced not only by the speech itself, but by the reader or listener-observer. Effective elevated language must relate itself to the understanding of those who would respond. Adaptation to the audience is a basic principle. This principle applies concretely to the selection of words that represent not only the message but the way that message addresses itself to the receivers. A relatively sophisticated audience will respond best to stylistic maturity and precision. Strongly imaginative-emotional-aesthetic listeners or readers attend more completely to the language of pictures—much connotation and coloring. Mass television and radio audiences respond best to directness of expression, com-

[37] Genung, *op. cit.*, 13.
[38] *Ibid.*, 15.
[39] Edmund Gosse, article "Style," in *Encyclopaedia Britannica* (1929–40).

parative simplicity, and sometimes crass or pseudo-sentimentality, or melodramatic softness.

As the audience marks the style so does the personality of the communicator. Georges Louis Leclerc de Buffon is often quoted as stating that "style is the man." [40]

The personal quality makes for language that reveals the speaker's or writer's inner ideas, attitudes, sentiments, ideals and other traits. Before his visible audience, his very bearing, gestures, vocal inflections and his methods of unfolding his ideas and their supports, all reveal the inner man. At his best in such communication he is attempting to adhere to his thinking, experiences, hopes and motivations. Again, he consciously or unconsciously develops in his essay or other prose or poetry, the heart and residue of his experiences, his training, and the summation of his total career. Unless he has well mastered his vocabulary, he has failed to compose accurate, clear, and stimulating statements. He may dissemble sincerity and conceal his real purpose, but audiences sooner or later will detect the genuineness or artificiality of his phrases and appeals.

Language and Disposition

Style, as structure, involves words, phrases, clauses, sentences, paragraphs, and larger units of the composition. These arbitrary divisions of language serve an effective rhetorical purpose. Caution, however, needs to be made in any assumption that these divisions and separations are more than arbitrary handling of connected language. A word, for example, can often be better understood if it joins with related words as sometimes is indicated by hyphens or other mechanical connections. The rhetorical principle is that of our recognition of a succession of thought units in a given communication. Phrases, clauses, and sentences, composed of such thought sequences, can be somewhat differentiated in a speech by the voice, or in a writing by the mental activity of the reader. The punctuation marks, the capital letters and periods, the indentations for paragraphs usually help to an understanding of the ideas.

Classical rhetoric classified the structure of language as:

1. *Electio verborum*, chiefly the treatment of individual words
2. *Compositio verborum*, the structure of the phrases, clauses, sentences

Diction (*electio verborum*) deals with the selection of words but also with their connection and arrangement. Diction is concerned with the choice of words, their accuracy, present use, intelligent and scholarly use. Selection is governed by the speaker's knowledge, his familiarity with the

[40] Buffon, "Discourse on Style," in Lane Cooper, *Theories of Style* (New York, Macmillan, 1907).

language, his approach to his subject, his identification with the audience, and the kind of response he would elicit.

Word arrangement governs the way the words are related and developed to secure the speaker's purpose. The laws of grammar operate, but these forms in turn really yield to rhetorical ends and methods. Fairly well standardized are the syntactical principles dealing with number, mood, case, tense, and the collocation—the intelligent placing of words and clauses; the application of retrospectic reference (the discrimination, coordination and restriction of antecedents); prospective reference; the relations in sentence structure of conjunctions and other correlation devices; the use of negation, language copiousness, economy of words, repetition, and other devices that help to express the aims of the discourse.

Structure, as a principle of language usage, becomes a problem of sentence formation, including simple, complex, and compound types, periodic, loose, and balanced structure, and the informative, exclamatory, imperative, and interrogative forms.

Structure calls for systematic assembly of sentences into paragraphs and their combinations. Since a paragraph is really an abbreviated discourse, the same constructive methods apply to both paragraphs and the discourse as a whole.[41]

Historical and Philosophical Concepts of Style

Greek and Roman writers of antiquity analyzed style not only in its structural aspects, but according to the effectiveness which a teacher would inculcate and a speaker would demonstrate. Aristotle, in the *Rhetoric*, felt that the excellent qualities of style were clearness and appropriateness.[42] Most of his successors analyzed style under four qualities: appropriateness, correctness, clearness, and embellishment.[43]

These four stylistic traits apply both the words and their combinations. Since the later rhetoricians deviate little from this classical analysis, we will follow this convenient and satisfactory four-point division. Like most divisions, these overlap, but do provide elements by which we may explain much of rhetorical effectiveness—or lack of it.

Audience Adaptation (Appropriateness). The style of the discourse should be appropriate to the speaker, the audience, to the subject.

Style, rhetoricians have agreed, should relate to the subject. Aristotle suggests that when weighty matters are discussed, the manner should also be serious; when trivial topics are bandied about, the manner should be correspondingly lighthearted. To Aristotle language is appropriate if it

---

41 For further discussion of structure in the discourse, see Chap. 9 on "Structure."
42 Aristotle, *Rhetoric*, III, xii.
43 Cicero, *De Oratore*, III, 37, 52, 55; Quintilian, *op. cit.*, VIII.

expresses emotion and character and if it corresponds to the subject. We must neither speak casually about weighty matters nor solemnly about trivial ones. Nor must we add ornamental epithets to commonplace nouns or the effect will be comic. The aptness of language is the one thing that makes people believe in the truth of the story.

Adapt the subject to the *speaker or writer*. Audiences want direct contact with a speaker (or writer). If the speaker is naturally formal or informal, he will remain so, except that he will cross out words that call attention to themselves. The speaker's or writer's language, as we indicated above, should express his own experiences, attitudes, interests, his intellectual and emotional activity, and the other elements that express individuality (or personality).

According to Quintilian, the speaker or writer must adapt his discourse to his character, or at least to that character which he would present to his audience. He should not boast or speak arrogantly, for example, or engage in buffoonery, or disregard of authority. His style should be fitting of his age and public reputation. The style of older men is more precise and controlled than that of younger ones. The latter, according to Quintilian, express more daring and exuberance.[44]

Cicero suggests also a style that would normally be identified with the speaker's or writer's profession. The philosopher, historian, poet, soldier, lawyer, and other representative groups all have certain stylistic marks —or should have—of their trade or profession.[45]

These classical approaches as they deal with personality apply to later speakers and writers. The columnists, editorial writers, college professors, business men, labor leaders, preachers, radio and television talkers —all have styles that identify each with his group.

Adaptation also requires close identification between the communicator and his audience. That audience may be a selected one—a few chosen experts. It may be millions, if television is the medium and the speaker is the President of the United States. The rhetorical problem is for the speaker to understand the individual and collective personalities of those who listen, their probable attitudes toward the broadcaster and his ideas, their interests, experience, knowledge, and thinking habits. According to the specific analysis of the audience, the language will be idiomatic or learned, standard or colloquial—national, regional, humorous, technical, or popular.

What of the oral style? Repetition and insertion of introductory, transitional and summarizing phrases, are more characteristic of speeches than of written material. Readers obviously do not need so much help

---

[44] Quintilian, *op. cit.*, IX, i.
[45] *The Orations of Marcus Tullius Cicero,* tr. C. D. Yonge, Vol. 4 (London, H. G. Bohn, 1852), Chap. 21 ff.

in following the thread of the thought. The language of the speaker should usually be simpler than that of the writer. Aristotle regarded written style as "more finished" and indicated other differences.[46] Quintilian recognized similarly the differences and asserted that writing would have to be recast for speaking purposes.[47]

William Hazlitt, in his essay on "The Difference between Writing and Speaking," comments on the time factor as important: quickness and facility of perception in the oral situation. He doubts whether a speaker rises above mediocrity of expression. "An orator can hardly get beyond commonplaces; if he does he gets beyond his hearers." [48]

The differences between written and spoken style are those of degree rather than kind. Despite Charles Woolbert's important analysis, the two types often merge with little discrimination between the oral and literary factors in the given document.[49] Expression is governed heavily by the speaker's purposes in a given situation. Word choice and other stylistic elements will be influenced by the audience and occasion and will vary with these speaking conditions.

Style and the Occasion. The specific audience and occasion will affect strongly the language.

Cicero, in commenting on style as adjusted to specific situations remarks that panegyric situations require one kind of oratory; judicial proceedings, another; common conversations, another; reproof situations, another; disputations, another; and historical expositions and narrations, still another.[50] College debates, memorial services, farewell dinners, Red Cross drives, and all other gatherings have their distinctive language requirements.

Aristotle regards the style of oratory in deliberative assemblies as really "just like scene painting." The bigger the throng, the more distant the point of view; so that in the one and the other, high finish of detail is superfluous and seems the better way. Forensic style, if addressed to a single judge, has little room for rhetorical artifices. "It is ceremonial oratory that is most literary, for it is meant to be read." [51]

Correctness. Correctness refers to word choice and usage. It is a problem of much more than a study of vocabulary. Aristotle, for ex-

---

[46] *Aristotle, op. cit.,* 1413b, 9.

[47] Quintilian, *op. cit.,* XII, 4, 43.

[48] William Hazlitt, "Table Talk," in *Miscellaneous Works of William Hazlitt* (Philadelphia, 1848), Vol. 2, 175 ff.

[49] Charles H. Woolbert, "Speaking and Writing—A Study of Differences," *Quarterly Journal of Speech Education,* VIII (June, 1922), 209–217.

[50] Cicero, *De Oratore,* III, lv.

[51] Aristotle, *op. cit.,* III, xii.

ample, believed that correctness was the basis of a worthwhile style. According to him, the constituent elements should include: [52]

1. Proper use of connecting words
2. Use of specific words
3. Avoidance of ambiguity
4. Accurate handling of the genders
5. Correct handling of plurality, fewness, and unity.

George Campbell, in his *Philosophy of Rhetoric*, develops a detailed analysis of style that has been taken over almost bodily in later treatises and texts.[53] Campbell's tests of word effectiveness are three:

1. To what extent must the word be understood, to enlarge numbers of reputable writers and speakers?
2. Are the words in national uses opposed to provincial or foreign use?
3. Are they in present use?

Campbell confesses difficulty in defining "present"—and is broadminded about rejecting either old or new words. He sets forth nine canons of usage. These aim to establish purity of diction, though Campbell recognizes that good use is not always uniform in its decisions. These nine canons state:

The first canon, then, shall be, When use is divided as to any particular word or phrase, and the expression used by one part hath been preoccupied, or is in any instance susceptible of a different signification, and the expression employed by the other part never admits a different sense, both perspicuity and variety require that the form of expression which is in every instance univocal be preferred. . . .

The second canon is, In doubtful cases regard ought to be had in our decisions to the analogy of the language. . . .

The third canon is, When the terms of expression are in other respects equal, that ought to be preferred which is most agreeable to the ear. . . .

The fourth canon is, In cases wherein none of the foregoing rules gives either side a ground of preference, a regard to simplicity (in which I include etymology when manifest) ought to determine our choice. . . .

The fifth and only other canon that occurs to me on the subject of divided use is, In the few cases wherein neither perspicuity nor analogy, neither sound nor simplicity, assists us in fixing our choice, it is safest to prefer that manner which is most conformable to ancient usage.

The sixth canon is, All words and phrases which are remarkably harsh, and unharmonious, and not absolutely necessary, may justly be judged worthy of this fate [that is, merit degradation]. . . .

The seventh canon is, When etymology plainly points to a signification different from that which the word commonly bears, propriety and simplicity both require its dismission. . . .

[52] *Ibid.*, 1407a.
[53] George Campbell, *op. cit.*, 154 ff.

The eighth canon is, When any words become obsolete, or at least, are never used, except as constituting part of particular phrases, it is better to dispense with their service entirely, and give up the phrases. . . .

The ninth canon is, All those phrases which, when analyzed grammatically, include a solecism, and all those to which use hath affixed a particular sense, but which, when explained by the general and established rules of the language, are susceptible either of a different sense or of no sense, ought to be discarded altogether.[54]

Accuracy calls for a maximum attempt to mirror the reality they are intended to symbolize. A high degree of correspondence between the symbol and the referent is the communicative aim. Overpreciseness may rob the discourse of spontaneity but is preferable to semantic obscurity. The accurate phrasing means absence of ambiguity, archaicisms, slang, localisms, foreign terms, inconsistency of meaning, exaggerated or all-inclusive language, immaturity of expression, emotional distortions, and the undue heightening of language. Heightened language need not be condemned, but it is not to be substituted for facts and thought.

Clearness. Proper audience adaptation depends on clearness, just as accuracy is a matter of the speaker-writer determining for himself what the symbol is that which best relates to the referent. Aristotle remarks, "let excellence of style be defined as to consist of its being clear; style to be good must be clear, as is proved by the fact that speech which fails to convey a plain meaning, will fail to do just what a speech has to do." [55] Clearness is the effort of the communicator to make himself understood to others. Whether the aim is to inform, persuade, or inspire, he who speaks does so in vain unless he is understood. The distinction between accuracy and clearness is not always distinct. Both use the choice of word and their arrangement.

Aristotle suggests that clearness is attained by using words that are current and ordinary, by using metaphors and familiar illustrations, and by avoiding redundancy. He would select specific words, avoid ambiguities, and avoid over-long suspension of thought through parenthetical devices.[56]

Quintilian said that clearness is the first virtue of style. In this matter of clearness or perspicuity, "Let there be proper words in proper places" and a clear order. "Let not the conclusion be too long protracted; and let there be nothing either deficient or superfluous." [57]

What are these barriers to clearness?

Campbell suggests three ways in which perspicuity or clearness may

54 *Ibid.*, 154–169.
55 Aristotle, *op. cit.*, III, ii.
56 *Ibid.*, III, v.
57 Quintilian, *op. cit.*, VIII, ii.

be violated. One way is that of obscurity. (1) It may result from some defect in the expression, as when obscurities result from undue ellipsis, or from excess of vocabulary, or from bad choice of words. (2) It may result from faulty arrangement of words. As Campbell states it:

A discourse . . . excels in perspicuity when the subject engrosses the attention of the hearer, and the diction is so little minded by him that he can scarcely be said to be conscious that it is through this medium he sees into the speaker's thoughts. On the contrary, the least obscurity, ambiguity, or confusion in the style, instantly removes the attention from the sentiment to the expression, and the hearer endeavours, by the aid of reflection, to correct the imperfection of the speaker's language.[58]

(3) Obscurity may result from the same word in different senses. (4) References to pronouns and other relatives may be uncertain. (5) Sentence structure may be unduly complicated, as in periodic structure. (6) Technical words and phrases may obscure the meaning for lay readers or listeners. (7) Unduly long sentences may work against perspicuity.

In addition to obscurity, the second violation of perspicuity or equivocation arises from double meaning. Here the fault is "not that the sentence conveys darkly or imperfectly the author's meaning, but that it conveys also some other meaning which is not the author's." [59] Campbell illustrates from particles, conjunctions, pronouns, and other parts of speech. He distinguishes double meanings (expressions with more meanings than originally intended) from such equivocations as those which arise from bad construction, which he calls ambiguities.

The third general offense against perspicuity is that which gives no meaning at all—to Campbell, the "unintelligible." The speaker may confuse his thought, "commonly accompanied with intricacy of expression; secondly, "affectation of excellence in diction; and thirdly, total want of meaning." [60]

This want of meaning reveals itself in puerile expression (a writer may run into specious verbosity), the learned (learned nonsense), the profound (in political writings), the marvelous (it astonishes by the boldness of the affirmations).[61]

Aids to clearness lie partly in the definition of terms. Concrete language will promote clearness as well as accuracy. Many abstract words have emotional appeal, but their connotations may be so different to the individuals as to produce little or no common reaction. (See section below for further comment on concreteness and economy of style.) [62]

[58] Campbell, *op. cit.*, 221.
[59] *Ibid.*, 226.
[60] *Ibid.*, 243.
[61] *Ibid.*, 248.
[62] See section above on "Definition."

Embellishment (Interest). The fourth constituent of style is ornamentation or embellishment. The modern equivalents of these ancient terms are interest and impressiveness. C. S. Baldwin, for example, describes the qualities of style as "clearness and interest." [63]

The problem for the communicator is both to secure understanding through clearness and to hold attention and arouse interest. These qualities, far from being merely decorative or ornamental, are indispensible. "They and they alone will ensure adequate response to the effort to convince, persuade, entertain, impress, and actuate." [64]

Attention and interest are practically identical. As James Winans states, "the two terms are synonymous." [65]

Interest and attention relate to the speaker or writer's poise, his ability to appeal to interests and motives of his readers or hearers, their interests, for example, in change, novelty, curiosity, conflict, humor.

What qualities of the speech or writing help to create and sustain interest? These choices and arrangement of language include:

1. Concreteness
2. Conciseness
3. Illustrations
4. Parallelism
5. Rhythm
6. Variety
7. Figures of speech
8. Originality

Concreteness, as discussed above, is both a mark of clearness and of interest. Conciseness, also relates to clearness but becomes an important means of arousing or killing off interest. Language excessiveness is the bane of amateur would-be writers and of many talkers. Wordiness replaces ideas. Campbell, as cited above, warns against both prolixity and undue abbreviation. Conciseness does not consist of telegraphic brevity. The number, character, and arrangement of words must be determined by the thought. The essential thought should be uttered and enforced by suitable rhetorical considerations (securing of interest).

Economy of Language

Herbert Spencer has set forth the philosophy of economy in style. According to Spencer, good style should make minimum demands upon

---

[63] C. S. Baldwin, *English Composition—Oral and Written* (New York, Longmans Green, 1909).

[64] Baird and Knower, *op. cit.*, 142.

[65] James Winans, *Public Speaking* (rev. ed.; New York, Century Co., 1917), 53.

the hearer or reader's ability or power of reception. Maximum energy, rather, should be used to grasp the thought. Spencer said:

To so present ideas that they may be apprehended with the least possible mental effort, is the desideratum towards which most of the rules . . . point. When we condemn writing that is wordy, or confused, or intricate—when we praise this style as easy, and blame that as fatiguing, we consciously or unconsciously assume this desideratum as our standard of judgment. Regarding language as an apparatus of symbols for the conveyance of thought, we may say that, as in a mechanical apparatus, the more simple and the better arranged its parts, the greater will be the effect produced. In either case, whatever force is absorbed by the machine is deducted from the result. A reader or listener has at each moment but a limited amount of mental power available. To recognise and interpret the symbols presented to him requires part of this power; to arrange and combine the images suggested requires a further part; and only that part which remains can be used for the realization of the thought conveyed. Hence, the more time and attention it takes to receive and understand each sentence, the less time and attention can be given to the contained idea; and the less vividly will that idea be conceived. How truly language must be regarded as a hindrance to thought, though the necessary instrument of it, we shall clearly perceive on remembering the comparative force with which simple ideas are communicated by mimetic signs. . . . No phrase can convey the idea of surprise so vividly as opening the eyes and raising the eyebrows. A shrug of the shoulders would lose much by translation into words. Again, it may be remarked that when oral language is employed, the strongest effects are produced by interjections, which condense entire sentences into syllables. And in other cases, where custom allows us to express thoughts by single words, as in *Beware, Heigho, Fudge,* much force would be lost by expanding them into specific verbal propositions. Hence, carrying out the metaphor that language is the vehicle of thought, there seems reason to think that in all cases the friction and inertia to the smallest possible amount. Let us then inquire whether economy of the recipient's attention is not the secret of effect, alike in the right choice and collocation of words, in the best arrangement of clauses in a sentence, in the proper order of its principal and subordinate propositions, in the judicious use of simile, metaphor, and other figures of speech, and even in the rhythmical sequences of syllables.[66]

Rhythm

Still another technique that enhances embellishment is rhythm. Rhythm has been a classical characteristic of "elevated," or emotional, prose. It is an effective instrument for transmitting emotional stimulation to the audience.

[66] Herbert Spencer, "The Philosophy of Style," *Westminster Review,* new series, Vol. 58 (October, 1852), 436–37.

According to Wayland Parrish, "Rhythm is a rhetorical device which consists of effects repeated at regular intervals of time, and is intended to give distinction of style or leisure to the audience." [67]

The sources and explanations of rhythmical prose originate in the emotional activity of the speaker or writer whose language correlates with an emotional accompaniment. It is the same impulse that produces music, poetry, and other forms of art. In rhythmical prose the structure of sentences, their arrangement in the paragraph, fall into a combination of metrical feet and of meter "unmeasured" but never neglected.

J. F. Genung in speaking of rhythm in prose describes meter as "measured rhythm," peculiar to verse, and "unmeasured rhythm," ever varied, and yet never neglected, as "equally natural to artistic prose." [68] Rhythmical prose stems from the simple effort to please the ear by the easy flow of accented and unaccented syllables, and by the musical regularity, yet variety, of natural pauses.

As in other categories, the rhythms of prose and that of poetry fade into each other. Just as poetry and prose become hardly distinguishable, so does the same rhythmical pattern pervade both. Rhetoricians are loath to attempt hard distinctions between rhythm of prose and that of poetry.

Variety

Still another agency of interest is variety of language. The greatest vice of mediocre speech makers and writers is repetition. Although repetition is much more permissible in speaking than writing, the constant use of a barren vocabulary soon palls on readers or listeners. The efficient speaker or writer strives always to inject some variety into word usages. Sentence structure needs variety. Simplicity of construction, with predicate following a subject, produces maximum clearness but corresponding dullness. For increased suspense and accelerated movement, periodic structure correlates with the heightened mood. Balance structure, too, gives emphasis, as do questions, and commands.

These variations, however, need not be artificially framed. Ideas rather than deliberate framing of these rhetorical patterns should be the end.

Variety in word employment will lead to a censorship of hackneyed terms. Some slight originality is hoped for, as ideas are framed in words slightly different from those used over and over by thousands of speakers and writers. Hackneyed phrases stem from the habit of imitation. A new phrase catches on. Immediately a host of unimaginative word-

---

[67] Wayland Maxfield Parrish, "The Rhythm of Oratorical Prose," in *Studies in Rhetoric and Public Speaking in Honor of James Albert Winans* (New York, Century Co., 1925), 217–232.

[68] Genung, *op. cit.*, 169.

mongers duplicate it. Presently, listeners or readers will show their bore-dom—sometimes they are oblivious of the reason for their negative re-action. Most prominently treated in older rhetorical writings has been figurative language.

Problems of Connotation

To hold attention and sustain interest, the language of vividness, of connotation, is important. Suggestions in addition to the literal meanings help to quicken the imagination and emotions and to stamp the thought as vivid. For acceptance of belief or deep feeling concerning a subject, the language of emotion and imagination must be substituted for the merely objective and disinterested.

Figurative language, by no means the exclusive possession of poets and old fashioned orators, accomplishes practical ends. Figures of speech, although not always recognized as such, pervade the speech and energetic writings of the bulk of speakers and writers.

Cicero and Quintilian gave considerable space to figurative expression. The figures of antiquity were classified as tropes, figures of thought (*figurae sententiarum*) and figures of language (*figurae verborum*). Tropes were the changing of a word or sentence from its proper significa-tion to another meaning.[69] Figures, on the other hand, were for emphasis by phrases differently couched "from what is plain or common." The trope converted the word or sentence to another sense. The figures did not change the sense but merely aimed to "illustrate, enliven—or embel-lish" it.

As Quintilian admitted, it was "not easy to tell the difference between tropes and figures." [70] Later rhetoricians ignored these categories and substituted "figures of speech" for "tropes" and allowed the large list of figures of thought and of language to diminish in number and to go largely unnamed.

What were formerly listed as figures of thought or of language would include an exclamation to express strong passion; doubting, to express hesitation; the retracting or recalling what we have spoken or resolved; the granting or yielding up of something in order to gain a point, "which we could not well secure without it." [71]

Quintilian, for example, lists as figures of thought the rhetorical ques-tion, anticipation, hesitation, consultation, simulation of any passion,

[69] Thomas Gibbons, *op. cit.*, 3.
[70] Quintilian, *op. cit.*, 1, iii.
[71] Lester Thonssen and A. Craig Baird, *Speech Criticism* (New York, Ronald Press, 1948). For illustration of figures of thought and language, see 420–422. The present author is heavily indebted to Dr. Thonssen for approaches and details of this chapter.

apostrophe, illustration, irony, mimicry, intimation, and so on.[72] Figures of language would include parallelism, antithesis, climax.

Thus we retain, under "figures of speech," the metaphor (direct identification of the objects, ideas, and relationships under comparison); similes (comparison of one object or idea with another of different kind or quality); personification, analogy, allegory, metonymy, synecdoche, irony, hyperbole, and others. The defect of many former rhetoricians lay in their undue encouragement of the use of figurative embellishments.

To hold attention and develop interest, then, language must be accurate, clear, impressive, vivid. Needed are words that suggest as well as denote. Language effectiveness is skill in choosing words, those best adapted to a given audience, to the speaker or writer's personality, to the occasion, and to the subject—words that are current, intelligible, and varied. Definitions will clarify ideas. The vocabulary will be suited to idea. Sentence structure will vary in length, complexity, and arrangement. Prolixity will be avoided. Impressiveness will come partly through rhythm, figurative terms, and word and sentence variety.

Classifications of Style

Both ancient and recent rhetoricians have attempted to classify style according to general characteristics. If it is completely devoid of life, it is dry; if unduly pervaded with emotional abandonment, it is florid. If it is unduly compressed, it is concise; if it multiplies words, it is diffuse.

According to the *Ad Herrennium*, style was to be classified as plain, or middle, or grand. Cicero took over these same distinctions.[73] The plain style was without the "fetters of rhythm," and had little "oratorical furniture."

The moderate style was more fertile, somewhat more forcible, but nevertheless was tamer than the highest class of oratory. There was not much vigor but the greatest "quantity of sweetness." The third or grand style was the sublime. It was copious, dignified, ornate, vehement, earnest. This most copious speaker, if he is nothing else, "appears scarcely in his senses." [74]

Quintilian divided style into Attic, Asiatic, and Rhodian. The style of the Attic orators was "compressed and energetic," whereas that of the Asiatics was "inflated and deficient in force." These Asiatic stylists were redundant and without restraint. The Rhodian style was intermediate between the other two. The name Rhodian was derived from the island

---

[72] Quintilian, *op. cit.*, IX, i, 4.
[73] Cicero, *Orator*, in *The Orations of Marcus Tullius Cicero*, translated by C. D. Yonge (London, H. G. Bohn, 1852), Vol. 4, 400 ff.
[74] *Ibid.*, 409–10.

of Rhodes—where Aeschines was exiled. The Rhodian schools were accounted somewhat deficient in vigor and spirit, though nevertheless not without force. Their expression resembled "not pure springs, nor turbid torrents, but calm floods." [75]

The development of "mass audiences" of the later twentieth century called for oral and written language best adapted to these millions, who followed radio, television, and press.

Dr. Rudolph Flesch in his *Art of Plain Talk* [76] contended that "the plain and simple talk is what we need." To him this plain talk was mainly a matter of language structure and spacing the ideas. Dr. Flesch became specific. If we should wish to write so that the average person may understand us, our sentences should average seventeen words in length. Six personal references should attend every one hundred words. He also advised the use of verbs. "Two sentences are better to understand than one with extra stuff in it. Avoid the use of empty words and phrases." Dr. Flesch attacked "rhetoric" as often getting in the way of plain talk and of understanding. His advice was: Do not use rhythm, or periodic sentences, or rhetorical questions, or metaphors, without accompanying explanation.

He provided a yardstick by which to measure the effectiveness of language and made clear that if the address was to the average reader or listener, the writing style should aim at those with about eighth grade education rather than to those of cate high school or college level.

Flesch was not to be taken too seriously for his standards of style. His critics rightly attacked this entire approach, by insisting that the language should not be lowered to the plain people, but rather that the educational level of the people should be raised. They were to be trained to use, interpret, and understand language as written and spoken by intelligent communicators.

The Golden Mean

The main problem in the management of style is to strike a proper balance of language in consideration of the principles and requirements relating to accuracy, correctness, clearness, adaptation to the speaker, speech, audience, occasion, and combinations to language that contribute to attention and interest.

Aristotle's golden mean philosophy suggests the proper control of these language factors to secure effective results. The Aristotelian principle would warn against excessive use of elements to establish a point; the excessive use of examples, figures of speech, rhythm, of illustrations,

[75] Quintilian, *op. cit.*, XII, x, xix.
[76] Rudolph Flesch, *The Art of Plain Talk* (New York, Harper, 1946).

long sentences, repetition, or other elements that properly used would help
toward clearness, propriety, or embellishment.

Aristotle's mean calls for the speaker's (or writer's) good judgment in
the use of these language materials, to secure maximum interest and comprehension. This judgment is governed by the specific situation, the purposes of the speaker, his temperament and his communicative experience.

Aristotle's doctrine of the mean is that of the Greek mind with its concern for proportion in all applications. To Aristotle, both excess and
deficiency were to be avoided. To Aristotle

[the mean] is neither too much nor too little for us. But this is not one and
the same to all; as, for example, if ten is too many, and two too few, six is
taken for the absolute mean, for it exceeds two as much as it is exceeded by
ten. But this is the mean according to arithmetical proportion. But the relative mean is not to be taken in this manner; for it does not follow, that if ten
pounds are too much for any person to eat, and two pounds too little, the
training-master will prescribe six pounds; for perhaps this is too much or too
little for the person who is to eat it. For it is too little for Milo, but too much
for one just commencing gymnastics; and the case is similar in running and
wrestling. Thus, then, every person who has knowledge shuns the excess and
the defect, but seeks for the mean, and chooses it; not the absolute mean, but
the relative one.[77]

Summary

Language has been a principal agency for the transmission of a speaker's or writer's ideas, his communicative purposes, and his means of developing attention and interest and securing results. (Delivery also
becomes a supplement of language.)

Ancient, medieval, and modern rhetoricians have all given much prominence to the role of language. Aristotle, Cicero, Quintilian, medieval
rhetoricians, and Wilson, Ward, Campbell, Blair, Whately, and the twentieth century writers and teachers have all contributed much to this constituent of communication.

Newer insights into the role of language in communication have been
the writings of I. A. Richards, Kenneth Burke, Susanne Langer, Alfred
Korzybski and the later semanticists. The focusing has been on meaning,
with the analysis of words in the thing-symbol-thought relationship.
The thing (actual referent, "event," source of the stimulation, assumed

---

[77] Aristotle, The "Nicomachean Ethics" of Aristotle, II, vi, tr. R. W. Browne
(London, 1850). Cf. Donald Bryant, "Aspects of the Rhetorical Tradition: Emotion,
Style, and Literary Association," Quarterly Journal of Speech, XXXVI (October,
1950), 326–332. See also his "Aspects of the Rhetorical Tradition: The Intellectual
Foundation," Quarterly Journal of Speech, XXXVI (April, 1950), 169–176; and
"Rhetoric: Its Functions and its Scope," Quarterly Journal of Speech, XXXIX (De-
cember, 1953), 404–424.

and not objectively verified) becomes the symbol, evoked by a sign (or signs) that reconstructs the "event" in association with the past experiences of the respondent. (See again Chapter 3 for discussion of "facts.") The symbols, the naming of words and their contexts, become the means of embodying the reference or "idea."

Style is the usage of language for communication. Such usage of words is "inextricably interwoven" with invention, including logical and emotive materials, and with disposition (structure).

The chief traits of style are accuracy or correctness, clearness or perspicuity, adaptation to the abilities and interests of the agent, the audience, the occasion, and the message itself, and the embellishment, quality of the discourse to develop interest and secure the desired response. Typical problems of style have to do with economy of language, figurative usages, and the golden mean, the proper balance of style in relation to the occasion, speaker or writer and the audience.

9

Structure

Disposition, Arrangement, and Proportion

Classical rhetoric recognized structure or arrangement as the second part of rhetoric. It was almost inseparable from invention, and under the title of *dispositio*.

Dispositio has often been translated as "arrangement" and apparently limits itself to the order of points, the parts of a speech, and a few elementary theories and suggestions concerning planning.

English rhetorical theory did little to promote an adequate explanation of the term. Wilson, in his *The Arte of Rhetorique* (1555), gave a few pages to the subject; he included the parts of speech under invention.[1]

George Campbell, in his *Philosophy of Rhetoric* (1776) almost completely ignored *dispositio*. Hugh Blair's *Lectures on Rhetoric and Belles Lettres* (1783) called *dispositio* the "conduct of a discourse" and merely named and described the parts.[2] Whately, in his *Elements of Rhetoric* (1828), explained arrangement as a means of ordering logical arguments.[3] William Sandford's *English Theories of Public Address*, 1530–1828, considered *dispositio* as arrangement of material.[4] John Genung, in his *Practical Elements of Rhetoric*, discussed under Invention, the general process in the ordering of materials, including the determination of the theme, and the construction of the plan.[5] Charles Baldwin's *Ancient Rhetoric and Poetic*, pointed out the inadequacy of arrangement as the

[1] Thomas Wilson, *The Arte of Rhetorique*, ed. G. H. Mair (Oxford, Clarendon Press, 1909), 156–160.

[2] Hugh Blair, *Lectures on Rhetoric and Belles Lettres*, 3 vols. (8th ed.; London, T. Cadell Jun. and W. Davies, and W. Greech, Edinburgh, 1801), Lectures XXXI and XXXII.

[3] Richard Whately, *Elements of Rhetoric*, ed. Douglas Ehninger (Carbondale, Ill., Southern Illinois University Press, 1963).

[4] William Sandford, *English Theories of Public Address* (Columbus, Ohio, H. L. Hedrick, 1931), 16–19.

[5] John F. Genung, *Practical Elements of Rhetoric* (Boston and New York, Ginn, 1886), 217–282.

proper concept of *dispositio* and suggested rather that disposition referred to the plan of the whole composition.[6]

What was the classical concept of the term?[7] Aristotle conceived *dispositio* as chiefly planned adaptation to the audience and speech. To him the parts of the speech were not important features of arrangement. The thesis and proof were the only essential "parts." He treated briefly proem, statement, argument and epilogue, but chiefly stressed the principles of adaptation. He advised concerning the selection, and order, adaptation of materials of the speech, according to the audience, the subject and the speaker, the opponent.[8]

To Cicero, *dispositio* was the adapting of the product of *inventio* to the particular situation. He discussed two main parts of the process: the grouping of ideas invented in the natural order (exordium, narration, proof, and peroration). The main object of disposition, however, was the exercising of prudence and judgment. The construction of each speech was determined by the specific audience problems involved.[9]

Dispositio involves three matters: the selection of the materials, arrangement, and proportion. These are governed by matters of the speech situation and by the variable conditions involved. Five factors or conditions form the "situation": purpose of the speech, the subject (cause), kind of speech, age .(age, function, composition, mood of the audience), and the speaker (age, reputation, personality, limitations, capabilities).

Quintilian considered disposition as arrangement, but refused to draw up a lot of rules on rhetoric or lay down rules for the parts of the speech. Like Cicero, he said that *dispositio* included selection, elimination, ordering, massing or proportioning, and coloring. The time, place, speaker, purpose, and audience would determine the proper handling of disposition.

In general, these classical rhetoricians, including Aristotle conceived of τάξις or *dispositio* as planned adaptation.

What, then is the appropriate translation or designation for this second part of rhetoric? According to Russell Wagner, "arrangement" and "planning" hardly cover the case. "Composition" and "speech construction" are equally objectionable. "Organization" comes closest to a satisfactory term, but implies commitment to plan or outline. "Structure"

---

[6] Charles Baldwin, *Ancient Rhetoric and Poetic* (New York, Macmillan, 1924), 67.

[7] Marilyn Nesper Hewlett, *"Theories of Speech Arrangement as Developed by Selected Ancient Rhetoricians"* (unpublished M.A. thesis, State University of Iowa, 1947).

[8] *The "Rhetoric" of Aristotle*, tr. Lane Cooper (New York, Appleton-Century-Crofts, 1932), III, xiii–xix.

[9] Cicero, *De Oratore*, tr. E. W. Sutton and H. Rackam, 2 vols. (London, Heineman, 1942), Vol. 1, 436 ff.; *De Partitione Oratoria*, in *The Orations of Marcus Tullius Cicero*, tr. C. D. Yonge (London, G. Bell & Son, 1913), Book IV, 486–527.

also implies much more than "outline" but is often confused with syntax. Dr. Wagner suggests that the term be called "disposition," in view of the full meaning as contained in rhetorical classics. He defines the term as "the functional selection and use of materials for a particular purpose." [10]

We shall here identify structure with disposition. This term deals with the principles of selection, orderly arrangement, and proportion of the parts of the discourse.

Problems of Selection and Analysis

In disposition (structure), selection and analysis are basic in the incorporation of the subject matter in the means of communication; in the framing of the purpose and materials; and in the pointing of the way toward thematic development in the subdivisions.

Selection of the materials of a given discourse is centered in the theme or thesis, whether it is framed mentally or otherwise recorded. The purpose of the speaker or writer is to reduce his thesis to a clearcut statement that embodies both his over-all idea and his rhetorical aim of informing, entertaining, persuading, convincing, inspiring, or combining some of these ends. This theme, the working idea or plan of the discourse, is sufficiently definite for the writer or speaker to refer to at every step in his preparation. It is a "nucleus-thought, expressed or implicit, which must be in his mind as a central point of reference, a constant determinator and suggestor of the scope and limits of his subject." [11] It is the germ of the whole work and the essence both of the speaker's or writer's thought and his specific audience purpose.

The theme and its analysis must be heavily affected by the subject itself. Since the choice of purpose and topic is made, the whole vista of materials is open. The reading, thinking, interaction with people and events, including the communicator's previous experiences, all openly or subtly play for inclusion and primacy in what is to be uttered.

Obviously, the theme as phrased is not the subject. The latter is the class-idea on which the more specific topic is based. The principle is both that of appropriating to the full the materials comprising the subject and simultaneously limiting the scope of treatment to avoid undue comprehensiveness. The aspects to be selected will be partly affected by the writer or speaker's view of what is best said; and how familiar is the audience with the subject.

Such theme as related to limited aspects of the broad field will be modi-

---

[10] Russell H. Wagner, "The Meaning of Dispositio," in *Studies in Speech and Drama in Honor of Alexander Drummond*, ed. Herbert A. Wichelns (Ithaca, N.Y., Cornell University Press, 1944), 285–294.

[11] Genung, *op. cit.*, 249.

fied as fresh materials come into view. The preliminary point of view becomes somewhat modified as the discourse evolves. Thus the theme both precedes and follows the development of the materials.

The comprehensive statement is exact, suggestive, and brief. Not only is it limited and brief, but it incorporates the speaker's approach to the problem and perhaps reveals his speaking motives.

The selection and analysis are also shaped by the communicator's approach to his specific audience. Aristotle assumed and explained that each speaker should become a judge of people. He himself became a psychologist in advising the most suitable means of influencing others. In communication it is axiomatic that the speaker or writer must adopt his theme and analysis to the peculiar needs of each audience. His purpose, to illustrate, may be not only to justify before a certain audience an increase in state income taxes, but to relate such increases to the economic advantage of the urban, agricultural, relatively illiterate or unsophisticated, strongly partisan or politically neutral attitudes of those who listen.

In addition to the subject itself, the personality of the speaker and the identification of speaker with his audience, the occasion itself is a major determinant, or should be, in what is included, excluded, and expanded.

The occasion may call for ceremonial or epideictic discourse, the eulogy of some important figure, a historic event enshrouded in a century of previous tributes.

The occasion may be that of a strong political appeal over the radio or television, or before a cheering face-to-face audience prior to a national election. Or a broadside may be distributed to stir several million readers. The occasion may be that of a congressional or other legislative debate on some critical issue. The scene may be that of a court room, with plea to jury or judge. The situation may be that of a religious service with an appropriate sermon; or stockholders' gathering with the leader defending corporation policies; or a school or college administrator addressing a state educational convention.

Each occasion thus markedly affects the theme and selection of materials for this event relating to a specific time, place, and audience.

What of the analysis? Communication is initially the discovery and selection of the materials to illuminate and enforce certain speaking purposes. This discovery and selection constitute analysis or division of the discourse.

The starting point, as discussed above, is the reduction of the nebulous areas of the subject to a clear-cut thesis. In exposition or informational speaking or writing the thesis may be merely a topic statement. In controversial types, it is a resolution for debate, or an impartial question for discussion.

The background of facts, ideas and principles, flitting or persistently emerging as mental hypotheses or declarations, later fall into recognizable relationships and order.

The second step in operational analysis is the focusing on essential questions (or topics framed as sentences), about which the general theme revolves.

The third step is one of selection for actual communication from the deposit of relevant ideas. If the queries on the topic have been comprehensive and specific, the speaker or writer has assembled more explorative subtopics than can be handled in the brief time to be given to the auditors or readers. Some of these inquiries or topic-statements are trivial; some are irrelevant; others are quasi-logical; still others, although important, are not of primary consequence to the immediate hearers or readers. Only those questions of major concern and applicability are selected.

The fifth step is the framing of these ideas into proper language as a basis for full development. These declaratory or interrogative sentences make up the so-called partition of the discourse. These are the issues in debate, the *stasis* of Roman rhetoric, the divisions of a lecture or article. To repeat, these need not be formally presented as suggested in some treatises that indicate first the "division" of the subject (presumably in a series of questions), followed by the "partition" (statement that indicates what the speaker or writer will establish).

Such rigidity is seldom or never called for, but the mental processes of arriving at the field to be covered however much the method may be covert, is that suggested by all representative rhetoricians, classical and modern.[12]

Logical and Quasi-Logical Methods of Division. By what principles are the materials to be divided? How are the suitable units of the subject arrived at? The management of the discourse in general and of its details calls for satisfactory division of the data and ideas. The representative methods of grouping these materials for basic divisions comprise the following: [13]

1. Chronological or historical
2. Spatial
3. Definitional
4. Classificational
5. Logical
6. Psychological
7. Some combination of such divisions

[12] For full discussion of analysis, see Chapter 3. Note especially analysis of problems of policy and problems or topics dealing with fact.

[13] See Chapter 2 above for such divisions. See also Lester Thonssen and A. Craig Baird, *Speech Criticism* (New York, Ronald Press, 1948), 395–397.

The chronological (time or historical method) for example, may arrange the materials from the past, to the present, or to the future. Or the order may be from the present to the past. Many speeches use the time order, and texts on speech and written composition illustrate the method.[14]

The topographical or space order means arranging materials according to any pattern of space—from near to far, bottom to top, inside to outside, etc.

The definitional method develops from the exploratory question at the outset, "What do the terms mean?" This inquiry may set up the sole or chief pattern for the entire discourse. Thus the definitional details may be illustrated by examples, specific instances, testimony, etymology, and other specific means.[15]

The classificational or topical method calls for grouping the materials as social, political, educational, economic, and otherwise. By classification the material may be divided according to the occupational, political, religious or other groups involved in the issues. The divisions may be according to logical, ethical, political, psychological, philosophical categories, as in the divisions of rhetoric. Or the division may follow the types of argumentative elements, such as testimony, causation, analogy, specific instances, and deductive statements. Or a classification may be made according to fallacies, such as false division, false use of facts, false reasoning from general propositions, ignoring the question, and begging the question.[16]

Still other methods may be psychological, in which audience attitudes may be classified as emotional, motivational, sentimental, and so on.

These various methods are suggestive only. Any one of them lends itself to further subdivisions. They overlap, but may provide a useful approach to constructive presentation and interpretation of a subject.

Order in Disposition

In what order are the parts of a speech to be developed? According to Plato, "Every speech ought to be put together like a living creature, with a body of its own, so as to be neither without head, nor without feet, but to have both a middle and extremities, described proportionately to each other and to the whole." [17] Plato thus outlined the beginning, middle, and end of a speech.

[14] William Norwood Brigance, *Speech* (New York, Appleton-Century-Crofts, 1952), 213 ff.

[15] See Chapter 3 for methods of definition.

[16] A. Craig Baird, *Argumentation, Discussion and Debate* (New York, McGraw-Hill, 1950), 163–165.

[17] *Phaedrus*, in *The Works of Plato*, ed. Henry Cary (London, H. G. Bohn, 1854), Vol. 1, 342–343.

The principle of number and order of parts, within this beginning, middle and end, is that of function rather than of any arbitrary assignment of numbers and their order. Aristotle wrote that "the only indispensable parts of a speech are the statement of the case and the proof." He agreed that if additional parts were needed the total should not exceed four: the exordium, statement of the case, proof, and the peroration.

Rhetorica ad Herennium (published about 86 B.C.), sometimes attributed to Cicero, provided a pattern of the teaching of rhetoric in Rome during the days of Cicero. According to this rhetoric, invention was developed in six divisions of the address: *exordium, narratio, divisio, confirmatio, confutatio,* and *conclusio.*[18]

The *exordium* rendered the audience attentive and friendly; the *narratio* stated the facts; the *divisio* or *partitio* outlined the main points to be developed; the *confirmatio* developed the constructive argument; the *confutatio* consisted of rebuttal; and the *conclusio* or *peroratio* gave the conclusion.

This division heavily influenced later rhetoricians in their treatment of *dispositio.*

Cicero in *De Partitione Oratoria* listed four parts, including *partitio* with *narratio,* and combining *confirmatio* and *refutatio.* Quintilian discussed at length the parts of *dispositio* as relating to forensic speaking.[19]

In the preface to Book VII, Quintilian explained that any rules concerning arrangement must be general:

The whole of this book, therefore; will be devoted to arrangement, an art the acquisition of which would never have been such a rarity, had it been possible to lay down general rules which would suit all subjects. But since cases in the courts have always presented an infinite variety, and will continue to do so, and since through all the centuries there has never been found one single case which was exactly like any other, the pleader must rely upon his sagacity, keep his eyes open, exercise his powers of invention and judgment and look to himself for advice. On the other hand, I do not deny that there are some points which are capable of demonstration and which accordingly I shall be careful not to pass by.[20]

He defined the matters to be considered concerning *dispositio* as "the distribution of things and their parts in advantageous places."

Later rhetoricians were inclined to elaborate on four, five, six, or even more parts, especially as forensic speaking and writing were dealt with. In his *Lectures on Rhetoric and Oratory,* John Quincy Adams developed

18 Cf. Augustus S. Wilkins, *M. Tulli Ciceronis "De Oratore,"* 3 vols. (3d ed.; Oxford, Clarendon Press, 1890–93), Vol. 1, 56–64.

19 The *"Institutio Oratoria"* of Quintilian, tr. H. E. Butler, 4 vols. (London, Heinemann; New York, Putnam, 1921–22), 223.

20 *Ibid.,* p. viii.

successive lectures on the proposition and partition (XIX), confirmation, ratiocination (XX), induction (XXI), confutation (XXII), digression and transition (XXIII), and conclusion (XXIV).[21]

Later writers of public address (in the first quarter of the twentieth century) taught that the forensic discourse, specifically argumentation and debate, should be formally developed. The introduction of such forensic discourse, should contain (1) immediate cause for discussion, (2) definition of terms, (3) brief history of the case, (4) statement of admitted or waived matter, (5) conflicting arguments, (6) statement of issues and or statement of what a speaker proposes to prove.[22]

Function of the Parts of a Discourse. What principles govern the selection of materials, their sequence and emphasis, in rhetorical order?

The structure of a given discourse depends on the occasion and type of the communication. Deliberative, epideictic and forensic speaking, each has a distinctive structure, in line with its purpose. Forensic speaking, for example, designed for the court room and judges and juries, is usually more complete in number of parts and in the completeness of each part than is the case with other types. The legal practices and tradition require a statement of facts and other elements not always so precisely treated in deliberative or epideictic speaking.

The Introduction. In written discourse, too, expositional and argumentative writing are structurally more formal than the more entertaining-interesting types.

What of the introduction? Its purpose is normally to gain attention; state the subject; in some cases define it; and announce the main issues or points to be developed. Announcement of the subject may be assumed in many cases. Definitions or explanations may or may not be necessary, according to what is to be talked about and the speaker's plan to expand in detail definitional details in the course of his speech. Severe defining may create mechanics that deaden audience interest.

The main points to be treated may be listed at the outset. Here again the mechanics of the expression may mar an interesting style. To withhold such listing of the propositions to be enlarged upon will often create suspense and heighten interest. The alternative is the preliminary bald statement in the interest of clearness. Thus speakers, expositional or argumentative, often map out just what they intend to develop. A spe-

21 John Quincy Adams, *Lectures on Rhetoric and Oratory* (Cambridge, Hilliard & Metcalf, 1810).

22 G. P. Baker and Henry Barrett Huntington, *The Principles of Argumentation* (rev. ed.; Boston, Ginn, 1905); William T. Foster, *Argumentation and Debating* (new ed.; Boston, Houghton Mifflin, 1932); James Milton O'Neill and James Howard McBurney, *The Working Principles of Argument* (New York, Macmillan, 1932); James M. O'Neill, Craven Laycock, and Albert L. Scales, *Argumentation and Debate* (New York, Macmillan, 1928).

cialized audience, listening to a scientist in their field explaining his latest discovery, will want only clear-cut and direct presentation. Attention and interest in the subject are automatic and need no rhetorical aids.

Should the unfolding be chiefly deductive or inductive? Direct utterance of the main propositions to be followed by their details is deductive. In induction, the specific items in turn merge into succeeding points, with the cohesive pattern moving toward a logical climax. The summarizing and transitional statements link together the successive parts. Rules cannot prescribe specific choices of deduction or induction. The subject, audience, and the rhetorical judgment of the communicator will determine the method.

The responsibility for clearness will often lead the communicator to line up at the outset his topics or issues. An audience thus conditioned to the main ideas will thus recall more completely the successive topics or propositions than if the compositional contour is blurred. Older sermonizers told their audiences in the introductions of their sermons the propositions to be developed. These were followed with such development and final summaries as would enable listeners to relate days later the ideas of that sermon.

This introduction, whatever the occasion, audience, and theme, should stimulate attention and interest. The psychological (ethical and motivative) elements are not to be withheld for a later section of the discourse but immediately expressed. A reference to the author himself, to the immediate occasion, the audience, the sponsors of the program, and early identification of the subject with the needs of the audience, all help to set the proper atmosphere and speech movement. These approaches are psychological as well as logical.

Here, again, as in other rhetorical applications in the introduction, all should be brief, for audiences want the main body to get under way. In some cases, as Henry Grady, of Georgia, in his address on the "New South" (delivered in New York City, December 22, 1886), spent about one fourth of his time upon the introduction. His audience problem justified his long opening. He had to ingratiate himself with his Northern audience; to adjust to preceding speeches that were not entirely complimentary to his Georgia; to inject humor into this dinner occasion; and to refer to his own limited abilities to meet the demands of this significant occasion.

Main Body. The main body of any discourse, whether long or short, should meet the expectations suggested by the introduction. Or if no preliminary revelation of the main lines of thinking is given, these main ideas, whether announced or gradually unfolded, are to be logically, persuasively, and interestingly framed.

If the address is argumentative and refutative, the constructive and refutatory content may be presented in the Ciceronian order with the constructive arguments first. Or the refutation, if a formidable case has preceded, may come immediately, especially if a speaker has the extempore skill of direct rebuttal. Or construction and refutation may be closely blended. William Jennings Bryan's "Cross of Gold" speech, before the Democratic National Convention at Chicago, July 9, 1896, was a direct refutation of the speech by David Hill of New York, and others who, preceding Bryan, supported the gold standard. Bryan's own silver, low tariff, income tax and other platforms were interwoven with his eloquent indictment of the opposing currency position.

In the amplification of any dominant method, such as the chronological or logical development, it becomes again a matter of selecting those details that best enforce the preferred pattern of organization. History may proceed chronologically forward or backward. Logic may amplify testimony, statistics, analogies in any sequence. Causal materials may deal in order with effect to cause (a posteriori reasoning), or from cause to effect (a priori reasoning). And so with the other methods. Furthermore, as we have already stated, this order of presenting supporting details may combine procedures—historical, logical, and other—in a given speech or article. The only principle is that each mode must justify itself and be clearly integrated with these other methods of division.

This amplification of the main body of discourse will also carry with it motivational materials, some of them almost identical with the factual and other content procedures. A passage developing need, or practicability, may supply figures and illustrations that buttress the proposition. These logical materials, however, may carry for the audience important emotional involvements.

Some sections of a discourse may more directly suggest emotional and imaginative reactions. The general tone may "elevate" itself into "true oratory." But where such passages are to appear (assuming that the creative process is not artificial) cannot be arbitrarily designated. The older rhetorical admonition, to expound logic and follow it with emotional passages, cannot be artistically or practically defended.

The insertion, too, of "ethical proofs" cannot be arbitrarily assigned to a given section. Whether the personal qualities of the speaker or writer, the adulation of his friends and cause, and the castigation of opponents, shall be placed first, last, or elsewhere, or blended with the evolution of the whole, is a matter for the discretion of the communicator. The critic will decide whether the method chosen was efficacious or ineffective.

As the structure of the body proper is governed by these principles of underlying thought and psychological elements, so it is affected by the language through which these logical and emotional appeals are made.

The language that supports disposition should be primarily accurate and clear. Sufficient application of transitional and other terms is made to assure unity and coherence. The extent to which connotative usages are introduced to further effective disposition is again a matter for the judgment of the writer or speaker.

Conclusion. What of the order in the conclusion? The end of the discourse may have a function other than that of adding a final note to the listener's knowledge of the topic. Conclusions often include such devices as summaries, series of questions, prophecies, quotations, brief anecdotes, and striking statements. The function of the conclusion, if it involves more than "just stopping," is to recapitulate and thus to help the audience recall. The conclusion, more often, however, aims to make clear what has been said. Speakers, moreover, here indicate an action step, or personal reference to the speaker himself; or pay farewell compliment to the listeners. These procedures are persuasive. Some of them may be blatant and amateurish. Who is to say what logical, expositional, motivative elements are to be included or excluded in this final action? The style and content should at least enhance what has gone before and should supply a final capstone to the speaker's contribution of information, conviction, persuasion, or inspiration. The one principle here is economy of materials. When the speech or article is done, the author should stop.

Proportion

Proportion, the third principle of disposition (structure), deals with the position and space of the content.

Its aim is to set out the most important ideas and parts so that a listener or reader can properly appreciate their relative importance. The aim is to secure emphasis.

Such proportion is partly a matter of position. What is presented at the beginning or at the end may be more easily remembered than what is here or there treated. The span of attention, as we have stated above, is limited.

The trained speaker (or writer) will place at the beginning ideas or information of genuine importance to the success of his theme. These preliminary materials, as we have suggested above, may comprise a somewhat formal explanation of the plan of treatment, or a fairly complete statement of the purpose of this speech or article. Uncertain movement or excursiveness at the start destroy proper proportion and emphasis. Either the speaker may be unsure of what he has to say, or he may be prolix in his approach to the heart of his theme. Proportion calls for a significant beginning. The end should similarly be couched impressively. The summaries and restatement of the major points add up to satisfactory proportion. Like the beginning, however, the end should be neither too long nor too short. The tendency of some speakers (and writers) to multiply the final words works against the maximum proportion in the conclusion of the article or speech.

A second means of proportion is by space. Obviously we are more impressed by what a speaker or writer talks most about. What is before the attention longest should penetrate further than that which is briefly revealed.

Thus repetition of ideas—in one place or in a number of selected passages—through explanation, illustration, logical detail, through comparison and contrast with other ideas or information—all will help the more important concepts to be impressive.

This principle of proportion may be illustrated in many an important speech. Abraham Lincoln, in his First Inaugural Address, for example, balanced the need for reconciliation between the free and slave states with his affirmation of federal supremacy in protecting rights—and his warning that war would follow defiance of the federal authority. He used well the distribution of his theme and space to stress his major points.

Charles W. Eliot's "The Solid Satisfactions of Life," [23] an address to the new students at Harvard University on October 3, 1905, developed his theme by a clear structure. He discussed and recommended for cultivation three sources of solid satisfactions in life:

1. Health
2. Capacity for hard work
3. Honorable conduct

The third, which he regarded as most important, he placed last; enlarged on it, and stressed it again in the final paragraph of his conclusion. He, like Lincoln, used well the space for his significant ideas.

Our observation in the previous chapter on the Golden Mean in style applies equally well to the structure of the discourse. Selection is a problem in discriminating between the important and the trivial; between excess and paucity of materials; between ideas and data; between economy of space and number of points to be treated. These applications of satisfactory disposition involve at every turn the principle of avoiding superficial and scanty materials. True art reveals a fitness of materials and proper balance in position and prominence.

[23] Charles W. Eliot, *The Training for an Effective Life* (Boston, New York, Houghton Mifflin, 1915), 1–9.

Synthesis and the Outline

Disposition begins with analysis and ends with synthesis. Analysis locates the specific subject in an area of ideas. It drafts a theme and frames relevant and significant questions or statements for further exploration and confirmation. Synthesis, in this process of following through with answers to the issues, concerns itself with the further dispositional problems of order and proportion. Synthesis thus integrates the parts of the subject, adequately phrases the several main and subtopics, and fills in the factual and persuasive details. Thus synthesis may delineate the forthcoming speech or article itself—except that the final communication, under immediate audience stimulus, may—and often does—reshape this preliminary pattern.

The concern for designing the details of what is to be uttered or written has led later rhetoricians—those interested in English composition and those writers and teachers of public speaking—to advocate extensive outlining of the subject—either for examination by others or for the author's own preparation.

Whether or not the increased attention to outlining is the tendency of the twentieth century technological civilization, this extension of disposition to include these blueprints is a strong tendency. Such outlines are of the organizational age with its card-filling, recording machines, elaborate indexing, and all the rest.

Outlining, a purely mechanical replica of the thought processes that underlie structure, may be dismissed as the fetish of mechanically minded communicators and their teachers. The wide instruction in such supplementary forms of disposition however, cannot be lightly dismissed. Experiences of translating structure into a visible demonstration may help much with the planning and thinking. But the principles of disposition as well as the mechanics of outlining must determine the worth of such rhetorical school. In many cases, the purpose and province of structure itself are hardly understood and the prospective communicator produces an outline that may or may not convey essential ideas and that may later clog the act of communication itself. The mechanical frame is explained and illustrated in detail by ten or fifteen rules, with special application to persuasive, informative, argumentative, discussional, and other types of speaking. Students of debate are encouraged to work out in detail briefs that comprise a complete digest of the entire case.

Accompanying the formal outline or brief may be a personal and informal arrangement with the specific audience in mind. This guide is a "speaker's outline," to remind him of the essentials to be uttered.

Speakers and writers through the centuries have used such notes.

They suggest again the importance of *disposition* in effective communication.[24]

Over-all Philosophy of Structure

Organization or arrangement is essential in any satisfactory speech or writing. The classical rhetoricians designated organization as second after invention among the five parts of speech. As *dispositio*, it deals with selection, unity, order or sequence, and proportion of the parts of a discourse. Thus it has broad application—much more than mere sequence. These are the principles by which it is to be viewed in all discourse.

Structure is no artificial quality in composition but rather is an expression of the order, symmetry, and unity common to all art forms and to the natural and aesthetic world.

Invention and disposition are hardly distinguishable and in some treatises are discussed together. They unitedly represent the "thought" in its logical, imaginative, and emotional concept and development. Together they verify, sift, and unfold the theme from its origin on through its organizing inventiveness.

The philosopher-rhetorician surveys the composition, oral or written, as a unified process of thinking and amplification. First is the critic's overview of the entire discourse, with the parts functioning together to produce the orderly effect. Second is the more detailed examination of the theme or purpose that governs every detail of the unfolding. This order and unity correlate within a grouping—historical, distributive, logical, or other—or with a combination of these modes of development.

Disposition begins with analysis and ends with synthesis. It locates the specific subject within an area of ideas. It drafts a thesis or theme and frames the statement for detailed expression. Synthesis also is involved. It attempts to deal with the issues or propositions or variety of concepts and concerns itself with accuracy, clearness, audience adaptation, and attention and interest in the introduction, main body, and conclusion (whether or not these divisions are marked or sharply discernable). Synthesis thus serves an integrative purpose.

What of outlining-either of a given article or one under planning? Systematic outlining, often elaborated into briefing for courtroom examination, or merely shaped as rough "speaker notes", is a secondary formalistic exercise. It nevertheless should suggest the underlying structure of the composition and its inventive quality.

[24] Donald C. Bryant and Karl R. Wallace, *Fundamentals of Public Speaking* (3d ed.; New York, Appleton-Century-Crofts, 1953–60), 145 ff.; William Norwood Brigance, *op. cit.*, 210 ff.; Alan H. Monroe, *Speech* (3d ed.; Chicago and New York, Scott Foresman, 1949), 261 ff.

10

Communication in Literature

Rhetoric in Relation to Literature

Rhetoric, oral and written, covers all effective communication. The communicator reacts to and affects an audience at a given time and place. He transmits ideas, by logical, emotional, and personal elements; by enforcement details; and by structure, language, and, in case of oral expression, delivery.

Literature, if similarly defined, also includes much or all of written discourse. The two sorts of communication overlap or merge and so make questionable dichotomous terms. All is rhetoric, or all is literature. Kenneth Burke, for example, analyzes the poetic and rhetorical components and concludes that with the common aims and techniques, "effective literature can be nothing else but rhetoric."[1] If, however, literature is restricted to belles lettres, then it is more properly a fine art as in poetry, fiction, and drama. Its aims are pleasure and its marks are beauty, universal and permanent appeal. Literateurs may view rhetoric as mundane, practical, prosaic, embodied in histories, biographies, essays, pamphlets, editorials, news reports, other miscellaneous types of exposition and argument, including public speeches. The distinction is somewhat that attributed to Aristotle's "rhetoric" and "poetic," or to Thomas De Quincey's "literature of knowledge" and of "power."[2]

Despite these divergencies these two types have such basic likenesses as to give them a near or complete identification. At least the best of rhetoric and the best of literature fall into a common pattern and their differences become merely casuistic.

---

[1] Kenneth Burke, *Counter Statement* (New York, Harcourt Brace, 1931), 265–266.
[2] Thomas De Quincey, "The Poetry of Pope," in *Collected Writings of Thomas De Quincey,* 14 vols. (London, A. & C. Black, 1896–97), Vol. 2, 54.

Rhetoric and Poetic

From the beginnings in classical Greece, poetry (literature) and rhetoric were hardly distinguishable. George Kennedy analyzed the techniques of persuasion in Greek literature before 400 B.C. to illustrate the rhetorical elements of artistic writing. He illustrated, from Sophocles' *Antigone* and *Oedipus the King,* from Aeschylus' *Eumenides,* Euripides' *Hippolytus,* Homer's *Iliad,* and the histories by Herodotus and Thucydides, their strongly rhetorical qualities.[3] Greek literature developed from oral communication and gradually was reduced to written versions. The specific rhetorical cast is obvious in the invention, organization, and style of the speeches that pervaded these plays, epics, and histories.

Donald Bryant, in his review of ancient Greek literature, concluded that the chief business of the poet is creation and the chief business of the orator is persuasion. This position did not deceive the ancients, who knew that the orator and the poet depend upon imaginative power in about the same way and use it for similar ends.[4]

Our inquiry here concerns the relationship of rhetoric to literature. What are their common elements and possible distinctions? We approach each as it expresses its purpose in communication; its transmission of thought (idea, ideology, truth, meaning, or complex of meanings); its emotional fabric or texture (feeling, mood, attitude, a complex of drives and motives, sentiments, stereotypes); its imaginative view and relation to the world; and its utilization of language (form) in the service of thought, emotion, and imagination.

Rhetoric and Literature as Communication

Communication is the common purpose of both rhetoric and literature. The transmission of ideas, emotions and imaginative insights from communicator to audiences is the nature of these two processes.

I hold with Wilbur Samuel Howell [5] that literature is an enterprise in communication, just as is rhetoric. The interpreters of some literature as devoid of communication point to poetry especially in the lyric as largely free from the purpose of adjusting to and affecting an audience. These critics assert that where the aim is to substitute, for the soliloquy

---

[3] George Kennedy, *The Art of Persuasion in Greece* (Princeton, N.J., Princeton University Press, 1963), Chap. 2.

[4] Donald Bryant, "Aspects of the Rhetorical Tradition II: "Emotion, Style, and Literary Association," *Quarterly Journal of Speech,* XXXVI (October, 1950), 326, 332.

[5] Wilbur Samuel Howell, "Literature as an Enterprise in Communication," *Quarterly Journal of Speech,* XXXIII (December, 1947), 419–426.

or inward expression, the appeal to audience comprehension and reaction, the discourse, poetry or prose, devolves into so much rhetoric. Even narratives, plays, tragic or comic, as they seek to inform, persuade, or inspire an audience lose their artistic character and become so much persuasion.

Howell cites John Stuart Mill in his "Thoughts on Poetry and Its Varieties"[6] as saying that "eloquence is heard, poetry is overheard. . . . [The poet's] act of utterance must be itself the end."

Those of us who identify all literature with communication cite at length the plays, tragic and comic, novels, poems, epic, lyric, and narrative, that possess obvious rhetorical intent to impress. The reading of any genuinely literary production enriches the reader's spirit and mind and leads him to recognize his experience as one with "beauty and truth."

All genuine literature produces identification between the author and the audience. Are the twenty-eight plays of Henrik Ibsen not strong in rhetorical as well as literary-dramatic values? *Brand* is the tragedy of a priest who argues for an impossible ideal in a world of compromise. *The Master Builder* concerns an individualist who assaults false ideals. Similarly, *Pillars of Society, The Doll's House, Ghosts, The Wild Duck,* and *Peer Gynt* are developed by situations and theses that Ibsen would present to his audience. Similarly, Bernard Shaw engages in the drama of satire with his *Caesar and Cleopatra, Major Barbara, Candida, Pygmalion,* and a long list of other stage plays that criticize nationalities, professions, church, law, army and medicine. Shaw is a rhetorician, a propagandist, and a stirring writer whose deep interest in communicating these ideas—is matched by his uncommon skill and artistry. Thus Molière, Maeterlinck, Ben Jonson, Shakespeare, whether their mood was heavy or light, romantic or realistic, symbolic or didactic, addressed their characters, plots and themes to immediate and wider audiences. The communicative spirit of literature extends also to ballads, odes, elegies, poems of love, patriotism, nature, religion, and even to "pure" lyrics. All are designed for more than recital by the solitary author himself. The sonnets of Shakespeare, Milton, Byron, Keats, Elizabeth Barrett Browning, and Longfellow are more than emotion set to music. The audiences again and again respond to the personal themes. The author's communicative impulse is steady.

Exactly what that communicative discourse says or how it utilizes its materials is questionable. The communicative stimulus, nevertheless, is there and so places in a common mold the purpose of the literary and the rhetorical writers.

[6] John Stuart Mill, *Dissertations and Discussions,* 4 vols. (Boston, W. V. Spencer, 1868), Vol. 1, 97.

Thought

Logical substance pervades both literature and rhetoric. The instrumental communication of rhetoric is basically intellectual. Rhetorical communication develops a theme (idea) and puts it in the language of listener-observers. The mind of the speaker-writer is more akin to that of the logician or the scientist with his facts and inferences than of the imaginative author. In literature, to be sure, the idea also appears in the inception, but it must not overload the movement. Postulates and facts may distort or side track the imaginative artistry. Aesthetic power is lessened as sheer intellectuality takes over. The assumption here does not imply that the formula for equating successful literature with a minimum amount of fact and reasoning approaches quantitative description. Where genuine literature lapses and rhetoric looms up as the mental temper dominates can be assessed only by an estimate based on a view of the total enterprise.

The age of Dryden, Pope, Johnson, and Burke was not an age of English literary creativity, because these vigorous writers were inclined to shape their prose and poetry to express primarily intellectual patterns. The poetic imagery of Browning and Matthew Arnold suffered from doctrinaire overtones that lessened the aesthetic effect. Speculative subtleties permeated the movement of "Dover Beach" and "My Last Duchess." The imaginative insights of these poems nevertheless elevated them to high compositional art.

Arnold's definition of culture as a record of the "best that is known and thought" does not commit us to a record of deduction and induction of theorems and syllogisms. Rather, its method is to illumine the thought and utterances with the vistas perceived by their creator but not limited to the sensory dimensions of the scene. *Henry IV* and *Henry V* are grounded in Holinshed, but the characterizations of Prince Hal and Falstaff, the plots and successive scenes dwarf the mere chronological spirit. Dickens exposed the social blights of early nineteenth century England, but his narrations are genuine and are a far cry from welfare documents.

The rhetorician's target is the mind, however that mind is conceived in its manysided rational, emotional and imaginative activity. The rhetorician presents his theses to enlighten, convince, persuade, impress. His aims and materials are to affect or change his listeners or readers. Here and there poetry heightens his discourse. But always the themes persist in language, structure and design. For him is the approximation of truth, or truth as he tries to unfold it. He may be the expounder, almost without his awareness, of the philosophical force of his time and culture, of realism or transcentalism, of orthodoxy or atheism, of platonism or pragmatism. His application enforces the fundamentals of these "truths," however erroneous they may be.

The literary artist, however, is governed by no such measurable boundaries of thought or restrictions on his personal involvement. He is faithful to the truth of life as he personally reacts to it. The personal factor in his appropriation of philosophical trust is a measure of his excellence.

René Wallek and Austin Warren hold such a view of literary worth. "A theoretical insight may increase the artist's depth of penetration and scope of treatment. But it need not be so. The artist will be hampered by too much ideology if it remains unassimilated." Literature, with its poetry, drama, and fiction and its criticism of culture and life, is to be judged, "not by the value of the material, but by the degree of integration and artistic intensity." [7]

Thus the intellectual element, always controlling in the best rhetoric, gives integrity also to the literary classics. But the thought (idea, mental rumination) in high art is not of the nature of systematic reflection spelled out in detail. For interpretation of the essential "truths" we need to discern the movement of the discourse itself—understand the nature of the emotional, imaginative and intellectual energy. Overshadowing intellectualism, to repeat, dwarfs the artistic quality. But the entire absence of such factor may produce only jangled emotional meandering.

Emotion and Imagination

Rhetoric, as we stated in Chapter 7, was a process of the "totality" of method and effect—informational, emotional, and actional. The principal datum of rhetoric—reason and logic—is insufficient to account for audience reaction. Human beings, as every critic observes, are largely dominated by non-intellectual attitudes and behavior. According to H. W. Hollingworth, "The members of an audience are more alike in their instincts and emotions than in capacity to follow logical reasoning: hence emotional appeals or topics will move uniformly, and generally influence them. The beliefs of an audience do not depend on evidence alone; they are definitely warped, even against the evidence, by desires and hopes." [8]

Although training, tradition, and personal experiences modify and curb these elemental responses, the drives, wants, desires, and marks of emotional thinking and acting continually assert themselves. And these

[7] René Wellek and Austin Warren, *Theory of Literature* (New York, Harcourt Brace, 1942, 1949), Chap. 10, "Literature and Ideas," 122–123.

[8] H. L. Hollingworth, *The Psychology of the Audience* (New York, American Book, 1935), 137–138.

individual impulses or attitudes, in some cases, become more marked as the group influence operates. Groups are relatively more emotional than the individuals. Charles Bird states that "with few exceptions crowd behavior is a regression to the uncontrolled and destructive activities or the volatile, superficial happiness of childhood." [9] The individual and the group tend to believe what satisfies their primary and secondary needs and wants.[10]

Rhetoricians and the psychologists alike recognize that "emotions" is a loose term to describe the combination of preceptive experiences that are the reaction to outward or inward stimuli. These "emotions," tangible reactions, become the basic (primary, physiological, biological) and the secondary (derived psychological, social, learned, habitual) wants and desires. Hence the emotional activities or reactions that deal with anger, pity, love, rage, fear, self preservation, assertiveness, accumulation of goods, comforts, personal and social convenience, intellectual and aesthetic satisfactions. These distinctions and categories obviously overlap. They do suggest the representative reactions of the individual and of groups. Prejudices, impulses, motives, sentiments, rationalizations, are to be reckoned with at every step of communication. By agreement of practically every student from Plato and Aristotle to the present, however, the intellectual element in rhetorical expression is paramount.

Genuine literature, as we discussed "thought" above, although recognizing the essential mental impulse that gives coherence to a composition, has as its principle of expression, emotionality. Stephen C. Peffer, a critic of the arts, explains that rhetoric differs from literature in that in the latter, "feeling is understood as the qualitative side of experience in contrast to the practical and logical." [11]

C. T. Winchester asks what gives permanence to literature? What leads us to preserve some fragile lyric and presently forget a treatise on calculus, or geology, or even philosophy? His answer is that the poem appeals to the emotions whereas the treatise appeals chiefly to the intellect. States he, "It is the power to appeal to the emotions that gives a book permanent interest, and consequently, literary quality." [12]

Thomas De Quincey classifies literature as that of knowledge and that of power. While the discourse of knowledge teaches, that of power cre-

[9] Charles Bird, *Social Psychology* (New York, Appleton-Century-Crofts, 1940), 357.

[10] A. Craig Baird, *Argumentation, Discussion and Debate* (New York, McGraw-Hill, 1950), 216.

[11] Stephen C. Peffer, *The Basis of Criticism in the Arts* (Cambridge, Mass., Harvard University Press, 1946), 77.

[12] C. T. Winchester, *Some Principles of Literary Criticism* (New York, Macmillan, 1900), 42.

ates deep sympathy with truth. "Power," as interpreted by De Quincey, means power over the feelings: emotional appeal. The literature of knowledge thus differs from creative literature. Said De Quincey:

In that great social organ which, collectively, we call literature, there may be distinguished two separate offices that may blend, and often do so, but capable severally of a severe insulation, and naturally fitted for a reciprocal repulsion. There is, first, the literature of knowledge; and, secondly, the literature of power. The function of the first is—to teach; the function of the second is—to move: the first is rudder; the second an oar or a sail. The first speaks to the mere discursive understanding; the second speaks ultimately, it may happen, to the higher understanding or reason, but always through affections of pleasure and sympathy.[13]

Note that De Quincey really attributes to all genuine literature this motivative power. The other type is often literature only by courtesy —actually, rhetoric. Some of De Quincey's literature of knowledge is no doubt genuine literature; much of it is otherwise, just as some of this literature of power may also be merely rhetoric. De Quincey's affirmation of genuine literature as having "higher understanding or reason" is well taken. De Quincey is in line with the thinking of this chapter that regards literature as possessing this "higher understanding" though always revealed in "affection," "sympathy," and the other appeals (emotions, drives, sentiments).

This quality of emotion pervades whatever the subject matter or literary genre. Aristotle's *Poetics* well illustrates the two sorts of utterances, their differences and their common elements. To Aristotle rhetoric deals with persuasive discourse, especially deliberative, epideictic, and forensic speaking. He could well have expanded his rhetoric to embrace expositional and entertainment applications. These, he apparently assumed, were secondary and, in the case of entertainment, trivial. The other category of discourse to Aristotle would be that of imagery and the other products of creative imagination, "the art of sharpening and expanding this vision." [14]

Literature and rhetoric would differ in their purposes. Rhetoric, to him, had the practical aim of persuading the Greeks of his time to adopt certain attitudes and decisions. Poetics or literature had as its chief end pleasure and aesthetic satisfaction. Its end was not primarily not to discuss life but to present it. How was—or is—literature to secure such satisfactory end? Chiefly, according to Aristotle, by providing the reader or

[13] De Quincey, *loc. cit.*
[14] Charles S. Baldwin, *Ancient Rhetoric and Poetic* (New York, Macmillan, 1924), 134.

observer-listener with the experience of imitation. Man was an imitator by nature. Literature, like rhetoric, was to take account of the factors, logical, emotional, that compose the ways of man and affect his conduct.[15] But literature, in this case the drama, must concentrate on the ways by which people react in their total personalities.[16] The *Poetics,* in dealing importantly with tragic drama, notes that the plot is generated and carried through by the human beings involved. In Aristotle's concepts tragic art is "imitating (presenting) men in action." And such experience of the dramatis personae issues in an emotional catharsis.[17] This dramatic climax in the case of some personage, caught in the midst of some "human error" deals with the effect of fear and pity that develops in this clash of motive with circumstance.[18]

Tragedy is thus thoroughly emotional. According to Aristotle, such drama offers not merely emotional excitement, but emotional satisfaction. "Tragedy reveals our motives and moves us onward through vicarious experience. We yearn toward our fellows, moved as we are, more deeply; we fear in some great crisis what obscurely threatens us day by day; and we know the inevitable end not with our minds, but with our awakened hearts." [19]

The presentation of heroism, virtue, vice, altruism, self-sacrifice, defiance of gods or men, fear, loyalty, and the other traits are at the heart of the literary method. Oedipus, Medea, Hamlet, King Lear, Cyrano de Bergerac, Candida, and the others of high tragedy and comedy represent character in crisis, with all the attributes that essentially compose literature in its highest expression.

The elegy, epic, and other poetry, prose drama, novels, and other fiction deal with the same human nature with its drives and emotional reactions. At what point does history or political philosophy become literature? Are essays by Lamb, Landor, De Quincey, Arnold, Huxley, Macaulay to be classified as rhetorical rather than literary? Attempts at inflexible categories, as we have said, must always fail. The descriptive continua include many examples that may fall into either category on the scale—according to critical judgment. The degree of emotion as a criterion cannot mark the difference. Chatham as parliamentary speaker was highly emotional. But he was not a speaker or writer of literature. Lewis' "Monk" seethed with horror but, in my opinion, it was not important literature. But neither did it rank as rhetoric.

---

[15] The *"Rhetoric"* and *"Poetics"* of Aristotle, tr. Rhys Roberts and Ingram Bywater (New York, Modern Library, 1954), 65.

[16] *Ibid.,* 234–235.

[17] *Ibid.,* 230, lines 20 ff.

[18] *Ibid.,* 230.

[19] Baldwin, *op. cit.,* 148.

Personality Expression

How do these respective types convey personality appeals? Does the personality of the literary author differ from that of the rhetorical communicator? Essentially, the differences are minor and the likenesses are basic. In each case the author-speaker-communicator reveals his individuality as a measure of his emotional-imaginative projection. Aristotle expounded ethical "proofs" as one of the three bases for establishing the thesis. Personality, however it is identified, also is foundational in literary creativeness. Even though the author is anonymous or a composite of several writers, as allegedly is the case of the Iliad, the personal quality reveals purpose, selection of materials, order of unfolding, and the wording.

The communicator's personality is obviously more direct and immediately effective in rhetoric than in most literature. The speaker or writer connects directly with his audience and their immediate problems. He utilizes his voice and physical assets to enforce his words and speaking aims. Equally so does he project a similar quality into his editorials, pamphlets, letters or other writing, even though he may be nameless. The letters of Junius were highly effective rhetoric with strong ethical proofs, even though the composer is still undetermined. In literature, as in other fine arts, the writer may be anonymous. Novels, plays, and poems may be enjoyed without knowledge of their authors. An anonymous creation of literary beauty is still a work of beauty. A persuasive document, however, has significance partly because it is Burke pleading for conciliation with the American colonies, or Thomas Jefferson with his inaugural address, or Ralph Waldo Emerson delivering "The American Scholar" at Harvard. The examples here cited may not be the best, for they verge on literature. Typical rhetoric serves its hour and usually dies with the week or year. Charles James Fox gave brilliant parliamentary debates "so potent for the hour; so impotent for posterity." The personal appeal usually fades with its author's voice. The literary voice, however nameless or obscure it may be, continues its firm tones and its impress. The Psalms, Job, and many another writing of universal recognition reflect the personal note that helps to explain the permanent appeal. Thus rhetoric in its mould and the literary art both are basically personal. Each fulfills its function through such individual quality—even though rhetoric is ephemeral and the best literature by comparison is ageless.

Moral Content

What of the moral content of literature and of rhetoric? According to Aristotle and his successors, rhetoric should incorporate ethical motives.

Superior rhetoric, as we analyzed it in Chapter 6, attempted to promote the happiness of mankind and a better society. Ethics in rhetoric correlates with valid logic and helps produce intellectual and moral integrity of the communication. Contemporary social and political conditions may largely affect the author's concepts of such direction, but the vigor of this moral quality is nevertheless there in every case.

Literature carries with it the aim of generating aesthetic pleasure and satisfaction and does so through an emotional-imaginative climate. It would seem a far cry from such literature to the ethical drive accompanying responsible speaking or rhetorical writing. The two kinds of expression, nevertheless, are ethically one.

Literature's mission is to reveal human nature in its genuineness—its Judas Iscariot, Iago, Satan, as well as its Joan of Arc. It combines realism and naturalism with idealism. Its purpose is not to preach, else it becomes rhetoric. Cleopatra, Medea, Lady Macbeth are not to be by-passed because they transgress the bounds of acceptable conduct. Literature's role is to depict the truth of life and have fidelity to the laws of human nature. Winchester assumes such truth as a literary dictum. "Let the poet show us if he will, the whole man, howsoever bad, if he will only show him truly. Art demands truth; morality demands nothing more." [20] This portrayal of complex characters and the world that governs and is governed by them is the "high seriousness" that Matthew Arnold attributes to genuine literature. The deep tragedy, the great epic, the comedy with its humor and irony, the novels of their contemporary world—"how can any of them be true if they ignore the deepest facts of human nature?" [21]

Fénelon, in his *Dialogues on Eloquence,* according to Wilbur S. Howell, felt that "good art is that which inspires men in the quest for wisdom, good laws, justice, and individual betterment, whereas bad art inspires men to favor their flatterers, follow their private inclinations—to seek personal power, wealth, reputation, no matter at what expense." [22]

This ethical import of great literature is thus the measure of its effective revelation and interpretation of the ways of mankind. Genuine literary discernment and expression thus express the truth—however elusive that term may be. Its "truth" is much wider and different from orthodox morality codes. Otherwise, James Joyce, D. H. Lawrence, Somerset Maugham, and the writer of the *Decameron* would have been banned by the moral guardians. Literature, like the best of rhetoric, aims at the emancipation of human nature and so opens the way toward the universe

---

20 Winchester, *op. cit.,* 115.
21 *Ibid.,* 116.
22 Wilbur Samuel Howell, "Oratory and Poets in Fénelon's Literary Theory," *Quarterly Journal of Speech,* XXXVIII (February, 1951), 7.

of "truth." Walter Pater expresses this relation of literary excellence to such a goal:

In the highest as in the lowest literature [rhetoric] then, the one indispensable beauty is, after all, truth:—truth to bare fact in the latter rhetoric, as to some personal sense of fact, diverted somewhat from men's ordinary sense of it, in the former [literature]; truth there [rhetoric] as accuracy, truth here [literature] as expression, that finest and most intimate form of truth, the *vraïe vérité*.[23]

Language in Literature and Rhetoric

Has literature as a fine art a style distinct from that of rhetoric, the practical art?

The literary artist expresses himself imaginatively and emotionally. His language is not ornamental but is the inevitable expression of the movement and concepts. The literary composer "writes passionately because he conceives vividly; he has a firm hold on it [the subject] and therefore he is luminous. When his imagination wells up, it overflows in ornament. He expresses what all feel but cannot say." [24]

Feeling impels the writer to embody such impulses in words. Technical skill is not enough to explain this heightening of language. "It isn't the way the words are strung together that makes the Gettysburg address immortal, but the feelings that were in the man." [25]

Thus through emotional-imaginative stimulus is developed the language of connotation, the figures of speech, negation, suspension, repetition, alliteration, inversion, euphony, rhythm, parallelism, and the other combinations of words, phrases, clauses, and sentences that convey the literary mood.[26] Robert Louis Stevenson commenting on style speaks of the key words, the web of the discourse, the fabric of composition. The heightening is there, but its value is determined by the proportion, balance, and vividness of the language. The golden mean of Aristotle decries ornamentation for its self alone, or the emotional excesses that vitiate the genuineness of the composition.

What of the language of rhetoric? Aristotle noted that the language of speech should be rhythmical. Stated he, "The form of a prose composition should be the metrical nor destitute of rhythm. The metrical

[23] Walter Pater, *Appreciations, with an Essay on Style* (London, 1889, 1927), 34.

[24] John Henry Newman, "Literature" (from *The Idea of a University*); reprinted in William T. Brewster, *Representative Essays on the Theory of Style* (New York, Macmillan, 1911), 125.

[25] "Words That Laugh and Cry," editorial in the *New York Sun*, March 16, 1890; quoted in R. W. Brown, *The Writer's Art* (Cambridge, Mass., Harvard University Press, 1921), 113.

[26] See Chapter 8 for detailed discussion of rhetoric and language.

form produces artificially and distracts attention by such mechanism." [27]
Robert G. Ingersoll, despite his power as a platform lecturer, often engaged in metrical prose that later students of public address put down as
affected, the marks of an earlier age that endorsed exuberance in American public address. Cicero endorsed rhythmical language, but suggested
that oratory should be mingled with and regulated with regard to the
rhythm, not prosaic nor on the other hand sacrificed wholly to rhythm.[28]
Aristotle believes that for political speaking a finished style would be
superficial. The forensic style, before a judge, would have opportunity
for more finish. The epideictic style would approach the genuinely literary and its proper function would be to be read rather than delivered.[29]

As the composition passes from every-day communication, from information or straight argument to more impassioned utterance, from plain
demonstration and logical progress to the climate of emotion, the style
becomes more complex and stimulating. The movement is from drabness
to illumination and beauty. George Henry Lewes cites beauty as the
goal in literary style. "The principle of Beauty is only another name for
style, which is an art, but as incommunicable as are all other arts, but
like them subordinated to laws founded on psychological conditions." [30]

In rhetorical and literary prose, we thus fail to indicate wide differences in the use of figures, tropes, rhythm, or the other marks of interesting and moving style. If the creator of the work is mightily moved by his
theme and is conditioned by his personality, the subject, the audience, and
the time and place, he may create that which has beauty and permanence.

But who is to impose a set of rules to separate rhetoric from literature?
Cicero, reflecting on the usage of rhythm in public address, observed:

. . . If the question is raised as to what is the rhythm of an oration, it is
any sort of rhythm; but one sort is better and more suitable than another. If
the question is what is the place of this rhythm? It is in every portion of the
words. If you ask where it has risen, it has risen from the pleasure of the
ears. . . . if the question is, when; always: if, in what place, it consists in
the entire connection of the words. If we are asked, What is the circumstance which causes pleasure, we reply, that it is the same as in verse; the
method of which is determined by art; but the ears themselves define it by
their own silent sensations, without any reference to principles or art.[31]

Can a uniqueness be noted in the language of the poetic as distinguished from the rhetorical? Samuel Howell suggests that the use of

[27] Aristotle, *op. cit.*, 180.
[28] Cicero, *Orator*, tr. C. D. Yonge, in *The Orations of Marcus Tullius Cicero*,
Vol. IV (London, H. G. Bohn, 1852), 442–443.
[29] Aristotle, *op. cit.*, 273.
[30] George Henry Lewes, "The Principle of Beauty," *The Principles of Success in
Literature*, in R. W. Brown, *The Writer's Art*, 209 ff.
[31] Cicero, *op. cit.*, 444–445.

symbolism marks a real difference between the literary style and that of the orator. Both types use connotative language, for example such figures as the metaphor, but the rhetorician (orator) would do so to illustrate concrete argument, whereas the literary writer would use such imagery to express the idea itself. The orator or rhetorician, according to Howell, uses words to illuminate factual matters, whereas the littérateur uses words to illuminate things that in turn illuminate factual matters.[32]

To all students of communication, including Howell, words are the signs of things. "Things" are "referents," and the meanings assigned to words reflect the meanings in turn assigned to their referents.

What is the nature of referents of rhetorical communication? They are presumably those of the words of our experience. Our practical communicative experience deals with our reactions to the language as it is based on our habitual and immediate experiences.

The literary creator, however, is more suggestive and imaginative. *Longinus On the Sublime*, "The Great Unknown," suggests the importance of height in style (ὕψος), through imaginative diction and rhythmical pace. The poetic style he contrasts with rhetoric but also explains their interdependence. Charles Sears Baldwin in his discussion paraphrases the Great Unknown:

> What life disperses and interrupts, poetry focuses and brings in to emotional sequence and momentum. Its essential processes are to realize these saliences imaginatively and to unify them. The parallel method of rhetoric is the converse; it is amplification. Poetry suggests in a flash; oratory iterates and enlarges. The one is intensive; the other, extensive. They all fall short without what we call heightening.[33]

> Height means direct lift [διάρμα]; amplification implifies multitude. As imagery means one thing with the orators and another with the poets, you must have observed that with the latter its function is vivid suggestion; with the former, precision.[34]

The literary meaning, initiated by the same words of the rhetorical utterance, may call up primary referents different from those in the given rhetorical discourse. The problem in understanding the contribution of language to the literature according to Howell, is that of understanding a second set of referents—those used by the inspired writers.

A full understanding and appreciation of any kind of utterance is greatly helped by a knowledge of the author's background, times, and the other insights related to his ideas and language. "But," as Howell

---

[32] Wilbur S. Howell, "Literature as an Enterprise," *Quarterly Journal of Speech,* XXXIII (December, 1947), 419.

[33] Baldwin, *op. cit.*, 127.

[34] *The Sublime,* tr. W. Rhys Roberts (2d ed.; Cambridge, 1899), Chap. 15.

states, "the major clues to an author's meaning are his own words, and it is in studying them that we must proceed with an eye to the differences between statements and symbols."

Most critics agree that communication of all kinds and levels uses imagery and connotation—crude though the figurative associations may be in much day-to-day communication. Howell's suggestion, however, that the real difference between the oratorical and poetic style lies in the particular use of language in each case and in the possible uniqueness of the poetic words is an isolated conclusion. Most of us would agree with Fénelon, the seventeenth century critic discussed by Howell.[35] Fénelon found the difference merely one of degree in that "poetry differs from simple eloquence only in this: that she paints with ecstasy and with bolder strokes. Prose has its paintings; albeit more moderated. Without them one cannot heat the imagination of a listener or arouse his passions." [36]

Summary

The differences between literature and rhetoric are secondary.[37] They are one in the general function of communication. If Arnold's word holds that literature as culture is a criticism of life and aims not only to see and learn but to make truth prevail, we can also conclude that rhetoric and poetics unite in serving mankind. The disagreements are obviously those of method. Rhetoric communicates in the market place and usually utilizes informational-persuasive materials and the applications of language, to clarify, adapt, and illuminate the thesis and its details. Literature, with its aim and quality of the pleasurable utilizes these same intellectual, emotional, and personal elements to its more aesthetic ends. Beauty and truth are the outcomes.

William Hazlitt, in the presence of Coleridge, with his mastery of both literature and rhetoric, explained: "I could not have been more delighted if I had heard music from the spheres. Poetry and philosophy had met together." [38]

[35] Wilbur S. Howell, "Oratory and Poetry in Fénelon's Literary Theory," *Quarterly Journal of Speech*, XXXIII (December, 1947), 1010.

[36] *Ibid.*, p. 7 (Fénelon's *Dialogues on Eloquence*, p. 28, as translated by Howell).

[37] G. M. A. Gruber, "Rhetoric and Literary Criticism," *Quarterly Journal of Speech*, XLII (December, 1946), 339–344.

[38] William Hazlitt, "My First Acquaintance with Poets," in *Selected Essays* (Cambridge, Mass., Cambridge University Press, 1958), 3.

11

Delivery

Rhetoric, as we defined it in Chapter 1, applies to all types of practical discourse, oral and written. Milton's *Areopagitica*, although in form an address as if to be delivered by an Athenian orator, was a pamphlet. The letters of Junius were treated by Chauncey Goodrich as "eloquence" in the best rhetorical manner. Thus *inventio, dispositio, eloquentia,* apply similarly to both written and spoken rhetoric. In this chapter we are reviewing delivery (*pronunciatio* and *actio*), the fifth of these rhetorical "parts." (*Memoria,* as a major constituent, was dropped several centuries ago.)

Significance of Delivery in Rhetoric

How important is delivery in rhetoric? To the ancient Greeks, rhetoric was pretty largely oral; therefore they recognized the need for effective utterance of their persuasions. But with their endorsement of the oral element as a significant agency in communication arose the question of the manipulation of voice and physical activity in the process. Enthusiasm for delivery implied an endorsement of demagoguery. Aristotle gave scant treatment of this oral art. To him the unsophisticated audiences required that speakers pay some attention to their delivery. Aristotle, however, apparently dismissed this part of rhetoric as hardly a subject for philosophical inquiry. Ideas, he believed, should be accepted on their own merits rather than as dependent on the supports of voice and bodily activity. Wrote Aristotle:

The subject [of delivery] has been hitherto neglected. . . . We have no systematic treatise on delivery in public speaking; and the real reason is that the whole subject of utterance was late in coming to the front. . . . [It] "is still popularly considered and indeed is rightly supposed to be something vulgar [inferior]. Still as the entire study of rhetoric has regard to appearance, it is necessary to pay due attention to declamation [delivery], not that it is right to do so but because it is inevitable. Strict justice indeed, if applicable to rhetoric, would confine itself to seeking such delivery as would cause neither pain nor pleasure. For the right condition is that the battle should be fought out on the facts of the case alone; and therefore every thing outside the direct proof is really superfluous, although extraneous matters are highly effective, as has been said, owing to the depraved character of the audience.[1]

Aristotle's words here are pretty harsh. He deprecates the low comprehensive level of Greek audiences and the necessity of providing them with vocal embellishments if they are to understand and respond to the messages.

Cicero, on the contrary, regarded delivery as of supreme value for forensic and other speaking situations. Wrote Cicero:

But all these parts of oratory [different types of speaking] succeed according as they are delivered. Delivery, I say, has the sole and supreme power in oratory; without it a speaker of the highest mental capacity can be held in no esteem; while one of moderate abilities, with this qualification, may surpass even those of the highest talent.[2]

Cicero repeated several times the anecdotes in which Demosthenes testified to the power of delivery. When asked what was of the first importance in delivery, the supreme Greek orator is said to have replied, "Delivery." When asked what were the factors of second and third importance, he is said to have stated in each case, "Delivery."

Cicero, in addition to repeating this tradition, commented on the story of Aeschines at Rhodes. Aeschines is reported to have read, at the request of the Rhodians, that outstanding speech he had delivered against Ctesiphon, in opposition to Demosthenes, and he was asked to read the next day the speeches Demosthenes had delivered in favor of Ctesiphon. And when he had read this, too, in a pleasing and powerful voice, and all expressed their admiration, he said, "How much more would you have admired it if you had heard him deliver it himself!" Cicero, in agreement declared, "Delivery is the dominant power in oratory."[3]

Quintilian followed Cicero's high endorsement of delivery. The Latin schoolmaster in his *Institutes of Oratory*, said:

We are fortunate if the judge catches the fire of our passion; he will not be melted by our yawning. Actors add charm to our greatest poets when heard far more than when read; they even get a hearing for worthless authors who are denied a place in libraries. If delivery can count for so much in fictitious themes, I dare affirm that even a mediocre speech will be more

---

[1] *The "Rhetoric" of Aristotle,* tr. J. E. C. Welldon (London and New York, Macmillan, 1886), III, 226.

[2] Cicero, *De Oratore, or On the Character of the Orator,* III, lvi, in *On Oratory and Orators,* tr. J. S. Watson (London, H. G. Bohn, 1855).

[3] *Ibid.,* III, lv.

effective, if delivered well, than the best speech, if poorly delivered. Demosthenes gave the palm to delivery as first in importance in speaking, and then added that it was second, and also third. This explains why he studied so diligently under the actor Andronicus and why Aeschines admired his delivery so extravagantly, as told by Cicero. Cicero records that Lentulus had a great reputation for his delivery, as did also Gracchus and Antonius and Crassus; but the greatest of all was Hortensius, whose writings, however, fail to show such charm. Words count for much in themselves; when voice and gesture and motion add their force, something like perfection comes from these combined qualities.[4]

Medieval rhetoric tended to transfer the content of *inventio* to dialectic and to limit the meaning of rhetoric to language or style, with incidental treatment of delivery. As Donald Clark stated it, "By the late Middle Ages rhetoric had come to mean style alone."[5] The influence of Pierre de la Ramee, Peter Ramus, the French philosopher, who was strong in reforming the liberal arts during the sixteenth century, also affected concentration on delivery. His *Dialecticae Libri Duo*, formulated into a system by Omer Talon, was translated into English in 1574. Ramistic dialectic was composed of Invention and Arrangement. Ramistic rhetoric was limited to Style and Delivery. Gradually during the seventeenth century delivery became more and more prominent, and in the eighteenth century was carried to extremes. John Bulwer's *Chirologia* and *Chironomia*, 1644, for example, became the first book in English limited to the treatment of gesture.[6]

This elocutionary tradition in England became an examination of delivery "so specialized in nature and content as to differ in kind from former studies."[7]

Delivery developed a new importance in England during the period of parliamentary growth, and in the pulpit Charles Palmer, Deputy Sergeant of the House of Commons, wrote that delivery "is the very life and soul of eloquence. The art of oratory is never so great and potent by the things that are said, as by the manner of saying them."[8]

The rising emphasis on delivery was explained by the more practical temper of the eighteenth century. There was greater emphasis on good delivery in political, forensic and religious speaking; increasing linguistic investigations of pronunciation; and increased inclusion of delivery as

---

[4] Quintilian, *Institutes of Oratory*, XI, ii, iii, tr. J. S. Watson, 2 vols. (London, H. G. Bohn, 1856).

[5] Donald Lemen Clark, *Rhetoric in Greco-Roman Education* (New York, Columbia University Press, 1957), 83.

[6] John Bulwer, *Chirologia* (London, T. Harper, 1644).

[7] Frederick W. W. Haberman, "English Sources of American Elocution," in Karl Wallace (ed.), *A History of Speech Education in America* (New York, Appleton-Century-Crofts, 1954), 105 ff.

[8] *Aphorisms and Maxims* (London, 1748), quoted by Haberman, *op. cit.*, 107.

part of general education. Typical of the elocutionary movement and of its leaders were Thomas Sheridan, with his lectures on elocution at Oxford, 1759, published three years later;[9] and John Walker, with his *Elements of Elocution*.[10]

Walker and Sheridan were actors, educators, lecturers, writers, and lexicographers—typical of the interests and practical needs of the late eighteenth century.

Gilbert Austin's *Chironomia* [11] was filled with rules for use of the voice and bodily action. Good delivery to Austin, both preacher and educator, was essential in effective communication. He believed that following his rules would improve the voice, and that the eyes, mouth, and bodily movements in general, including gestures, should receive detailed instruction. His work had immense influence both in England and in America.

The elocutionary movement in America was chiefly influenced by Dr. James Rush, with his *Philosophy of the Human Voice*.[12] It was the first and most complete scientific approach to the problem of voice, "the first great analytical inquiry into the physiology of vocal delivery." [13]

Ebenezer Porter, James Barber, William Russell, James Murdoch, Samuel Silas Curry, Andrew Comstock, Leland Powers, Robert Cumnock, Arthur E. Phillips, Thomas C. Trueblood, Robert I. Fulton, represented the development of this emphasis on delivery in the later elocutionary movement in America.

The English rhetoricians of the classical school with their chief attention to Invention, Disposition and Style, did not neglect delivery. Campbell gave a lecture on it; Ward cited Greek and Latin sources to stress that "this is the principal part of an orator's province from whence he is chiefly to expect success in the art of persuasion." Blair pronounced delivery as "most important," and Whately called it "the most important branch of rhetoric." [14]

Later writers on rhetoric in the twentieth century continued to give varied emphasis on delivery. Some ignored it completely; some developed a balanced distribution of invention, disposition, language and

---

[9] Thomas Sheridan, *Lectures on Elocution* (London, printed for J. Dodsley, 1781).

[10] John Walker, *The Elements of Elocution* (3d ed.; London, J. Johnson, 1806).

[11] Gilbert Austin, *Chironomia* (London, printed for T. Cadell and W. Davies, 1806).

[12] James Rush, *Philosophy of the Human Voice* (4th ed.; Philadelphia, Lippincott, Grambo & Co., 1855).

[13] Lester Thonssen, "James Rush," in *Rhetoric and Public Speaking* (New York, H. W. Wilson, 1942), 281.

[14] John Ward, *A System of Oratory*, 2 vols. (London, J. Ward, 1759), 314–316; Hugh Blair, *Lectures on Rhetoric and Belles Lettres* (8th ed.; London, T. Cadell Jun. and W. Davies and W. Greech, Edinburgh, 1801), 383 ff.; Richard Whately, *Elements of Rhetoric*, ed. Douglas Ehninger (Carbondale, Ill., Southern Illinois University Press, 1963), 339–390.

delivery; others concentrated entirely on delivery, or on voice, or on phonetics alone. Some treatises or texts with the title of "Rhetoric," or "Rhetoric and Composition," ignored delivery. John Genung's *Principles of Rhetoric* [15] is such example. A long array of school or college texts of the next century used the same title, but limited the contents to written composition.

Other teachers of speech and writers of texts gave scope to voice, articulation, and bodily action in relation to full exposition of the other elements of public speaking, such as selection of subjects, analysis, forms of support, organization, language, audience adaptation, and types and occasions of speaking.[16] Some of these teachers in their writings placed delivery first; others interspersed it with other topics; still others put it at the end.

Lew Sarett and William Trufant Foster's *Basic Principles of Speech* [17] developed in order, first, the principles of delivery, Part I (twelve chapters), followed by Part Two, Composition (nine chapters). James M. O'Neill and Andrew Thomas Weaver's *The Elements of Speech* [18] was arranged in six parts: I, What Speech Is; II, The Mechanics of Speech; III, Speech Composition; IV, The Psychology of Speech; V, Types of Speech; VI, Kinds of Public Speeches.

Alan Monroe's *Principles and Types of Speech* [19] gave part one to delivery; part two, to composition; parts three and four, to types of speeches.

Others in the elocutionary tradition, expounded only delivery. Charles Woolbert's *The Fundamentals of Speech* [20] announced itself as "a behavioristic study of the underlying principles of speaking and reading, a textbook of delivery."

Irving Lester Winter's *Public Speaking*,[21] despite its title, limits itself to delivery, with a considerable body of selections for student practice.

The major concepts of rhetorical theory, with only *memoria* abandoned, were carried on by many later rhetoricians. There were offshoots in a large body of material given exclusively to delivery, or to phonetics, or to oral reading. Other writings concentrated on special types of

[15] John F. Genung, *Principles of Rhetoric* (Boston, Ginn, 1886).

[16] Loren Reid, *First Principles of Public Speaking* (2d ed.; Columbia, Mo., Artcraft Press, 1962); Donald Bryant and Karl Wallace, *Public Speaking* (2d ed.; New York, Appleton-Century-Crofts, 1960); Eugene White and Clair Henderlider, *Practical Public Speaking* (New York, Macmillan, 1954); Giles Gray and Waldo Braden, *Public Speaking* (2d ed.; New York, Harper, 1963).

[17] Lew Sarett and William T. Foster, *Basic Principles of Speech* (Boston and New York, Houghton Mifflin, 1936).

[18] James M. O'Neill and Andrew Thomas Weaver, *The Elements of Speech* (New York, Longmans Green, 1926).

[19] Alan Monroe, *Principles and Types of Speech* (Chicago, Scott Foresman, 1949).

[20] Charles Woolbert, *The Fundamentals of Speech* (New York, Harper, 1926).

[21] Irving Lester Winter, *Public Speaking* (New York, Macmillan, 1912).

public speaking, including debating, discussion, persuasion, radio and television talks, business and professional speaking. In each case the principles were accompanied by chapters or extended sections on delivery. Thus, though the hard core of classical rhetoric persisted, the tremendous changes of twentieth century civilization, with technology, scientific, liberal education, cultural, professional and scientific and industrial growth, and the political changes, inevitably led to rhetorical specialization. The principles were derived from the centuries of rhetorical theory and practice. The applications registered the needs and demands of the times.

History of the Philosophy of Delivery

A philosophy of delivery calls for a review of the range of concept and the significance of the elements involved.

What comprises the area of delivery?

To Aristotle and the Greeks it was ὑπόκρισις, a term that referred to voice placing and volume, pitch, rhythm; a term closely related to style (diction, λέξις); as a concept expressing the concrete presentation of communication in contrast to the abstract formulation of the process.

To Cicero, delivery was *pronuntiatio* (a term applying mainly to the voice) or *actio* (bodily activity, especially gestures). Cicero used *actio* as the comprehensive term to cover both voice and bodily action.[22] Quintilian thus summarized the concept:

Delivery is called *pronuntiatio* from the use of the voice, and more often *actio* from the gesture. Cicero describes *actio* as *sermo* (speech), *vox* (voice), and as *eloquentia corporis* (*motus*), "eloquence of the body" (movement). By whatever name we call it, delivery produces desired emotions by voice, look, bodily *carriage*.[23]

Quintilian, the schoolmaster, expounded in detail the nature and methods of improving the use of voice and bodily activity in speech.

Medieval and modern students of rhetoric have continued to identify delivery with vocal and physical expression, that is, what the audience hears and what it sees. Advances of the present century, however, have contributed more knowledge concerning these areas than existed during all the preceding centuries. Physiology and anatomy have given much added insight into the speaking mechanism. Acoustics has opened the way to a much better understanding of speech sounds, and has helped with the foundation of speech science. Phonetics, linguistic, regional, and experimental, has established concrete approaches to the control of

[22] Cicero, *op. cit.*, III, lvi, lix, lx, lxi; *Orator*, vi, viii, ix.
[23] Quintilian, *op. cit.*, XI, iii.

articulation and pronunciation. Psychology, in the modern sense, unknown to Aristotle, has penetrated into the ways of individual personality, group behavior, and through methods of measuring opinions and attitudes, an evaluation of persuasive methods and results. These various disciplines with their systematic exploration of the details of delivery have enlarged the understanding of the communicative act itself—even if such knowledge has not produced more impressive public speakers than ever before existed. At least the general population, according to modern science and education, has improved its communicative efficiency through the substitution of constructive habits.

Areas of Delivery

In view of the history of rhetoric and the later applications, what then are the areas that comprise delivery? They are,

1. The speaker's preparation for his speech or speeches
2. Method of communication in relation to the composition of the material
3. Method of voice usage, including rate, pitch, intensity, quality
4. Articulation and pronunciation
5. Physical activity, including movement, posture, gestures
6. Speaking personality

These elements are judged in terms of audibility and intelligibility, variety, vocal fluency, vocal pleasantness, vocal meaningfulness (good will, purpose), vocal flexibility, rapport with audience and circular response.[24]

Preparation for Delivery

Adequate explanation of the scope and method of delivery lies partly in an understanding of the speaker's method of immediate and wider preparation. What of his education and experience that would relate to his platform methods and effectiveness? Franklin D. Roosevelt, for example, had much early training in French, German, and other languages. Did such linguistics contribute anything to his skills before audiences? At Groton Academy the program was essentially classical—Latin, Greek, English literature, Mathematics, with daily required religious services. Did such curriculum contribute more to his speaking skills than would have more studies in economics, modern history, and English composition and speech making? (Groton required debating.) The same questions would apply to his educational experiences at Harvard. Is it significant that there he had a course in "Forms of Public Address," under George P. Baker, the leading teacher of argumentation

---

[24] A. Craig Baird and Franklin H. Knower, *General Speech* (3d ed.; New York, McGraw-Hill, 1963), 162–221.

and public speaking? His academic record there was "average." Do superior school and college grades predict superior speaking powers? [25]

More specifically, how did Roosevelt prepare his talks? The evidence would cite the advice to him from many people on the content of a given speech. He kept a voluminous speech file. From the suggestions, including materials from such notes, he would draft the outline of his address. He tells us that for a given speech he would often develop five or six successive drafts. He would study, review, and read aloud each draft, criticizing, inserting dictated or personally written changes. "Because of the many hours he spent in its preparation, by the time he delivered a speech, he knew it almost by heart." [26]

Robert Sherwood, Samuel Rosenman, Harry Hopkins, and Raymond Moley were among the so-called ghost writers. But "decisions as to ideas and the final language in which they were to be couched were inevitably made by Roosevelt himself." [27]

John Kennedy had also his speech collaborators, including Theodore Sorenson, Arthur Schlesinger, Jr., but again the preparation of specific speeches was largely the product of Kennedy himself.

What happens as a speaker delivers his message?

Actual delivery involves two speeches, the one which the audience directly hears and may later read, and the "speech behind the speech" reflecting wide array of the speaker's earlier education, family influences, travels, reading, writing, important contacts with specific people, military and civilian career, and a considerable number of other factors that directly affect the materials selected, the composition of the address, and the habits of its author in his platform methods.

Such perspective on preparation of the speech may imply fullfledged biographical research. But, as Lester Thonssen suggests, the biographical details must be closely related to the man as a speaker.[28]

Delivery and the Composition of the Material

Analysis of delivery as related to the speaker's previous oral or written composition for the occasion concerns itself with the impromptu, extempore, memorized, or manuscript-reading presentation of the materials.

Impromptu delivery is theoretically without previous preparation of

[25] For detailed study of F. D. Roosevelt as speaker, see Ernest Brandenburg and Waldo W. Braden, in A History and Criticism of American Public Address, Vol. 3, ed. Marie Hochmuth (New York, Longmans Green, 1955), 458–530.

[26] Ibid., 465.

[27] Ibid., 471.

[28] Lester Thonssen and A. Craig Baird, Speech Criticism (New York, Ronald Press, 1948), 435.

ideas, language, vocal or other agencies to adjust to the audience. It is without previous planning or notice. It is on the spot communication—a dinner occasion, an informal conversation, a legislative debate in which instant and unexpected reply is called for, or a press conference or question period in which often irrelevant queries are addressed to the speaker.

Extempore speech, on the other hand, grows out of a careful assembling of materials, organization, and even phrasing. The speaker may use notes to guide his delivery. In his selection of ideas, their arrangement, the evidence, and other illustrative details, he takes pre-stock of the needs and interests of his prospective listeners. In actual presentation he may omit or add to ideas. He may reshape the order of his discourse. Chiefly his extempore skill lies in his oral language. Extemporization by no means implies lack of preparation.

The extempore speaker, especially sensitive to the audience, and the effort at circular (two way) response centers on his ideas rather than on words. The language develops spontaneously. If he is a seasoned speaker, he will adequately clothe his purposes and content with effective vocabulary.

Franklin D. Roosevelt was excellent in extemporization, despite his constant reading of speeches. He made many changes in the prepared manuscripts. Robert Sherwood testifies that "those who worked with him on speeches were all too well aware that he was no slave to his prepared text. He could and did ad-lib at will, and that was something which always amused him greatly." [29]

Impressive speeches have grown spontaneously from seeming impromptu expression. Notable, was David E. Lilienthal's expression of his beliefs as given before a session of the Joint Congressional Committee on Atomic Energy, February 4, 1947. The question before the committee was whether Lilienthal should be confirmed as chairman of the Commission. Senator Kenneth McKeller of Tennessee, ancient foe of Lilienthal, accused the latter of communistic leanings. One point of the questioning cut Lilienthal deeply—the reference to the European origin of his parents (they were born in Czechoslovakia). Pursuing this line of inquiry, the Senator asked, "The truth is that your sympathies were very leftist, are they not?" The witness gave an extemporaneous, unrehearsed expression of his defense and his beliefs, "one of the most moving and eloquent definitions of democracy heard on Capitol Hill in many a year." This Lilienthal creed was widely reprinted, was lauded in many an editorial and radio commentary, and included in anthologies.[30]

[29] Brandenburg and Braden, *op. cit.*, 480.
[30] A. Craig Baird, *Representative American Speeches: 1946–47* (New York, H. W. Wilson, 1947), 150–158.

Extemporization has been generally preferred to the other methods of delivery. Its weaknesses are tendencies to garrulity, haphazard selection of words, glibness at the expense of solid preparation of ideas. The timing may also suffer. Organization balance may be absent. The groping for effective words may block the real communication. The advantages of such delivery nevertheless are obvious: the audience integration, the flexibility of ideas as uttered at the time and place. Good extemporization assumes a mature language facility and a speaker thoroughly steeped in his subject and its appeals to a given audience.

The third method of delivery in relation to the composition is the oral reading of the speech. When the occasion, politically or educationally important, depends on accurate recording of what is said, the manuscript presentation is often used. The politician, for example, may distribute to the press his speech before the address—and he usually follows closely the text that may already be on the way to the press.

Such reliance on the manuscript is satisfying to those who struggle to reduce their message to the time limits and who strive meticulously for the effective phrases. In addition the speaker is relieved of the strain of audience adjustment, for he has already anticipated the moods and attitudes of his prospective listeners. He has previously caught the inspiration of the forth appearing audiences. He has embodied these factors in audience identification. As he reads, his words come alive as if coined on the spot.

Too often, however, the manuscript delivery becomes much reading of words without the living communication. Many oral readers lack the skill to equate their manuscript with the flexible situation called for. Harry Truman and other extempore speakers have admitted their inadequate reading of a speech. They have felt a void in their audience projection. William Jennings Bryan, before the Democratic convention in Chicago on July 8, 1896, evoked tremendous applause and approval in his completely extempore oration. It included direct refutation of preceding speeches. A month later on August 12th in his formal acceptance speech in Madison Square Garden, New York City, he read his manuscript and filled it with logic rather than with passionate appeal. One third of his bored audience walked out.

A fourth relationship exists between the speaker and his composition —that of the memorized delivery. Such speeches are those to be repeated often (such as Conwell's "Acres of Diamonds," delivered about six thousand times). Sales talks and popular lectures are examples. Albert J. Beveridge, U. S. Senator and the stirring debater and speaker during the decade after 1898, wrote many of his formal speeches. He wrote his "Star Empire" address in full and carefully revised the manuscript. The final revision he memorized and practiced it before delivery.

Memorization for him was easy. Said a commentator, "I was a reporter for the *Indianapolis Star* for several years that Mr. Beveridge was engaged in public affairs. He practically did not deviate at all from the typewritten manuscript in delivering his addresses, although he did not keep a note before him. After preparing a speech he seemed to know it by heart, even as to the very language." [31]

The memorized delivery usually suffers from an obvious malady: it sounds memorized and therefore uncommunicative. The concentration on words creates a barrier to the transfer of ideas and to the flexible oral phrasing. A few successful speakers, with unusual retentiveness, have delivered with ease their memorized compositions. Robert G. Ingersoll, for example, could repeat verbatim long passages from Shakespeare and other sources. His own speeches he easily memorized and often delivered with few or no notes. On the other hand he was completely at home with extemporization in the courtroom, in popular lectures and in his speeches of tribute.

Most speakers falter at this tax on their memory. They spend an undue amount of time on such preparation, and in the delivery itself break their communication as they struggle for the prepared words.

The ideal speaker, we assume, has the ability to adapt his discourse to the requirements of a specific audience. With his full preparation and his memoriter skill, he can extemporize, or read his document, or repeat it from memory, in every case with full audience identification and response. Much depends, as we have said, on the personality of the speaker, the specific demands of the speaking situation. The goal in every case is maximum communication. The means cannot be arbitrarily determined.

Voice

Perhaps the most significant aspect of delivery is the use of voice. Voice, with its attributes of rate, pitch and pitch variation, loudness or intensity, and quality, has been given the central position in oral communication with bodily action, by the representative rhetoricians, including Aristotle, Quintilian, Thomas Wilson, Hugh Blair, Richard Whately, Rush, and later authorities in this field. Specialists in phonetics, like Grant Fairbanks, have added much to the later knowledge of voice.

Quintilian, for example, discussed in detail the proper management of voice. Power of voice is estimated by quantity and quality. Quantity is on a continuum from much to little. Moderate intensity is the aim of excellent delivery. Quality varies from clear, or husky, full or weak,

[31] Cited by Herold T. Ross in "Albert J. Beveridge," in N. W. Brigance, *History and Criticism of American Public Address* (New York, McGraw-Hill, 1945), Vol. 2, 35.

smooth or rough, hard or flexible, sharp or flat, with long or short breath. The tone should be sweet, not grating. The middle tones should be cultivated. Variety of tone and avoidance of monotony are needed. The bawling tone is to be avoided, or that without animation, or the straining of the voice, the panting, coughing, or singing tone.[32]

The good voice meets the standard of audibility. Intensity and pitch are properly controlled. It has fluency, a matter partly of rate as determined by the types of materials presented under specific speaking conditions. The satisfactory voice is pleasant, free from qualities that interfere with audience acceptability. Such voice also supports the speaker's meanings. This voice is flexible, steady, authoritative, credible, clear, simple. It is free from arbitrary and mechanical variations.[33]

Pronunciation and Articulation

Classical rhetoricians, despite their focussing on *pronunciatio* as including both voice, and the details of its production, were not too precise in their treatment of vowels and consonants and the other articulatory aspects. Quintilian, for example, commented that pronunciation should be "easy, clear, agreeable, polished, and free from rustic or foreign taints." [34] He was vague in the meaning of these terms and the methods of achieving clearness and other articulatory excellence.

With the more systematic study of voice, in eighteenth century England, some English rhetoricians had considerable insight into these problems. George Campbell and others of that time were promising precursors of the later knowledge of articulation. Campbell divided delivery into "grammatical pronunciation" and "rhetorical pronunciation." Grammatical pronunciation consisted of "articulating audibly, and distinctly, the letters, whether vowels or consonants, assigning to each its appropriate sound, in giving the several syllables their just quantity, and in placing the accent, or as some call it, the syllabic emphasis, in every word, on the proper syllable." Rhetorical pronunciation was "giving such an utterance to the several words in a sentence, as shown in the mind of the speaker's strong perception, or as it were, feeling of the truth and justness of the thought conveyed by them, and in placing the rhetorical emphasis in every sentence, on the proper word, that is, on the word which by being pronounced emphatically, gives the greatest energy and clearness to the expression." [35]

With the increased knowledge of anatomy, the experimental concen-

---

[32] Quintilian, *op. cit.*, XI, iii.
[33] Baird and Knower, *op. cit.*, Chap. 11.
[34] Quintilian, *op. cit.*, XI, iii.
[35] George Campbell, *Lectures on Systematic Theology and Pulpit Eloquence* (Boston, W. Wells and T. B. Wait, 1810), 197 ff.

tration on pronunciation and articulation, and electrical recordings and other mechanical aids, twentieth century knowledge of this area of delivery was greatly widened.

Articulation refers to the systematic modification of vocal tones to form vowel and consonant sounds used in speech.[36] Sounds unacceptable to auditors are misarticulated. Pronunciation, a broader term than articulation, refers to the acceptable utterance of a language sound, that which occurs in individual words without substitutions, additions, omissions, inversions, or misplaced accents.

Physical Activity

Ancient rhetoric and all later rhetorical theory since agree that *actio* or physical activity in speaking deals with posture, gestures, and bodily movements. The speaker's action, his position, appearance, manner, movements, habits of physical adjustment to his audience as he speaks— serve important communicative purposes apart from the vocal symbols. Such physical activity, although a supplement rather than a substitute for speech, is nevertheless an integral part of the total speech act. Its improper functioning may do much to destroy effective communication.

Gestures, and other physical expressions, for example, serve a major function in "orienting the listener to the linguistic expression of an idea. They provide a setting, a climate for the language which expresses a feeling or attitude." [37]

Quintilian, among the classicists, was especially interested in bodily action in delivery. He reviewed systematically the movements of the head, eyes, face, nose, neck, arms, hands, fingers, dress, feet, bodily stance, position, stage movement, and other aspects of action, and provided numerous rules for speaking improvements.

John Ward, among English rhetoricians, also gave elaborate advice concerning the management of eyes, and all other bodily expressions.[38]

Hugh Blair questioned the value of Quintilian's detailed rules for bodily action, and suggested that "the study of action in public speaking, consists chiefly in guarding against awkward and disagreeable motions; and in learning to perform such as are natural to the speaker, in the most becoming manner." [39]

Physical activity before an audience presumably provides clues concerning the speaker and so helps or hinders his communicativeness; signals his purposes in the speech; and through government and direction

---

[36] Baird and Knower, *op. cit.*, Chap. 12.
[37] *Ibid.*, 199.
[38] John Ward, *op. cit.*, I, 342–359.
[39] Blair, *op. cit.*, 448.

of these bodily expressions, aids in holding attention, conveying meaning, and stimulating the listener to the desired response to the speaker's
speaking aims.

Personality

Behind the voice, articulation, language, bodily activity is the personality of the communicator. These techniques of vocal and bodily
expression obviously refer basically to the intellectual and psychological
self of the agent, as his communication reaches the auditors and observers who are to react. Even before the speaker begins, his traits
begin to stand out. His appearance, dress, momentary mannerisms,
movements, eyes, face—all furnish initial clues to the man himself.

As his speech develops, the various elements of delivery continue to
reflect the mind, and emotions, and habits of the communicator. The
speaker-audience relationship becomes evident in the audience projection or lack of it, the familiarity of the speaker with his ideas, his
fumbling with notes, his striving to recall, or, on the other hand, his
close correlation between his utterances and his message.

His voice is an important index of the person. The voice and body
reflect stage fright, tight tones, breathiness. The rate may be unduly
accelerated or retarded as his intellectual or emotional processes function haphazardly. His pitch intensity, and other voice elements, again,
mark his personality.

Similarly pronunciation and articulation will make plain his culture,
geographically and educationally. The slurring of words and the general sloviness becomes so much evidence by which the student may
decipher something of what lies behind the speech as delivered.

The bodily character, nervousness (or lack of it), excessive, or no
gestures, physical stolidity, random movements and uncontrolled or impressive posture—again are of the inner man.

Thus reacting observers and listeners, consciously or otherwise, read
into the delivery the warmth of personality (or lack of it), enthusiasm
or indifference, aggressiveness, or unassertiveness, mental and emotional
power or weakness, belief or uncertainty, modesty or boastfulness, op-
timism or pessimism, vanity of self deprecation, strong or weak conviction, mental and moral courage or its absence, selfishness, altruism.
Speakers may dissemble some of these traits. Trained psychologists will
be more alert to note some of them. Our assumption, however, is that
these personality factors govern directly these outward attributes of
delivery and so become the major agencies in the employment of voice,
pronunciation, bodily action, and audience projection.

Philosophical Perspective

Delivery, like the other elements of the rhetorical parts, is to be identified with the whole. "The whole man speaks." Communication is a single total process with idea, supports, language, and delivery functioning as a unit. All of these powers of the individual—thought, organization, words, delivery—act together "spontaneously at the moment of expression." The binding factor is the purpose in each case to affect an audience response. This end or aim is also not simply to ensure audience reaction to the communicative agent, but to do so in a purposeful direction. The ends of rhetoric, as we have stated, are to contribute knowledge, instruction and guidance that make for a "good society." These ends, then, become the foundation for an understanding of the true character of rhetoric "as truth."

This goal, in turn, determines the selection and development of invention, disposition, language, and delivery of a given discourse. But these are means rather than the end. In their application they are techniques and not ends. Delivery, then, is a technique to further the purpose of the speaker. In that purpose the voice and bodily action must serve but be subservient to the ideas being presented. Invention and ideas are uppermost. What are these concepts that the speaker would transfer? They represent his thinking or reason in its classificational, causal relationships. They constitute the propositions stated or implied to be delivered.

Reason, we have agreed, is "logical proof," and is interwoven with "pathetic proof" (emotion), and "ethical proof" (personal factors). Invention, with its mental, emotional, and personal details, is the one justification for the speech. Delivery in the communicative process has an ancillary role. In some rhetorical examples it is absent. In other situations it is essential if the message is to be addressed to a listening-observing audience. If it properly serves the communicative thesis and details, it is to be neither artificially exuberant nor utterly expressionless. The rhetorical principle, then, is that of the primacy of sound and creative thinking and its interpretation through motivative appeals, structure, and language.

The question of delivery has from the beginning divided rhetoricians. As we suggested above, Aristotle questioned the need for strong emphasis on delivery if the audience is sophisticated. Whately discounted training in delivery because, if the techniques and rules were closely followed, bad mechanistic results would follow.

The issue was joined in the development of the English elocutionary movement. The two schools of thought were illustrated by Thomas Sheridan and John Walker.

Sheridan advocated the "natural" manner of delivery. He objected to the techniques that interfered with "spontaneous delivery." Said he in his lectures on *Elocution,* protesting against artificiality in delivery:

. . . by which all public speakers are to guide themselves is obvious and easy. Let each, in the first place, avoid all imitation of others; let him give up all pretensions to art, for it is certain that it is better to have none, than not enough; and no man has enough, who has not arrived at such perfection of art, as wholly to conceal his art; a thing not to be compassed but by the united endeavours, of the best instruction, perfect patterns, and constant practice. Let him forget that he ever learned to read; at least, let him wholly forget his reading tones. Let him speak entirely from his feelings; and they will find much truer signs to manifest themselves by, than he could find for them. Let him always have in view, what the chief end of speaking is; and he will see the necessity of the means proposed to answer the end. The chief end of all public speakers is to persuade; and in order to persuade, it is above all things necessary, that the speaker, should at least appear himself to believe, what he utters; but this can never be the case, where there are any evident marks of affectation or art. On the contrary, when a man delivers himself in his usual manner, and with the same tones and gesture, that he is accustomed to use, when he speaks from his heart; however awkward that manner may be, however ill-regulated the tones, he will still have the advantage of being thought sincere; which of all others, is the most necessary article, towards securing attention and belief; as affectation of any kind, is the surest way to destroy both.[40]

Opposed to Sheridan with his philosophy of minimum training in delivery was John Walker, with his *Elements of Elocution,* and many other books on pronunciation, elocution, and composition. He led the "mechanistic" school which laid great stress on following many specific rules. Walker said,

Elocution, in the modern sense of the word, seems to signify that pronunciation which is given to words when they are arranged into sentences and form discourse. . . .

Elocution, therefore, according to this definition of it, may have elements or principles distinct from those of pronunciation in its most limited sense; and we may consider the elements of elocution, not as these principles which constitute the utterance of single words, but as those which form the just enunciation of words in dependence on each other for sense: at this point the present work commences. The delivery of words formed into sentences, and these sentences formed into discourse, is the object of it; and as reading is a correct and beautiful picture of speaking; speaking, it is presumed, cannot be more successfully taught, than by referring us to such rules as instruct us in the art of reading. . . .

The sense of an author being the first object of reading, it will be neces-

[40] Sheridan, *op. cit.,* 375.

sary to inquire into those divisions and subdivisions of a sentence which are employed to fix and ascertain its meaning: this leads to a consideration of the doctrine of punctuation. . . .

Punctuation may be considered in two different lights; first, as it clears and preserves the sense of a sentence, by combining those words together which are united in sense, and separating those that are distinct; and secondly, as it directs to such pauses, elevations, and depressions of the voice, as not only mark the sense of the sentence more precisely, but give it a variety and beauty which recommend it to the ear; for in speaking, as in other arts, the useful and agreeable are almost always found to coincide; and every real embellishment promotes and perfects the principal design.[41]

Whereas the "naturalists" insisted that basic principles of delivery came from nature herself and that therefore the speaker needed to look within himself for guidance, the "mechanists" believed that naturalism needed to be developed through elaborate rules that would embody "nature."

The mechanistic approach received strong reinforcement in the United States in the nineteenth century, partly under the influence of François Delsarte (1811–1871), a French teacher of singing and dramatic art. According to him since audiences can view only the external activities and hear only the tones, therefore these elements should be heavily attended to. The training of the voice and bodily action were most important. His school prepared and applied an elaborate system of gestures and vocal control instructions to express properly the shades of emotion and thought.

Such "scientific" system would provide the key to the proper audible and bodily interpretations. Teachers of elocution in America reflected somewhat these Delsartean methods. James Rush, James Murdock, Robert Fulton, and Thomas Trueblood, though they insisted on naturalness, logic, and content, nevertheless were strongly identified with superficial and mechanical treatment of delivery. "Elocution" thus fell into disrepute and the large number of private teachers of "elocution and dramatic art" lost their leadership.

Samuel Silas Curry (1847–1921), with his School of Expression in Boston, was identified with the "natural" school. He emphasized the trained mind and imagination, the need to work "from within outward," and to function in speaking as a "unified person." Delivery should be primarily for the training of the mind and for the development of creative thinking. He criticised the followers of James Rush because they were "imitative." Murdock, Curry stated, had put too much emphasis on voice and with artificial tones. The Delsarte system he questioned as placing too much emphasis on pantomime. Curry did recognize in

41 Walker, *op. cit.*, 6, 12, 148–149.

Delsarte some worthwhile principles of training. He objected to "elo-cution" and substituted "expression." Complete adherence to his ap-proaches would encourage a loose handling of content and haphazard delivery. This Boston speech teacher embodied, however, a transition in his philosophy and methods to the more balanced treatment and methodology later expressed in the emerging speech departments of the American colleges and universities.[42]

Conclusion

Delivery is a process of audible, intelligible, and pleasurable recep-tion. At its best, circular response, unbroken, occurs.

Such maximum reception and response depend upon effective voice, articulation, bodily expression and speaking personality. These tech-niques in turn function from the speaker's lively sense of communica-tion, his insight into the personalities and attitudes of his listener-observers, and their corresponding reciprocity in the communicative activity.

Such communication, with its audience projection, is a single opera-tion by the total person. He realizes and appropriates at every turn the purposes and content of his emerging theme. His social and other aims for the "better society" govern his invention, structure, language, and the techniques of the communicative act itself. Delivery is a subordinate but necessary vehicle in the oral situation.

[42] For discussion of the elocutionary movement, see: Clarence W. Edney, "Eng-lish Sources of Rhetorical Theory in Nineteenth Century America," Chap. 4; Fred-erick W. Haberman, "English Sources of American Elocution," Chap. 8; Mary Margaret Robb, "The Elocutionary Movement and Its Chief Figures," in Karl Wal-lace (ed.), *A History of Speech Education in America* (New York, Appleton-Century-Crofts, 1954). Cf. also Mary Margaret Robb, *Oral Interpretation of Literature in American Colleges and Universities* (New York, H. W. Wilson, 1941).

Projects and Questions

The following problems and exercises suggest brief inquiries, discussions, limited oral and written reports, and wider problems for investigative papers. Many of the topics are broad. Each may be amended, limited, or otherwise adapted to meet individual or group study needs. Or the student may frame other related problems that invite treatment and interest and that promise specific answers.

Chapter 1: Boundaries and Applications

1. Trace the contribution of technological developments in the expansion of communication. Include attention to the development of worldwide communication via satellites.

2. "Speech is the recognized key that distinguishes human beings from animals." Discuss or develop in a paper.

3. Is speech "the one essential civilizing agency"? Discuss.

4. "As the source of all improvements, public speaking was itself improved by industry and application, by observation and experience." (See John Quincy Adams, "Inaugural Oration," *Lectures on Rhetoric and Oratory*, p. 15.) Discuss.

5. "Rhetoric does more harm than good. Socrates, for example, taught how to make the worse cause seem the better." (See Quintilian's *Institutes of Oratory*, III, xvi.) Criticize in a paper.

6. Does Aristotle's justification of rhetoric indicate modifications that would make his four propositions more acceptable to the conditions of modern democratic state? Develop in a four-member panel, each to deal with one proposition.

7. In a paper, apply to the field of sociology or psychology language as the center of the thinking.

8. "Some schools of eloquence embody a national consciousness and so the spoken history of the time." Discuss.

9. Do important speakers shape history or do the events themselves produce the speakers? Does the free will of the orator determine historic changes, or does the environment explain largely the power of the speaker? Develop as a panel discussion, oral report, or paper.

10. "If error and injustice prevail, then such unfortunate conditions are due to the weakness of the speakers themselves." Discuss.

11. "Things that are true and things that are better, are by their very nature easier to prove and to believe in." Discuss.

12. What program may be followed to deal with "sham rhetoricians"?

13. Define rhetoric according to Aristotle and compare his definition with that of one or more of the following: Blair, Campbell, Whately, Genung. Frame your own definition. Be prepared to expand your own comprehensive definition.

14. Write a paper on rhetoric as dealing with one or more of the following elements: (1) art; (2) adaptation; (3) the medium of language and delivery agencies; (4) the character of the audience; (5) affective human nature and attitudes; (6) relation of, to the preservation and progress of a free society and a "good" society.

15. One can "place in terms of rhetoric all those statements by anthropologists, ethnologists, individual and social psychologists, and the like, that bear upon the persuasive aspects of language, the function of language as addressed, as direct or round about appeal to real or ideal audiences, without or within." (See Kenneth Burke, A Rhetoric of Motives, pp. 43–44.) Analyze Burke's concept of rhetoric.

16. "If I had to sum up in one sentence the difference between the 'old' rhetoric and the 'new,' a rhetoric invigorated by fresh insight which the new sciences contributed to the subject, I would reduce it to this: '. . . The key term for the "new rhetoric" would be identification, which can include a partially unconscious factor in appeal'." (See Kenneth Burke, "Rhetoric—Old and New," Journal of General Education, V [April, 1951], 203.) Discuss Burke's view of rhetoric and identification.

17. Evaluate Chauncey Goodrich's approach to the concept of rhetoric as oral and written.

18. How shall practical communication be distinguished from literary communciation?

19. Interpret, and defend or reject, Quintilian's conclusion that "rhetoric is the science of speaking well."

20. Evaluate Donald Bryant's definition of rhetoric as "the rationale of informative and suasory discourse."

21. Comment on delivery as a major factor in the concept of rhetoric.

22. Discuss rhetoric applied to texts on English composition.

23. How does the rhetorical aim of discussion differ from that of debate?

24. Is rhetoric to be judged by effect rather than by the artistic excellence of the communicative act? Use this question for group discussion.

25. Discuss the "perfection" approach to determine speaking effectiveness as compared with the "results" approach.

26. Analyze and suggest modifications of the statement that "the speaking situation, therefore, involves at least five factors."

27. Expound and evaluate Wendell Johnson's explanation of the various functions that comprise the communicative process.

28. Review the classical concept of the five "parts" of a given discourse. What has happened to these "parts" in modern rhetorical practice?

29. To what extent should literary considerations of permanence and beauty enter into the judgment of a speech?

30. Comment on Thomas Carlyle's remarks on the "Stump Orator," in Latter Day Pamphlets: "First, that excellent speech, even really excellent, is not and never was, the chief test of human faculty, or the measure of a man's ability, for any true function whatever; on the contrary, that excellent silence needed always to accompany excellent speech, and was and is a much rarer and more difficult gift."

Chapter 2: Relationships to Categories of Learning

1. What is philosophy? In your discussion, comment on philosophy as: (1) inquiry; (2) the evaluation of information; (3) analysis; (4) tentative goals; (5) inferences and beliefs, including cause and effects, hypotheses and assumptions; (6) other aspects of the concept of philosophy.

2. What is the relation of philosophy to the systematization of thought and understanding?

3. Discuss: "Philosophy is a movement or direction toward the best answer rather than an area of ultimate knowledge."

4. Discuss: Philosophy is a search for the truth (the meaning of life, the significance of the world, and of concepts and standards of value).

5. Construct a working concept and definition of each of the following: (1) metaphysics, (2) epistemology, (3) aesthetics, (4) ethics, (5) politics, (6) logic.

6. Differentiate rhetoric from public speaking, speech, oratory, composition, communication.

7. What is the relation of logic or dialectic to rhetoric?

8. What does psychology contribute to rhetoric?

9. Discuss: "Ethics is the chief element in any satisfactory rhetorical system."

10. Discuss: "Rhetoric is the pedagogical instrument for learning the important uses of language."

11. Investigate and report: The general semanticists "offer what amounts to a new philosophy of rhetoric."

12. Evaluate: "What is needed is a new philosophy of rhetoric that takes account of the later influences of such philosophers as Descartes, Peirce, Dewey, Whitehead, Russell, Black."

13. Evaluate: "For twenty-three hundred years, little or no progress or change has occurred in the philosophy of rhetoric."

14. Do you agree with the statement that Campbell "came closest to a philosophy of rhetoric"?

15. "Aristotle's rhetoric forms the best synthesis of rhetorical elements of any rhetoric before or since his time." Develop as a paper or in oral discussion with others familiar with the history of rhetorical theory.

16. "Rhetoric is the counterpart of dialectic." Evaluate.

17. Discuss: "The philosophy of rhetoric remains an unexamined realm." (See Maurice Natanson, "The Limits of Rhetoric," *Quarterly Journal of Speech,* XLI (April, 1955), 135.)

18. "There is no true rhetoric without the dialectic." (See Richard Weaver, *Ethics of Rhetoric,* p. 15.)

19. Prepare a paper in which you analyze and react to Maurice Natanson's "Limits of Rhetoric," *Quarterly Journal of Speech,* XLI (April, 1955), 133–139.

20. Analyze and evaluate Donald Bryant's "Rhetoric: Its Function and Its Scope," *Quarterly Journal of Speech,* XXXIX (December, 1953), 401–424.

21. Differentiate the scientific and rhetorical approaches to communication. What common attitudes have the scientist and the rhetorician?

22. What possible contribution to rhetoric is the mathematical or symbolic logic of Russell and of Alfred North Whitehead? (The question calls for mature investigation.)

23. Discuss the contribution of Charles Woolbert to contemporary rhetorical theory.

24. Discuss: "Rhetoric is the offspring of ethics."

25. What is the relationship of discussion to the art of communication or rhetoric?

26. Differentiate oratory from rhetoric and from general public speaking.

Chapter 3: Analysis, Definition, and Fact

1. What is the relation of analysis to the method of the philosopher?

2. Define "issues" and defend or reject the explanation of issues which labels them: as "fundamental" questions; those as dealing with "truth or falsity"; those as assuming "propositions" to be verified or rejected.

3. Has the system of analysis proposed by Hermogoras become outmoded?

4. Explain the concept of *status* as used by Quintilian and criticize its application.

5. Modern American rhetoricians have vigorously questioned the method of stock issues. How valid is the condemnation of such method of analysis?

6. How do the use of topics and the framing of issues differ from those used by Quintilian or other classical rhetoricians?

7. Explain and evaluate John Dewey's pattern of reflective thinking.

8. Evaluate the "motivated sequence" as a method of organization and analysis of communication.

9. What are "facts"?

10. What is "evidence"? Its relation to "proof"?

11. Explain and evaluate the relative reliability of circumstantial and testimonial evidence.

12. Compare and contrast Quintilian and Aristotle in their treatment of evidence.

13. What are the chief "sources of fact"?

14. What are the tests of competency as a source of evidence?

15. Discuss the problems of minimizing prejudice in the use of evidence.

16. What has the "thought-word-thing" test of relationship to do with the concept of fact and its applications?

17. What is a "referent"? Its relation to the symbol and to the thought?

18. "Observation is the scientific scrutiny of a phenomenon." Discuss.

19. Appraise "dichotomy" as a scientific basis for classification.

20. What divisions, if any, are necessary for scientific classification?

21. What is the scientific attitude toward incomplete evidence?

22. Explain the "abstraction ladder" of S. F. Hayakawa in his *Language in Thought and Action*, p. 169.

23. "In any definition the definition (a) has fewer characteristics than the object, as represented by our nervous system, and (b) the object itself has fewer characteristics than the actual event." Discuss. (Consult Wendell Johnson's *People in Quandaries*, p. 472.)

Chapter 4: Logic and Reason in Discourse

1. What is the place of the intellectual element in communication as compared wtih the psychological, aesthetic, vocal, or other aspects of the process?

2. What is "logical" thinking? In your analysis, refer to reflective thinking

as a systematic procedure; as identified with situational stimuli; as a movement or process; as identified by systematic stages; as concerned with language, facts, analysis, structure, inferences.

3. What is "inference" in relation to an "order" system and to "the implicative whole"?

4. What are typical theories related to the testing of induction?

5. How does the scientist deal with inductive testing? What is the relation of his methodology to the general theory of knowledge? (In your brief discussion, cite any sources that throw light on this problem of the nature of induction and its evaluation.)

6. What are "facts"? How tested? Relation to inference? Relation to "truth"? (Refer to John Dewey and similar sources.)

7. Discuss "causation" as philosophical concept. What, for example, is the relation of causality, to "interaction"? to the "continuity of events"? to an "inferential whole"? to the "complexity of phenomena"?

8. Distinguish mathematical from logical analogy.

9. Discuss briefly the chief defects and fallacies of analogical reasoning in communication.

10. Defend or condemn (briefly) analogy as a scientific method. (Refer to Karl Wallace and others who discuss this problem.)

11. Prepare a report on probability as equivalent to relativity.

12. Analyze and evaluate three aspects of probability as related to the theory of communications: (1) based on observation and enumeration of happenings and failures; (2) calculation of chances; (3) application to aggregates and individual instances in aggregates. (Refer to Corax and to Aristotle in their rhetorical treatment of probability.)

13. What are Mill's canons of causality? Discuss briefly Mill's "method of agreement and method of difference." What place, if any, have such canons in the foundational concepts of public address?

14. What is deduction?

15. Diagram the Aristotelian system to indicate the (1) truth, (2) scientific demonstration, (3) dialectic demonstration, (4) rhetorical proof through the enthymeme, probability, "signs," and examples.

16. "It is quite true that syllogizing may prove a very interesting pastime, but we delude ourselves if we think it is likely to be of any real service in the serious business of reasoning." (See F. W. Westaway, *Scientific Method*, p. 169.) Comment on this conclusion. In your discussion refer to the point of view of F. C. S. Schiller, in his *Logic for Use*, or some similar source.

17. Comment on the approach to the problem of the enthymeme as discussed by Charles Mudd, and by Lloyd Bitzer. (See footnotes of this chapter for references.)

18. Explain Aristotle's general and special topics and his "twenty-eight" lines of argument.

19. Evaluate Brockriede and Ehninger's interpretation of Toulmin's suggestions concerning the uses of argument.

20. What are some principles to be applied to the use of hypotheses?

21. What is the coherence theory of truth? The pragmatic theory? The correspondence theory? (Refer to such sources as D. S. Robinson's *Principles of Reasoning*, Chap. 26.) Expound your own theory.

22. What is the psychological and logical basis of refutation in communication?

23. Classify representative fallacies. Differentiate those related to definition, language, facts, analysis, inferences, emotional appeals.

24. Evaluate logical proof as treated by Richard Whately in his *Elements of Rhetoric*.

25. Discuss the places of the enthymeme in rhetorical theory.

26. Prepare a paper in which you evaluate the treatment of deduction by one of the following: Schiller, Dewey, Toulmin, McBurney.

27. Evaluate Charles Woolbert's treatment of logic in a system of persuasion.

28. Discuss probability in mathematics or logic. (See, for example, D. S. Robinson, *Principles of Reasoning*, Chap. 17.)

Chapter 5: Politics and Public Address

1. Write a paper dealing with the relation of politics to rhetoric as reflected in Aristotle and similar sources of that time.

2. What is the philosophical concept of "politics"?

3. What is the relation of rhetoric to politics, and the relation of both politics and rhetoric to ethics?

4. Discuss the end of government. (Let your analysis take account of Karl Wallace on "Rhetoric, Politics, and Education," in Donald Bryant [ed.], *Rhetorical Idiom*.)

5. Discuss types of political life favorable to rhetoric.

6. Discuss the problem or rhetoric, public policy, law and justice. (Let your analysis include consideration of Lippmann's *Public Philosophy*.)

7. Analyze the communicative process in its political context.

8. Discuss the interdependence of rhetoric and modern democracy.

9. Evaluate Walter Bagehot's discussion of rhetoric and politics. (See Drummond and Hunt's *Persistent Questions in Public Discussion*, and other sources for Bagehot.)

10. Prepare a term paper on general education, rhetoric, and political education in the United States.

11. Prepare a paper on freedom of speech in the United States during World War II.

12. Evaluate John Stuart Mill's "Of Liberty of Thought and Discussion."

13. Discuss the "forensic mind," with special reference to Richard Murphy's "The Forensic Mind," in *Studies in Speech and Drama in Honor of Alexander Drummond*.

14. Evaluate Graham Wallas' political concepts in relation to communication. (See "Group Cooperation" in *Our Social Heritage*.)

15. Discuss Plato's *Republic* in relation to the problem of communication.

16. Evaluate John Locke on representative government in relation to the problem of communication.

17. Discuss one of the following issues dealing with politics and communication (organize a panel, or let each topic be assigned to a member of the group): (1) What form of government is best? (2) What of the worth of each member of society? (3) Does each have a duty to support the state? (4) What of the rights of the minorities? (5) What is the problem of developing mature public opinion? (6) What is the nature of liberty? (7) What is the best kind of education for democratic ends and free speech and press?

18. Outline the theory that relates democratic government to freedom of speech, press, and thought. In illustration of your discussion, cite the philosophy of one of the following: Plato, Locke, Hobbes, John Stuart Mill, Walter Lippmann.

19. Comment: "The modern media of mass communication do not lend themselves easily to a confrontation of opinions." (See Walter Lippmann, *The Public Philosophy*, p. 128.)

20. Comment: "Students of Aristotle's *Rhetoric* have long been aware of the two chief passages which explicitly associate rhetoric with politics and ethics. . . . If the two passages do nothing more, they flatly assert a relationship between politics and rhetoric which in mid-twentieth century the two fields, both blessed and cursed with their specialism, have half-forgotten and often ignored." (See Karl Wallace, "Rhetoric and Politics," in *The Rhetorical Idiom*, p. 79.)

21. "As rhetoric and politics become more scientific, they draw further apart." Discuss.

22. Analyze in detail Everett Lee Hunt's "Rhetoric and Politics," as read at a meeting of the Pennsylvania Speech Association, University of Pittsburgh, October, 1963.

23. Discuss one or more of the following statements as paraphrased from Thonssen and Baird's *Speech Criticism*, Chapter 18: (1) Are classical treatises the yardsticks for excellence in oratory? (2) Is there a final philosophy of discourse? (3) How can a closer union between politics and public address be established? (4) Comment: "The enemies of all liberty flourish and grow strong in the dark of enforced silence." (5) Comment: "The revival of certain features of the Isocratic doctrine is overdue." (6) Comment: "The closer union of politics and public address will ensure for speeches a more permanent place in historical records." (7) Comment: "There is a logic of discourse, the goal of which is the attainment and protection of personal liberty." (8) What is a basis of tolerance? (9) What are the limits of free speech?

Chapter 6: Ethical Responsibilities

1. "The nature of personality and its relation to the ethics of the speaker." Discuss.

2. Interpret "ethics" in Aristotle's *Rhetoric* and in his *Ethics*.

3. Discuss Quintilian's treatment of ethics in his *Institutes of Oratory*, Book XII.

4. Weigh the practical implications of the concept of ethics in communication.

5. Analyze the problem of ethical responsibilities and mass communication.

6. Discuss the "social context" theory of the ethics of oral communication, with special reference to Brembeck and Howell's *Persuasion*, Chap. XII.

7. Report on Bryant and Wallace's contribution to the role of ethics in their *Fundamentals of Public Speaking*, (rev. edition), Chap. XVII.

8. Discuss John Dewey's outline of a critical theory of ethics as applied to communication. (See his *Outlines of a Critical Theory of Ethics*, Hillory House, New York, 1957.)

9. Evaluate Franklyn Haiman's contribution to the role of ethics in public address. (See, for example, "A Reexamination of the Study of the Ethics of Persuasion," *Central States Speech Journal*, III [March, 1952], 4–9.)

10. Present a paper on Richard Weaver's concept of ethics in communication.

11. Evaluate Douglas Ehninger's discussion of "decision by debate," *Quarterly Journal of Speech*, XLV (October, 1959), 282 ff.

12. Evaluate Richard Murphy's analysis of the problem of ethics in communication. (See, for example, his "Preface to an Ethics of Rhetoric," in Bryant's *Rhetorical Idiom*.)

13. Discuss Robert Oliver's concept of ethics in communication. (See, for example, his *The Psychology of Persuasive Speech*, Chaps. 2, 3, 16.)

14. Compare and contrast Plato and Aristotle in their approach to the problem of ethics and rhetoric. Comment on Aristotle's concept of happiness (well-being); his description of "good things"; his doctrine of "the golden mean."

15. What of intelligence as a factor in personality and of ethics in persuasion?

16. What of the contribution of desirable behavior to persuasion through *ethos*? What of the speaker's attitudes and interests as factors? His aggressiveness? His self-sufficiency? His objectivity or lack of sensitivity? What of his good will as a trait of social behavior and source of appeal?

17. What is "high moral character" and how important is it in persuasion through *ethos*?

18. How can sincerity, honesty, and similar ethical traits be detected or measured?

19. Compare and contrast the theory of ethics in persuasion as expounded by Brembeck and Howell and by Oliver.

20. Evaluate Charles Woolbert's contribution, if any, to the theory of ethical responsibility in communication.

Chapter 7: Emotional Response

1. Discuss at length the relative place of thought and emotion in communication. Cite Aristotle, Woodrow Wilson, or others on the problem of dealing with the behavior patterns of human beings in speech or writing.

2. What is "pathetic proof" in Aristotle's system? Its relation to "ethical proof"?

3. Discuss the conviction-persuasion dichotomy or duality and the philosophy of monism. (Refer to studies by E. Z. Rowell, and by Dewey and other philosophers and psychologists.)

4. "Students of speech have depended largely on the philosophers, psychologists, social psychologists, and sociologists for the raw material out of which they have constructed their own theories of persuasion." (See Brembeck and Howell, *Persuasion*, Chap. 4, p. 58.) Discuss.

5. Evaluate Charles Woolbert's concepts of persuasion. (Was Woolbert a Watsonian behaviorist?)

6. Evaluate the psychological contribution by Winans to persuasion in his *Public Speaking*.

7. Summarize and appraise the communicative philosophy of Brembeck and Howell in their *Persuasion*.

8. Evaluate in an extended paper Kenneth Burke's concepts of persuasion.

9. What is the relation of emotion to language?

10. Explain the place of suggestion and stereotypes in communication.

11. Compare and contrast Robert Oliver's concepts of persuasion with those of Wayne Minnick in Minnick's *Art of Persuasion*.

12. What was N. W. Brigance's contribution to the concept of persuasion in communication?

13. Discuss concepts of emotion in recent rhetorical theory.

14. What is propaganda? Differentiate "good" from "bad" propaganda.

15. Discuss propaganda, public opinion, and communication.

16. Analyze the problem of propaganda and democratic government.

17. Develop a paper on "professional public relations and propaganda." (Read Stanley Kelley's *Professional Public Relations and Political Power*.)

18. Discuss: "ancient rhetoric and modern propaganda." (See Everett Hunt's "Ancient Rhetoric and Modern Propaganda," *Quarterly Journal of Speech*, XXXVII [April, 1953], 157–60.)

19. Discuss the role of prestige and personality factors associated with ethics. (See L. W. Doob, *Public Opinion and Propaganda*, pp. 371–373.)

20. Discuss psychological warfare as operating at present between nations—its methods as related to communication.

21. Discuss speech education and the teaching about propaganda.

22. Analyze the devices of the Institute of Propaganda. (See footnote reference in this chapter, to C. W. Miller.)

23. Analyze in detail the relationship of fallacies as treated in any volume on reasoning (that is, Robinson's *Principles of Reasoning*, or in a text on argumentation and debate. See, for example, footnote 40 of this chapter.)

24. Comment on Irving Lee's "Conceptions of Emotional Appeals in Rhetorical Theory," *Quarterly Journal of Speech*, VI (October, 1939), 66–86.

25. Discuss: Wendell Johnson's "The Spoken Word and the Great Unsaid," *Quarterly Journal of Speech*, XXXVII (December, 1951), 419–430.

Chapter 8: Language and Style

1. "Language is the most important form of human communication." Discuss.

2. "Language is verbal systematic symbolism." Explain. (See Joshua Whatmough, *Language*.)

3. Discuss: "Language is purposive activity of human beings."

4. "Scientists realize that the very tabulations of their measured conclusion are helplessly dependent upon language." Interpret and evaluate.

5. Explain language as related to (1) symbol, (2) thought, and (3) referent.

6. Explain language as denotative and connotative.

7. "Thought is as wide as the communicator's vocabulary." Discuss.

8. What was the scope of character of Aristotle's treatment of language in his *Rhetoric*?

9. Review and criticize the basic principles and methods of Cicero's theories of language in his *De Oratore* and *Orator*.

10. Compare and contrast Quintilian's theory of language with that of Aristotle or Cicero.

11. Distinguish verbal from non-verbal types of communication.

12. Differentiate language from style.

13. Explain the relation of language to invention; to organization.

14. Discuss the relation of delivery to language.

15. Expound the contribution of *Ad Herennium* to the theory of language.

16. Trace the changes in emphasis on language in communication during the Middle Ages and the Renaissance.

17. Review of the treatment of language by Thomas Wilson in his *Arte of Rhetorique*.

18. How did Peter Ramus influence the treatment of language in the rhetorical system?

19. Review the treatment of language by John Bascom in his *Philosophy of Rhetoric*.

20. Compare and contrast the theory of language of George Campbell with that of Hugh Blair.

21. Expound and illustrate the semantic theory of language in "processes of abstraction."

22. Develop in a paper I. A. Richards' treatment of the metaphor.

23. What was Richards' theory of abstraction?

24. Give a report on Kenneth Burke's theory of rhetoric with special attention to his pentad format.

25. Review Kenneth Burke's philosophy of literary form.

26. What is Wendell Johnson's theory of abstraction? (In your discussion, refer also to Alfred Korzybski and to S. I. Hayakawa.)

27. Comment on language and sincerity.

28. Discuss: "Style is the man."

29. Present the problem of language and mass communication.

30. Differentiate oral from written language. (See, for example, Woolbert's article on this subject.)

31. Present a paper on Donald Bryant's contribution to the theory of style.

32. Analyze *rhythm* in style.

33. Comment on *genus* and *differentia* in definition.

34. Distinguish contextual and derivational modes of definition.

35. Expound as used by semanticists: "organism-as-a-whole," "multiordinal relations," "two-valued orientation," "time binding."

36. Expound the representative elements of style, including clearness, adaptation, embellishment.

37. Compare the Asian, Attic, and Rhodian types of style.

38. Discuss the "golden mean" in style.

39. Discuss Herbert Spencer's "economy of style."

Chapter 9: Structure

1. What is structure in relation to rhetoric?

2. Explain in detail *dispositio* as expounded by Russell Wagner.

3. Explain the relation of analysis to structure. What are the representative methods of analysis?

4. Interpret Aristotle's treatment of structure in discourse.

5. Analyze the principles of structure, including selection, order, relevancy, proportion.

6. Interpret *dispositio* in Cicero's treatises as rhetorical theory.

7. Compare and contrast the Ciceronian and Quintilian treatments of *dispositio*.

8. Explain the "parts of the speech" as treated in classical and in recent writings on rhetoric.

9. Explain the relation of *dispositio* to thought.

10. Discuss the relation of structure to language.

11. How many parts of the speech are essential? Within each part, what

principles govern the demands of the speaker, audience, occasion, speaker's purpose, the distribution of logical, emotional, and ethical elements, and the representative modes of development, such as classificational, logical?

12. How do audience conditions affect the character of the structure in a given discourse?

13. Do distinct characteristics of structure govern the argumentative, expository, descriptive, persuasive types of address?

14. Compare and contrast the treatment of structure by Alan Monroe and Norwood Brigance in their representative writings on communication.

Chapter 10: Communication in Literature

1. Comment: "Literature is a criticism of life."

2. "Literature is an expression of human experience in words well chosen and arranged." Comment.

3. "Rhetoric is speechmaking with significant and immediate social, and historical influence." Comment.

4. "The components of rhetoric, different from those of literature, comprise Inventio, Dispositio, Elocutio, Memoria, and Pronunciatio." Comment.

5. "Common elements of literature and rhetoric are information, persuasion, entertainment, inspiration." Discuss.

6. "Literature and rhetoric have a common theme—human experience; no subject is off limits." Discuss.

7. "The audience for literature is that of readers, functioning in comparative solitude, whereas the audience of the speechmaking is that of a definite group, limited in time and place, and under immediate conditions." Discuss.

8. "Literature deals with general truths, whereas rhetoric aims at interests of a particular group by means of particular truths." Discuss.

9. Evaluate the general methods of literature and of rhetoric in their use of words.

10. Discuss the difference between literature as a fine art and rhetoric as a practical art.

11. Compare and contrast literature and rhetoric in their treatment of ideas.

12. "Literature is a record of beauty rather than a record of facts." Comment.

13. "Literature is essentially emotional and imaginative, whereas rhetoric employs emotion only as a datum." Comment.

14. Compare and contrast literature and rhetoric in their use of ethical and personal appeals.

15. "With literature the moral element is secondary; with rhetoric high ethical motive should be active at all points." Comment.

16. Compare and contrast the literary and rhetorical elements of Aristotle's *Rhetoric* and his *Poetic*.

17. "The chief business of the poet is creation and the chief business of the orator is persuasion" (Donald Bryant). Discuss.

18. "Literature is an enterprise in communication, just as is rhetoric." Discuss.

19. Discuss Kenneth Burke's concept of the respective elements of literature and rhetoric.

20. Analyze René Wallek and Austin Warren's view of literary worth and compare it with your estimate of rhetorical worth.

21. Discuss the relative permanence of literature and of rhetoric. Refer to Winchester and others in their analysis of literary permanence.

22. What is Thomas De Quincey's concept of literature and how does it compare with your concept of rhetoric?

23. Report on Fénelon's *Dialogues on Eloquence* with special reference to his concepts of "good" and "bad" art.

24. Compare the stylistic qualities of a representative speech by Robert G. Ingersoll with the inaugural address by John F. Kennedy.

25. "The use of symbolism marks a real difference between the literary style and that of the orator." Discuss.

26. What is the contribution of *Longinus on the Sublime* to the theory of rhetoric?

Chapter 11: Delivery

1. Discuss the relative importance of delivery as one of the five "parts" of rhetoric (*inventio, dispositio, eloquentia, memoria* and *pronunciatio*).

2. In the historical changes of rhetorical "parts," what has happened to *memoria*? Why?

3. Discuss the importance of delivery in rhetoric.

4. Summarize and comment on Aristotle's treatment of delivery in his *Rhetoric*.

5. Compare the treatment of delivery in Cicero's *De Oratore* and Quintilian's *Institutes of Oratory*.

6. What are the specific elements that comprise the area of delivery?

7. Analyze the relation of the speaker's personality to his delivery.

8. Present a paper dealing with the elocutionary tradition in England before 1700.

9. Explain the rising interest in England in delivery during the eighteenth century.

10. Comment on Gilbert Austin's *Chironomia*.

11. Report concerning the elocutionary movement in America as represented by Curry or other exponent of delivery.

12. Compare the philosophy of Curry concerning delivery with that of Robert Fulton or Thomas Trueblood.

13. Compare and contrast the philosophy of the "naturalistic" with the "mechanistic" approaches to delivery.

14. Summarize the representative methods of delivery as related to the speaker's composition of his address.

15. Review the treatment of delivery by rhetorical theorists, for example, Brigance, Bryant, Wichelns, Wallace, Woolbert, Gray. Construct your own philosophical principles concerning delivery in rhethorical theory.

Bibliography

ADAMS, JOHN QUINCY. *Lectures on Rhetoric and Oratory.* 2 vols. New York and Cambridge: Hilliard & Metcalf, 1810.

Ad Herrenium. In M. *Tulli Ciceronis "De Oratore,"* introd. A. S. WILKINS. Oxford: Clarendon Press, 1890–93.

ALLPORT, F. H. *Social Psychology.* Boston: Houghton Mifflin Co., 1924.

———. *Personality.* New York: Henry Holt & Co., Inc., 1937.

ARISTOTLE. *The Art of Rhetoric,* ed. JOHN H. FREESE. London: William Heinemann, Ltd., 1926.

———. *The Basic Works of Aristotle,* ed. RICHARD MCKEON, tr. W. RHYS ROBERTS *et al.* New York: Random House, Inc., 1941.

———. *The "Rhetoric" of Aristotle,* tr. LANE COOPER. New York: D. Appleton Co., 1932.

———. *The "Rhetoric" of Aristotle,* tr. P. E. C. WELLDON. London and New York: Macmillan & Co., Ltd., 1886.

———. *The "Rhetoric" and "Poetics,"* ed. FRIEDRICH SOLMSEN. New York: Modern Library, 1954.

———. *The Works of Aristotle Translated into English,* ed. W. D. ROSS, 11 vols. Oxford: Clarendon Press, 1924.

AYER, ALFRED J. *Language, Truth, and Logic.* London: Victor Gollancz, Ltd., 1936.

BACON, FRANCIS. *The Advancement of Learning.* Oxford: Clarendon Press, 1891; London and Toronto: J. M. Dent & Sons, Ltd., 1915.

———. *"The Great Instauration"* and *"Novum Organum."* In *English Philosophers from Bacon to Mill,* ed. EDWIN A. BURTT. New York: Modern Library, 1939.

BAGEHOT, WALTER. "The Age of Discussion." In his *Physics and Politics.* New York: Appleton & Co., 1873.

BAIRD, A. CRAIG. *Argumentation, Discussion and Debate.* New York: McGraw-Hill Book Co., Inc., 1950.

BAIRD, A. CRAIG, and KNOWER, F. H. *General Speech* (rev. ed.), New York: McGraw-Hill Book Co., Inc., 1963.

BALDWIN, CHARLES SEARS. *Ancient Rhetoric and Poetic.* New York: The Macmillan Co., 1924.

———. *Medieval Rhetoric and Poetic.* New York: The Macmillan Co., 1928.

BARRETT, WILLIAM. *Irrational Man.* Garden City, N.Y.: Doubleday & Co., Inc., 1958.

———. *What is Existentialism?* New York: Grove Press, Inc., 1964.

BARZUN, JACQUES. *The House of Intellect.* New York: Harper & Row, 1959.

BEARDSLEY, MONROE C. *Thinking Straight.* Englewood Cliffs, N.J.: Prentice-Hall, Inc., 1950.

BERGSON, HENRI. *Creative Evolution,* tr. ARTHUR MITCHELL. New York: Henry Holt & Co., Inc., 1911.

————. *The Creative Mind: An Introduction to Metaphysics,* tr. MABELLE ANDISON. New York: Philosophical Library, Inc., 1946.

BERLIN, ISAIAH. *The Age of Enlightenment.* New York: Mentor Books, 1956.

BIRD, CHARLES. *Social Psychology.* New York: Appleton-Century-Crofts, Inc., 1940.

BLACK, JOHN BENNETT. *Art of History.* London: Methuen & Co., Ltd., 1926.

BLACK, MAX. *Critical Thinking: An Introduction to Logic and the Scientific Method.* Englewood Cliffs, N.J.: Prentice-Hall, Inc., 1946.

————. *Language and Philosophy.* Ithaca, N.Y.: Cornell University Press, 1949.

BLACK, JOHN W., and MOORE, WILBUR E. *Speech: Code, Meaning and Communication.* New York: McGraw-Hill Book Co., Inc., 1955.

BLAIR, HUGH. *Lectures on Rhetoric and Belles Lettres* (8th ed.). 3 vols. London, T. Cadell Jun. and W. Davies in the Strand and W. Greech, Edinburgh, 1801. Also 6th ed., London, A. Strahan and T. Cadell, 1796.

BLANCHARD, BRAND. *The Nature of Thought.* 2 vols. London: Allen & Unwin, Inc., 1939.

BLOOMFIELD, LEONARD. *Language.* New York: Henry Holt & Co., Inc., 1933.

BOAS, FRANZ. *Race, Language, and Culture.* New York: The Macmillan Co., 1940.

————. *The Mind of Primitive Man.* New York: The Macmillan Co., 1938.

BOGARDUS, E. S. *Leaders and Leadership.* New York: Appleton Century Co., 1934.

————. *Democracy by Discussion.* Washington, D.C.: American Council of Public Affairs, 1943.

BORING, EDWIN G., LANGFELD, HERBERT S., and WELD, HARRY P. *Introduction to Psychology* (5th printing). New York: John Wiley & Sons, Inc., 1944.

BRADEN, WALDO, and BRANDENBERG, ERNEST. *Oral Decision Making.* New York: Harper & Row, 1955.

BREASTED, JAMES H., and ROBINSON, JAMES H. *History of Europe, Ancient and Medieval.* Boston: Ginn & Co., 1920.

BREMBECK, W. L., and HOWELL, W. S. *Persuasion.* Englewood Cliffs, N.J.: Prentice-Hall, Inc., 1952.

BRIGANCE, N. W. *History and Criticism of American Public Address.* 2 vols. New York: McGraw-Hill Book Co., Inc., 1943.

————. *Speech.* New York: Appleton-Century-Crofts, Inc., 1952.

————. *Speech Composition.* New York: F. S. Crofts & Co., 1937.

BRINTON, CLARENCE CRANE. *The Shaping of the Modern Mind.* New York: Mentor Books, 1957.

BRITTON, KARL. *John Stuart Mill.* London: Penguin Books, Ltd., 1953.

BRYANT, D. C. *The Rhetorical Idiom.* Ithaca, N.Y.: Cornell University Press, 1958.

BRYANT, D. C., and WALLACE, KARL. *Fundamentals of Public Speaking* (3d ed.). New York: Appleton-Century-Crofts, 1960.

BRYSON, LYMAN (ed.). *The Communication of Ideas.* New York: Harper & Row, 1948.

BURKE, KENNETH. *Counter-Statement.* New York: Harcourt, Brace & Co., 1931.

————. *A Grammar of Motives.* Englewood Cliffs, N.J.: Prentice-Hall, Inc., 1945.

————. *Permanence and Change* (2d ed., rev.). Los Altos, Calif.: Hermes Publications, 1954.

————. *The Philosophy of Literary Form.* Baton Rouge, La.: Lousiana State University Press, 1941.

————. *A Rhetoric of Motives.* Englewood Cliffs, N.J.: Prentice-Hall, Inc., 1950.

York: Random House, Inc., 1939.

————. *Right Thinking.* New York: Harper & Row, 1946.

BUTCHER, S. H. *Some Aspects of Greek Genius.* London: Macmillan & Co., Ltd., 1893.

CAMPBELL, GEORGE. *The Philosophy of Rhetoric,* ed. LLOYD F. BITZER. Carbondale, Ill.: Southern Illinois University Press, 1963.

CARLYLE, THOMAS. *Latter Day Pamphlets.* New York: Harper & Bros., 1850.

CARTWRIGHT, DARWIN, and ZANDER, ALVIN. *Group Dynamics.* Evanston, Ill.: Row, Peterson & Co., 1953.

CASSIRER, ERNST. *Language and Myth,* tr. SUSANNE K. LANGER. New York: Doubleday Anchor Books, Inc., 1953.

CHAFEE, ZECHARIAH, JR. *The Inquiring Mind.* New York: Harcourt, Brace & Co., 1928.

CHASE, STUART. *Guides to Straight Thinking.* New York: Harper & Row, 1956.

————. *The Power of Words.* New York: Harcourt, Brace & Co., 1954.

CICERO. *The Orator,* in *The Orations of Marcus Tullius Cicero,* tr. C. D. YONGE. 4 vols. London: H. G. Bohn, 1852; G. Bell and Sons, 1913.

————. *De Oratore* (3d ed.), ed. A. S. WILKINS. 3 vols. Oxford: Clarendon Press, 1890–1893.

————. *De Oratore,* in *Cicero on Oratory and Orators,* tr. J. S. WATSON. New York: Harper & Bros., 1890.

————. *On Oratory and Orators, with Letters to Quintus and Brutus,* tr. and ed. J. S. WATSON. London: H. G. Bohn, 1855; New York: Harper & Bros., 1890.

CLARK, DONALD L. *Rhetoric in Greco-Roman Education.* New York: Columbia University Press, 1957.

COFFEY, P. *Epistemology: or the Theory of Knowledge.* 2 vols. Gloucester, Mass.: Peter Smith, 1938.

COLUMBIA ASSOCIATES IN PHILOSOPHY. *Introduction to Reflective Thinking.* Boston: Houghton Mifflin Co., 1923.

COMMAGER, H. S. *The American Mind.* New Haven: Yale University Press, 1950.

COOPER, LANE (ed.). *Theories of Style.* New York: The Macmillan Co., 1907.

COPE, E. N. *An Introduction to Aristotle's Rhetoric.* London, Cambridge: Macmillan Co., Ltd., 1867.

COPI, IRVING. *Symbolic Logic.* New York: The Macmillan Co., 1954.

CRANE, R. S. (ed.). *Critics and Criticism.* Chicago: University of Chicago Press, 1952.

CROCE, BENEDETTO. *Politics and Morals,* tr. SALVATORE J. CASTIGLIONE. New York: Philosophical Library, Inc., 1954.

CROWELL, LAURA. *Discussion, Method of Democracy.* Chicago: Scott, Foresman & Co., 1963.

DEWEY, JOHN. *How We Think.* Boston and New York: D. C. Heath & Co., 1933.

———. *Intelligence in the Modern World,* ed. JOSEPH RATNER. New York: Random House, Inc., 1939.

———. *Logic; The Theory of Inquiry.* New York: Henry Holt & Co., Inc., 1938.

———. *The Quest for Certainty.* New York: Minton, Balch, & Co., 1929.

———. *Reconstruction in Philosophy.* New York: Henry Holt & Co., Inc., 1920. Enlarged edition, Boston: Beacon Press, 1948.

DEWEY, JOHN, and TUFTS, JAMES H. *Ethics* (rev. ed.). New York: Henry Holt & Co., Inc., 1932.

Dionysius of Halicarnassus. *On Literary Composition,* ed. RHYS ROBERTS. London: Macmillan & Co., Ltd., 1910.

DOOB, LEONARD W. *Public Opinion and Propaganda.* New York: Henry Holt & Co., Inc., 1948.

———. *Propaganda.* New York: Henry Holt & Co., Inc., 1935.

DRAKE, DURANT. *Invitation to Philosophy.* Boston: Houghton Mifflin, 1933.

DRUMMOND, ALEX, and HUNT, E. W. *Persistent Questions in Public Discussion.* New York: Century Co., 1924.

EATON, RALPH. *General Logic.* New York: Charles Scribner's Sons, 1931.

ELSE, GERALD F. *Aristotle's "Poetics": The Argument.* Cambridge, Mass.: Harvard University Press, 1957.

EDMAN, IRWIN. *The Works of Plato.* New York: Modern Library, 1928.

EPICTETUS. *The Works of Epictetus* (rev. ed.), tr. THOMAS W. HIGGINSON. 2 vols. Boston: Little, Brown & Co., 1890.

FÉNELON, M. DE. *Dialogues,* tr. WILLIAM STEVENSON. Boston: Farrand, Mallory, & Co., 1810.

FLEMING, T. V. *Foundations of Philosophy.* London: The Shakespeare Head Press, 1949.

FLESCH, RUDOLPH. *The Art of Clear Thinking.* New York: Harper & Row, 1951.

FOGARTY, DANIEL. *Roots for a New Rhetoric.* New York: Teachers College, Columbia University, 1959.

FRYE, NORTHROP. *Anatomy of Criticism.* Princeton, N.J.: Princeton University Press, 1958.

GENUNG, JOHN F. *The Practical Elements of Rhetoric.* Boston: Ginn & Co., 1886.

GIDDINGS, P. M. *The Scientific Study of Human Society.* Chapel Hill, N.C.: University of North Carolina Press, 1924.

GOODRICH, CHAUNCEY A. "Essays." In *Select British Eloquence,* ed. A. CRAIG BAIRD. Carbondale, Ill.: Southern Illinois University Press, 1963.

GILBERT, ALLAN H. *Literary Criticism: Plato to Dryden.* New York: American Book Co., 1940.

GRAY, GILES W., and BRADEN, WALDO. *Public Speaking Principles and Practice.* New York: Harper & Row, 1951.

GRAY, GILES W., and WISE, CLAUDE M. *The Bases of Speech* (3d ed.). New York: Harper & Row, 1959.

GREENE, THEODORE M. *The Arts and the Art of Criticism.* Princeton, N.J.: Princeton University Press, 1940.

HADAS, MOSES. *Basic Works of Cicero.* New York: Random House, Inc., 1951.

HAIMAN, F. S. *Group Leadership and Democratic Action.* Boston: Houghton Mifflin Co., 1951.

HAYAKAWA, S. I. *Language in Thought and Action.* New York: Harcourt, Brace & Co., 1949.

———— (ed.). *Language, Meaning and Maturity.* New York: Harper & Row, 1954.

HIGHET, GILBERT. *Man's Unconquerable Mind.* New York: Columbia University Press, 1954.

HOBBES, THOMAS. *The English Works of Thomas Hobbes,* ed. SIR WILLIAM MOLESWORTH. 3 vols. 1839.

HOCHMUTH, MARIE. *A History and Criticism of American Public Address,* Vol. 3. New York: Longmans, Green & Co., Ltd., 1955.

HOLLINGWORTH, H. L. *The Psychology of Thought.* New York: Appleton-Century-Crofts, Inc., 1927.

————. *The Psychology of the Audience.* New York: American Book Co., 1935.

HOME (of Kames), HENRY. *Elements of Criticism* (rev. ed.), ed. JAMES R. BOYD. New York and Chicago: A. S. Barnes & Co., 1855.

HORACE. *Ars Poetica,* tr. T. A. MOXON. London: J. M. Dent & Sons, Ltd., 1941.

HOWELL, WILBUR S. *Logic and Rhetoric in England: 1500–1700.* Princeton, N.J.: Princeton University Press, 1956.

HOWES, RAYMOND F. *Historical Studies of Rhetoric and Rhetoricians.* Ithaca, N.Y.: Cornell University Press, 1961.

HUDSON, HOYT. *Educating Liberally.* Stanford, Calif.: Stanford University Press, 1945.

HUME, DAVID. *An Inquiry Concerning Human Understanding,* ed. SELBY-BIGGE. Oxford: Oxford University Press, 1951.

HUXLEY, T. *Evolution and Ethics.* New York: D. Appleton & Co., 1894.

————. *Man's Place in Nature.* New York: Hurst & Co., 1890.

————. *Science and Education.* New York: D. Appleton & Co., 1897.

JAEGER, WERNER. *Aristotle,* tr. RICHARD ROBINSON. London: Clarendon Press, 1934.

————. *Paidei; The Ideals of Greek Culture,* tr. GILBERT HIGHET. New York: Oxford University Press, 1943–45.

JAMES, WILLIAM. *Pragmatism.* New York: Longmans, Green & Co., Ltd., 1928.

————. *The Principles of Psychology.* New York: Henry Holt & Co., Inc., 1918.

————. *Psychology.* New York: Henry Holt & Co., Inc., 1893.

JEBB, R. C. *Attic Orators.* 2 vols. London: Macmillan & Co., Ltd., 1893.

———— (ed.). *Selections from the Attic Orators* (2d ed., rev.). London: Macmillan & Co., Ltd., 1927.

JESPERSEN, OTTO H. *The Philosophy of Grammar.* New York: Henry Holt & Co., Inc., 1924.

JEVONS, FRANK B. *A History of Greek Literature.* London: Charles Griffin & Co., 1886.

JOAD, C. E. M. *Guide to Philosophy.* New York: Random House, Inc., 1939.

JOHNSON, A. *The Historian and Historical Evidence*. New York: Charles Scribner's Sons, 1926.

JOHNSON, WENDELL. *People in Quandaries*. New York: Harper & Row, 1946.

KANT, IMMANUEL. *Critique of Practical Reason* (6th ed.), tr. T. K. ABBOTT. London: Longmans, Green & Co., Ltd., 1927.

KELLEY, STANLEY. *Professional Public Relations and Political Power*. Baltimore, Md.: Johns Hopkins Press, 1956.

KENNEDY, GEORGE. *The Art of Persuasion in Greece*. Princeton, N.J.: Princeton University Press, 1963.

KOFFKA, KURT. *The Growth of the Mind*, tr. R. M. OGDEN. London: Routledge & Kegan Paul, Ltd., 1924.

————. *The Principles of Gestalt Psychology*. New York: Harcourt, Brace & Co., 1935.

KÖHLER, WOLFGANG. *Gestalt Psychology*. New York: Horace Liveright, 1929.

KORZYBSKI, ALFRED. *Science and Sanity* (3d ed., rev.). Lakeville, Conn.: The International Non-Aristotelian Library Publishing Co., 1948.

LANGER, SUSANNE K. *Philosophy in a New Key*. Cambridge, Mass.: Harvard University Press, 1951.

LASKI, HAROLD. *Reflections on the Revolution of Our Time*. New York: The Viking Press, Inc., 1943.

LASSWELL, HAROLD D. *Democracy Through Public Opinion*. Menasha, Wisc.: George Banta Publishing Co., 1941.

————. *Propaganda Technique in the World War*. New York: Alfred A. Knopf, Inc., 1927.

LAWSON, JOHN. *Lectures Concerning Oratory* (3d. ed.). Dublin: G. Faulkner, 1760.

LAZARSFELD, PAUL F. *Communication Research*. New York: Harper & Row, 1949.

LEE, IRVING J. *How to Talk with People*. New York: Harper & Row, 1952.

————. *Language Habits in Human Affairs*. New York: Harper & Row, 1941.

———— (ed.). *The Language of Wisdom and Folly*. New York: Harper & Row, 1949.

LERNER, MAX. *Ideas Are Weapons*. New York: The Viking Press, Inc., 1939.

LEVIN, HARRY. *Contexts of Criticism*. Cambridge, Mass.: Harvard University Press, 1957.

LILLIE, WILLIAM. *Introduction to Ethics*. London: Methuen University Paperbacks, 1955.

LINTON, RALPH. *The Cultural Background of Personality*. New York: Appleton-Century-Crofts, Inc., 1945.

LIPPMANN, WALTER. *Essays in Public Philosophy*. Boston: Little, Brown & Co., 1955.

————. *Liberty and the News*. New York: Harcourt, Brace & Co., 1920.

————. *Public Opinion*. New York: The Macmillan Co., 1922.

LIVINGSTONE, R. W. *The Greek Genius and Its Meaning to Us* (2d ed.). London: Clarendon Press, 1915.

LOCKE, JOHN. *An Essay Concerning Human Understanding*. London: J. M. Dent & Sons, Ltd., 1947.

McBURNEY, JAMES H., and HANCE, KENNETH. *Discussion in Human Affairs*. New York: Harper & Row, 1950.

McBURNEY, JAMES H., and WRAGE, ERNEST. *The Art of Good Speech*. Englewood Cliffs, N.J.: Prentice-Hall, 1955.

McGRATH, EARL J. (ed.). *Communication in General Education.* Dubuque, Iowa: William C. Brown Co., 1949.

MAHAFFY, J. P. *A History of Classical Greek Literature* (2d ed., rev.). 2 vols. London: Longmans, Green & Co., Ltd., 1883.

———. *Social Life in Greece.* London: Macmillan & Co., Ltd., 1888.

MARITAIN, JACQUES. *The Degrees of Knowledge.* New York: Charles Scribner's Sons, 1938.

MILL, JOHN STUART. *Dissertations and Discussions.* Boston: W. V. Spencer, 1868.

———. *On Liberty.* Oxford: B. H. Blackwell, Ltd., 1946.

———. *The Philosophy of Scientific Method,* ed. ERNEST NAGEL. New York: Hafner Publishing Co., Inc., 1950.

———. *Six Great Humanistic Essays.* New York: Washington Square Press, 1963.

———. *Utilitarianism, Liberty, and Representative Government.* London: J. M. Dent & Sons, 1910.

MILLER, CLYDE R. *What Everybody Should Know About Propaganda: How and Why It Works* (4th ed., rev.). Princeton, N.J.: Commission for Propaganda Analysis, 1952.

MENCKEN, H. L. *The American Language.* New York: Alfred A. Knopf, Inc., 1931.

MONROE, ALAN. *Principles and Types of Speech.* Chicago: Scott, Foresman & Co., 1951.

MURPHY, GARDNER. *Personality.* New York: Harper & Row, 1947.

MURPHY, RICHARD. *Studies in Speech and Drama in Honor of Alexander M. Drummond.* Ithaca, N.Y.: Cornell University Press, 1944.

NEWMAN, JOHN HENRY. *The Idea of a University.* London and New York: The Macmillan Co., 1889.

NICHOLS, MARIE HOCHMUTH. *Rhetoric and Criticism.* Baton Rouge, La.: Louisiana State University Press, 1963.

OGDEN, C. K., and RICHARDS, I. A. *The Meaning of Meaning.* London: Routledge & Kegan Paul, Ltd., 1923.

OLIVER, R. T. *The Psychology of Persuasive Speech* (2d ed.). New York: Longmans, Green & Co., Ltd., 1957.

ORTEGA Y GASSET, JOSÉ. *What Is Philosophy?* New York: W. W. Norton & Co., 1960.

OVERSTREET, HARRY. *Influencing Human Behavior.* New York: W. W. Norton & Co., 1925.

PACKARD, VANCE. *The Hidden Persuaders.* New York: David McKay Co., Inc., 1957.

PARETO, VILFREDO. *The Mind and Society,* ed. ARTHUR LIVINGSTON, tr. BORGIOMO and LIVINGSTON. New York: Harcourt, Brace & Co., 1935.

PARRINGTON, V. L. *Main Currents of American Thought.* 3 vols. New York: Harcourt, Brace & Co., 1927–1930.

PEIRCE, CHARLES S. *Philosophical Writings of Peirce* (2d ed., rev.), ed. JUSTUS BUCHLER. New York: Dover Publications, Inc., 1955.

PERSONS, STOW. *American Minds.* New York: Henry Holt & Co., Inc., 1958.

PLATO. *The Dialogues of Plato* (3d ed.), tr. BENJ. JOWETT. 2 vols. New York: Random House, Inc., 1937.

———. *Phaedrus, Ion, Gorgias, and Symposium,* tr. LANE COOPER. New York: Oxford University Press, 1938.

————. *Republic,* tr. BENJ. JOWETT. New York: P. F. Collier & Son, 1901.

————. *The Works of Plato* (3d ed.), ed. IRWIN EDMAN and tr. BENJ. JOWETT. New York: Simon & Schuster, Inc., 1928.

POLLOCK, THOMAS C. *The Nature of Literature: Its Relation to Science, Language, and Human Experience.* Princeton, N.J.: Princeton University Press, 1942.

POPPER, KARL. *The Open Society and Its Enemies* (rev. ed.). Princeton, N.J.: Princeton University Press, 1950.

POTTER, SIMEON. *Our Language.* Baltimore, Md.: Penguin Books, Ltd., 1851.

QUINTILIAN. *Institutio Oratoria,* tr. H. E. BUTLER. 4 vols. London: William Heinemann, Ltd.; New York: G. P. Putnam's Sons, Inc., 1921–22.

RATNER, JOSEPH. *Intelligence in the Modern World: John Dewey's Philosophy.* New York: Modern Library, 1939.

REID, LOREN. *First Principles of Public Speaking.* Columbia, Mo.: Artcraft Press, 1962.

REID, LOREN (ed.). *American Public Address.* Columbia, Mo.: University of Missouri Press, 1961.

RICHARDS, I. A. *Basic English and Its Uses.* New York: W. W. Norton & Co., 1943.

————. *The Philosophy of Rhetoric.* New York: Oxford University Press, 1936; London: Kegan Paul & Trench, Tubner & Co., 1929.

————. *Practical Criticism.* New York: Harcourt, Brace & Co., 1929.

————. *Principles of Literary Criticism.* London: Routledge & Kegan Paul, Ltd., 1924.

ROBB, MARY MARGARET. *Oral Interpretation of Literature in American Colleges and Universities.* New York: H. W. Wilson Co., Inc., 1941.

ROBINSON, D. S. *An Introduction to Living Philosophy.* New York: Thomas Y. Crowell Co., 1932.

————. *Principles of Reasoning* (3d ed.). New York: Appleton-Century Co., 1947.

ROBINSON, J. H. *Mind in the Making.* New York: Harper & Row, 1921.

ROSS, E. A. *New-Age Sociology.* London: Appleton-Century Co., 1940.

ROSS, W. D. *The Right and Good.* Oxford: Clarendon Press, 1930.

RUSSELL, BERTRAND. *A History of Western Philosophy.* New York: Simon & Schuster, Inc., 1945.

————. *Basic Writings of Bertrand Russell,* ed. R. E. EGNER and LESTER DENNON. London: George Allen & Unwin, 1961.

————. *Human Knowledge, Its Scope and Limits.* New York: Simon & Schuster, Inc., 1948.

————. *Outlines of Philosophy.* London: George Allen & Unwin, 1927.

SABINE, GEORGE. *History of Political Theory.* New York: Henry Holt & Co., 1950.

SANDFORD, W. P. *English Theories of Public Address, 1530–1828.* Columbus, Ohio: Hedrick Co., 1929.

SANDFORD, W. P., and YEAGER, W. H. *Principles of Effective Speaking.* New York: The Ronald Press Co., 1963.

SANTAYANA, GEORGE. *Soliloquies in England.* New York: Charles Scribner's Sons, 1924.

SAPIR, EDWARD. *Culture, Language and Personality: Selected Essays,* ed. DAVID G. MANDELBAUM. Los Angeles: University of California Press, 1956.

————. *Language: An Introduction to the Study of Speech.* New York: Harcourt, Brace & Co., 1921.

SCHILLER, F. C. S. *Logic for Use.* London: G. Bell & Sons, Ltd., 1929.

SCHLESINGER, A. M., and WHITE, M. G. (eds.). *Paths of American Thought.* Boston: Houghton Mifflin Co., 1963.

SCHOPENHAUER, ARTHUR. *The Art of Controversy and Other Papers.* London: S. Sonnenschein & Company; New York: The Macmillan Co., 1896.

SELDES, GILBERT. *The Great Audience.* New York: The Viking Press, Inc., 1950.

SCHRAMM, WILBUR. *Communication in Modern Society.* Urbana, Ill.: University of Illinois Press, 1948.

————. *Mass Communication.* Urbana, Ill.: University of Illinois Press, 1949.

SHERMAN, MANDEL. *Basic Problems of Behavior.* New York: Longmans, Green & Co., Ltd., 1941.

SHOEMAKER, FRANCIS. *Aesthetic Experience and the Humanities.* New York: Columbia University Press, 1943.

SONDREL, BESS. *The Humanity of Words.* New York: World Publishing Co., 1958.

SOROKIN, PITIRIM A. *Social and Cultural Dynamics.* 2 vols. New York: American Book Co., 1937.

SMITH, R. V., and SINDEMAN, EDWARD C. *The Democratic Way of Life.* New York: Mentor Books, 1951.

SPENCER, HERBERT. *The Philosophy of Style.* New York: Appleton-Century-Crofts, 1871.

STEBBING, L. SUSAN. *Thinking to Some Purpose.* Baltimore, Md.: Penguin Books, Ltd., 1939.

STEEVES, H. R., and RISTINE, P. H. *Representative Essays in Modern Thought.* New York: American Book Co., 1913.

STEVENSON, C. L. *Ethics and Language.* New Haven: Yale University Press, 1944.

Studies in Rhetoric and Public Speaking in Honor of James Albert Winans. New York: Century Co., 1925.

SULLIVAN, J. W. N. *The Limitations of Science.* New York: Mentor Books, 1949.

THONSSEN, LESTER. *Bibliography of Speech Education.* New York: H. W. Wilson Co., Inc., 1939; Supplement, 1950.

———— (ed.). *Selected Readings in Rhetoric and Public Speaking.* New York: H. W. Wilson Co., Inc., 1942.

THONSSEN, LESTER, and BAIRD, A. CRAIG. *Speech Criticism.* New York: The Ronald Press Co., 1948.

THOULESS, R. H. *How to Think Straight.* New York: Simon & Schuster, Inc., 1941.

THUCYDIDES. *The Complete Writings of Thucydides,* tr. P. CRAWLEY. New York: Random House, Inc., 1951.

TOULMIN, S. E. *An Examination of the Place of Reason in Ethics.* Cambridge: Cambridge University Press, 1950.

————. *The Philosophy of Science.* New York: Hutchinson's University Library; Longmans, Green & Co., 1953.

————. *The Uses of Argument.* New York: Cambridge University Press, 1958.

TOYNBEE, ARNOLD J. *A Study of History* (abridgements of Vols. 1–4), ed. D. C. SOMERVELL. New York: Oxford University Press, 1947.

TRILLING, LIONEL. *The Opposing Self.* New York: The Viking Press, Inc., 1955.

THORNDIKE, EDWARD L. *Psychology of Wants, Interests, and Attitudes.* New York: Appleton-Century-Crofts, Inc., 1935.

UTTERBACK, WILLIAM E. *Group Thinking and Conference Leadership.* New York: Rinehart & Co., Inc., 1950.

VEBLEN, THORSTEIN. *The Theory of the Leisure Class.* New York: The Viking Press, Inc., 1924.

WALLACE, KARL (ed.). *History of Speech Education in America.* New York: Appleton-Century Co., 1954.

WALLAS, GRAHAM. *The Art of Thought.* London: Jonathan Cape, 1931.

———. *The Great Society.* New York: The Macmillan Co., 1914.

———. *Our Social Heritage.* New York: Yale University Press, 1921.

WARD, JOHN. *A System of Oratory.* 2 vols. London: J. Ward, 1759.

WARD, LESTER. *Dynamics of Sociology.* 2 vols. New York: D. Appleton Co., 1883.

WATSON, J. B. *Psychology from the Standpoint of a Behaviorist* (3d ed., rev.). Philadelphia: J. B. Lippincott Co., 1929.

WATSON, J. S. (tr.). *Institutes of Oratory* (Quintilian). 2 vols. London: H. G. Bohn, 1856.

———. "Brutus," in *Cicero on Oratory and Orators.* New York: Harper & Bros., 1890.

WEAVER, ANDREW. *Speech.* New York: Longmans, Green & Co., Ltd., 1923.

WEAVER, RICHARD M. *The Ethics of Rhetoric.* Chicago, Ill.: Henry Regnery Co., 1953.

WELLDON, J. E. (tr.). *The "Rhetoric" of Aristotle.* London: Macmillan & Co., Ltd., 1886.

WELLEK, RENÉ, and WARREN, AUSTIN. *Theory of Literature.* New York: Harcourt, Brace & Co., 1942.

WESTAWAY, F. W. *Scientific Method.* London: Blackie & Son, Ltd., 1931.

WHATELY, RICHARD. *Elements of Rhetoric* (various editions).

———. *Elements of Rhetoric,* ed. DOUGLAS EHNINGER. Carbondale, Ill.: Southern Illinois University Press, 1963.

WHATMOUGH, JOSHUA. *Language.* New York: Mentor Books, 1957.

WHITE, MORTON. *The Age of Analysis.* New York: Mentor Books, 1955.

WHITEHEAD, ALFRED N. *The Aims of Education and Other Essays.* New York: Mentor Books, 1956.

———. *Alfred North Whitehead—An Anthology,* ed. F. S. C. NORTHROP and MASON W. GROSS. New York: The Macmillan Co., 1953.

———. *The Function of Reason.* Princeton, N.J.: Princeton University Press, 1929.

———. *Science and the Modern World.* New York: The Macmillan Co., 1925.

WHYTE, H. W. *Is Anybody Listening?* New York: Simon & Schuster, Inc., 1950.

WIENER, NORBERT. *Cybernetics: or Control and Communication in the Animal and the Machine.* New York: John Wiley & Sons, Inc., 1948.

———. *The Human Use of Human Beings: Cybernetics and Society.* Boston: Houghton Mifflin Co., 1950.

WILSON, THOMAS. *Arte of Rhetorique*, ed. G. H. MAIR. Oxford: Clarendon Press, 1909.

WIMSATT, WILLIAM K., and BROOKS, CLEANTH. *Literary Criticism: A Short History*. New York: Alfred A. Knopf, Inc., 1957.

WINANS, JAMES. *Speech Making*. New York: Century Co., 1915.

WINCHESTER, C. T. *Some Principles of Literary Criticism*. New York: The Macmillan Co., 1900.

WITTGENSTEIN, LUDWIG. *Philosophical Investigations*. New York: The Macmillan Co., 1953.

WOODWORTH, ROBERT S. *Experimental Psychology*. New York: Henry Holt & Co., Inc., 1938.

YONGE, C. D. (tr.). *The Orations of Marcus Tullius Cicero*. 4 vols. London: G. Bell & Sons, Ltd., 1913.

ZIMMERN, ALFRED E. *The Greek Commonwealth* (3d ed., rev.). Oxford: Clarendon Press, 1922.

ZIPF, G. K. *The Psychology of Language*. Boston: Houghton Mifflin Co., 1935.

Index

239